D. H. Lawrence's *Sons and Lovers*

A CASEBOOK

CASEBOOKS IN CRITICISM

Nadine Gordimer's *Burger's Daughter:* A Casebook
Edited by Judie Newman

James Joyce's *A Portrait of the Artist as a Young Man:* A Casebook
Edited by Mark A. Wollaeger

Chinua Achebe's *Things Fall Apart:* A Casebook
Edited by Isidore Okpewho

Richard Wright's *Black Boy (American Hunger):* A Casebook
Edited by William L. Andrews and Douglas Taylor

William Faulkner's *Absalom, Absalom!:* A Casebook
Edited by Fred Hobson

Edith Wharton's *The House of Mirth:* A Casebook
Edited by Carol J. Singley

James Joyce's *Ulysses:* A Casebook
Edited by Derek Attridge

Joseph Conrad's *Heart of Darkness:* A Casebook
Edited by Gene M. Moore

Ralph Ellison's *Invisible Man:* A Casebook
Edited by John F. Callahan

Orson Welles's *Citizen Kane:* A Casebook
Edited by James Naremore

Alfred Hitchcock's *Psycho:* A Casebook
Edited by Robert Kolker

D. H. LAWRENCE'S
Sons and Lovers

◆ ◆ ◆

A CASEBOOK

Edited by
John Worthen and Andrew Harrison

UNIVERSITY PRESS

2005

OXFORD

UNIVERSITY PRESS

Oxford University Press, Inc., publishes works that further
Oxford University's objective of excellence
in research, scholarship, and education.

Oxford   New York
Auckland   Cape Town   Dar es Salaam   Hong Kong   Karachi
Kuala Lumpur   Madrid   Melbourne   Mexico City   Nairobi
New Delhi   Shanghai   Taipei   Toronto

With offices in
Argentina   Austria   Brazil   Chile   Czech Republic   France   Greece
Guatemala   Hungary   Italy   Japan   Poland   Portugal   Singapore
South Korea   Switzerland   Thailand   Turkey   Ukraine   Vietnam

Published by Oxford University Press, Inc.
198 Madison Avenue, New York, New York, 10016
www.oup.com

Oxford is a registered trademark of Oxford University Press

Library of Congress Cataloging-in-Publication Data
D. H. Lawrence's Sons and lovers: a casebook / edited by John Worthen and Andrew Harrison.
p. cm.—(Casebooks in criticism)
Includes bibliographical references and index.
ISBN—13 978-0-19-517040-5; ISBN—13 978-0-19-517041-2 (pbk.)
ISBN 0-19-517040-7; 0-19-517041-5 (pbk.)
I. Lawrence, D. H. (David Herbert) 1885–1930. Sons and lovers.   I. Worthen, John.
II. Harrison, Andrew, 1973–   III. Series.
PR6023.A93S6675 2005
823'.912—dc22   2004054702

1   3   5   7   9   8   6   4   2

Printed in the United States of America
on acid-free paper

Acknowledgments

We would like to thank the authors of the essays reproduced in this book for enthusiastically agreeing to us using their work. In addition, we are grateful to John Turner for his contribution, and to Eve Bachrach at Oxford University Press for answering all our questions so speedily and helpfully. Andrew Harrison would like to thank his family for their invaluable support during his work on the book.

Andrew Harrison
John Worthen

Credits

A Note on Primary References

All quotations from *Sons and Lovers* are referenced in parentheses in the main body of the essays. Page numbers refer readers to the Cambridge text of the novel, first published in a hardback volume edited by Helen Baron and Carl Baron (Cambridge: Cambridge University Press, 1992). This text has been subsequently reproduced (with identical pagination) in a widely available paperback edition with different editorial matter, first published by Penguin Books in 1994.

Contents

D. H. Lawrence's *Sons and Lovers*

A CASEBOOK

Introduction

ANDREW HARRISON

◆ ◆ ◆

IN A LETTER OF 19 May 1913 written in Irschenhausen, near
Munich, Germany, D. H. Lawrence announced to his literary
mentor, Edward Garnett, his receipt of an advance copy of his
third novel: '*Sons and Lovers* has just come—I am fearfully proud
of it. I reckon it is quite a great book. I shall not write quite in
that style any more. It's the end of my youthful period.'¹ There
are a number of reasons why the twenty-seven year-old author
might have wanted to use the publication of this novel to draw
a line under his early life and writings. For one thing, the novel
drew heavily on his childhood, youth and early manhood in the
industrial midlands of England, and indeed on the lives of his
parents and siblings. His mother's death from abdominal cancer
in December 1910 had devastated him, and his outpouring of grief
and subsequent depression had contributed to his own physical
collapse (involving double pneumonia) in the winter of 1911. The
novel recreated his mother's rapid decline in health and her
death, with its traumatic aftermath. It also fictionalized the earlier
tragic death of his elder brother, Ernest, and explored in analytical

mode Lawrence's complex and doomed relationships with several women: most notably with his childhood sweetheart, Jessie Chambers, and with Alice Dax, a Nottingham friend and suffragette with whom he had a brief affair. He had quickly realized that the writing of *Sons and Lovers* represented a coming to terms with his early life. Writing to his former teaching colleague, Arthur McLeod, five months after the novel's publication, he would reflect that 'one sheds ones sicknesses in books—repeats and presents again ones emotions, to be master of them'.[2]

Lawrence's circumstances had undergone a transformation in the spring of 1912. Illness had brought an end to his career as a schoolteacher, and, seeking advice on finding alternative employment as a lecturer in Germany, he had met Frieda Weekley, the wife of the Professor of Modern Languages at Nottingham University College. In May 1912 they had travelled together to Germany, and though Frieda had no intention at the time of leaving her husband and three children for Lawrence, that was the eventual outcome. The letter to Garnett in which, a year later, Lawrence celebrated the arrival of *Sons and Lovers* was written from the house of Frieda's older sister, Else Jaffe, and he wrote it as a professional author, who was making his living from writing. The material of *Sons and Lovers* had concerned itself with kinds of relationships and psychological responses that Lawrence was attempting to move beyond in the spring of 1913; it encapsulated forms of provincial English life that he had come to understand from a different perspective by that time.

The novel's composition had spanned a highly productive period in Lawrence's early writing and publishing life. When he began work on it during the autumn of 1910,[3] he had published two short stories and a small number of poems; by May 1913, he was the author of two novels and a book of poems, in addition to various travel sketches, short stories and reviews.[4] The letter to Edward Garnett reveals a new self-confidence in Lawrence as an author. By the spring of 1913, he felt able to defend his new novel project (entitled 'The Sisters') with energy and confidence, countering Garnett's criticisms. In the letter of 19 May, Lawrence is claiming the freedom to write differently, putting behind him the painstaking construction of scenes and marshalling of emotions associated with his third novel.

Though his interest had characteristically shifted to his latest writings by the time the copy of *Sons and Lovers* had arrived in Germany, the pride Lawrence took in a work that had absorbed his attention and his life for two years was to be amply vindicated by its critical reception and, of course, by its subsequent status in twentieth-century English literature. Almost a century later, it remains his most popular, his best selling and his most widely studied novel. One mark of its greatness resides in the fact that the very controversies over content and form which accompanied its original composition and editing have persisted and intensified in its critical afterlife.

Composition

Lawrence first began work on *Paul Morel* (his original title for *Sons and Lovers*) around the period when his mother's health was in rapid decline, and the novel's origins lay in his attempt to understand the course of his mother's life and its impact on his own psychological development. In a letter of 3 December 1910, written during a break from nursing her, Lawrence described to a friend how he saw his parents' marriage:

> Their marriage life has been one carnal, bloody fight. I was born hating my father: as early as ever I can remember, I shivered with horror when he touched me. He was very bad before I was born.
>
> This has been a kind of bond between me and my mother. We have loved each other, almost with a husband and wife love, as well as filial and maternal. We knew each other by instinct. She said to my aunt—about me:
>
> 'But it has been different with him. He has seemed to be part of me.'—and that is the real case. We have been like one, so sensitive to each other that we never needed words. It has

been rather terrible, and has made me, in some respects, ab-normal.[5]

Helen and Carl Baron have shown that Lawrence's earliest attempts at writing a version of his mother's biography had dwelt on her premarital life (they point to an early fragment of an abandoned novel entitled 'Matilda').[6] Lawrence appears to have focused his attention on an early, failed but fondly remembered relationship between his mother and a sensitive, artistic man. This plot is first explored in a cancelled passage from his first novel, *The White Peacock*[7]; it survives into the published text of *Sons and Lovers* in the guise of young Gertrude Coppard's relationship with John Field (16–17). Lawrence was clearly fascinated by the forces that shape a life: by fate and chance, by events which occur before we are born, and by the things we see, feel and respond to as we grow up.

His attempt to understand these forces through his writing is suggested by the plan of the novel written in his college notebook in 1910, though this includes the figure of his mother only incidentally, perhaps because the idea of analyzing her failed marriage seemed too painful to Lawrence before he began to witness her rapidly deteriorating health. None of the 100-page first draft (written between October and December 1910) survives, though several of the plotlines in the plan were carried over into the later versions[8] and are sufficient to suggest that Lawrence's main interest had already shifted from his mother's premarital life and the earlier relationship to the consequences of her marriage for the children. The incomplete second draft (written between March and July 1911), recently published as *Paul Morel*, was at least 355 pages in length, and the majority of it has survived. It is a very different novel from the final version. In it, the father kills his youngest son, Arthur, throwing a knife-sharpener (or 'steel') at him during an argument. The father receives a lenient prison sentence but dies shortly after his release. Lawrence showed this draft to his childhood sweetheart, Jessie Chambers, who claimed (after Lawrence's death) that she found the writing tired and forced.[9] She suggested that Lawrence keep to the story of his nuclear family and urged him to include in the novel the history of his elder brother, who had tragically died in London from erysipelas (inflammation and fever leading to pneumonia) in October 1901 at the age of twenty-three.

The first complete version of the novel, begun shortly before Lawrence himself came down with pneumonia in November 1911 and finished in June 1912, kept closer to Lawrence's experiences, introducing a new level of psychological realism to the story whilst developing the plotline into a structure that aimed at a wider understanding of family dynamics. He asked Jessie Chambers to help him by writing down her own memories of their early days together, and he sought her opinion of his work as he wrote. This draft also, however, cast a more detached, critical and analytical light on Paul Morel's relationship with Miriam, a character whom Jessie knew to be her fictional counterpart. The novel in which he was seeking to understand his own situation became the vehicle for his criticism of his early life, and the betrayal (as Jessie saw it) and the casting off of the woman he had known best as a young man became a necessary part of the process. In the course of writing this penultimate version, Lawrence also met and fell in love with Frieda Weekley. It seems likely that she helped him to understand (or see from an altered perspective) the broader patterns of his early development, and in particular the dangers inherent in possessive maternal love, and in the spiritual love offered to Paul by Miriam.[10] The third version was revised in Germany, from a manuscript littered (in the Miriam sections) with Jessie's marginal comments, some of them critical of what she saw as departures from the truth. The revised novel was sent off to the publisher Heinemann on 9 June 1912, but that firm rejected it at once on the grounds that it was too outspoken, lacking the degree of reticence required for a book to achieve success with the powerful libraries; it was also said to lack form or 'unity'.[11]

Lawrence was angered by Heinemann's decision and sent the manuscript to Edward Garnett, soliciting his advice. Garnett— who acted as literary advisor and reader for the publisher Duckworth—recommended certain changes, the exact nature of which is unknown, and Lawrence began rewriting the novel for the final time in Icking in south Germany in August 1912, moving to Lake Garda in the north of Italy the following month. Frieda Weekley replaced Jessie Chambers as Lawrence's private audience; lacking Jessie's personal investment in the novel, she could help Lawrence see its psychological development more objectively. Frieda wrote to Garnett on 7 September 1912 (from Lake Garda) that Lawrence was 'writing P.M. [*Paul Morel*] again, [he] reads bits to me and we fight like blazes over it'.[12] Having given up her children for the sake of a man she loved, Frieda was in an interesting position to comment upon mothers and love. She brought to the project an appreciation of Freudian psychoanalysis, which may have helped to convince Lawrence that what he was writing was not simply a transformed version of his family history but an exploration of broader affective dynamics akin to *Oedipus Tyrannus* or *Hamlet*. He came to understand the novel as 'the tragedy of thousands of young men in England'.[13] In the course of this final rewriting, in October 1912, Lawrence decided to rename the novel *Sons and Lovers,* shifting the emphasis away from his main character to the timeless psychological dilemma his situation may be seen to reveal.

It was under this title that he sent the novel back to Garnett on 18 November 1912; the following day Lawrence sent Garnett a long letter defending the novel against charges of formlessness (the key passage is reproduced here in 'Excerpts from Lawrence's Letters'). Garnett was not convinced; he demanded major excisions to suit the novel to the literary marketplace. He edited it down, cutting out some eighty passages and reducing the novel's length by one tenth; he also censored a few of the novel's sexual references (a process continued by the novel's printer in 1913). Lawrence was saddened by Garnett's insistence on the excisions, but accepted them as necessary to the book's publication, and therefore to his chances of obtaining a reasonable income from his efforts. The edited novel was published, with a dedication to Garnett, in May 1913.

Note on Texts

Opinions as to the nature and significance of Garnett's editing of the novel vary widely. The debate was reactivated in 1992 with the publication in the standard Cambridge University Press edition of Lawrence's works of the longer text, edited by Helen and Carl Baron; this text was reissued in paperback in 1994 with different editorial matter by Penguin Books.

The Barons argue in the introduction to the Cambridge edition that Lawrence only accepted Garnett's excisions under duress, because of his financial situation; although he dedicated *Sons and Lovers* to Garnett, the decision to do so was taken before he knew the extent of the cuts that Garnett had made to the text. The Barons also suggest that since commercial strictures over length do not apply to modern critical editions there can be no good reason for reproducing the shorter text when Lawrence clearly expected and hoped to see the longer text published. Critics who find themselves in agreement with this stance argue for the validity of Lawrence's defence of his novel to Garnett, seeing in the 'restored' version a complexity of structure and a significant stress upon Paul's brother William lacking in the 1913 text. In addition, Helen Baron has argued that Garnett's cuts removed passages that attested to the young Lawrence's interest in evolutionary theory as it was expounded in works by Herbert Spencer: Garnett's version of the novel obscured and impoverished the intellectual debates staged in the longer version.[14]

Before 1992, it was generally accepted that the significant cuts Garnett made to the text were aesthetically justified, sharpening the focus of the plot and removing extraneous detail. Mark Schorer articulated this position in the introduction to his 1977 facsimile of the final manuscript of the novel.[15] Post-1992 proponents of the 1913 text, while they may personally subscribe to the earlier aesthetic judgement, are more likely to defend the earlier published version on the grounds that a negotiation of the literary marketplace is an integral feature of a book's nature as an historical document.

The preference for one text over the other partly rests on whether we value the novel more as an individual work with its own logic and structure or as a social artefact, shaped by a complex series of negotiations between the author, society, literary culture and commerce. While we have chosen to adopt as our point of reference the new, longer version of the novel reissued in the widely available Penguin paperback edition, we wish to draw attention to the importance of this debate over texts in our selection of essays and in the Suggested Reading section. In particular, two of the essays collected here represent the different sides of the debate: the essay by Michael Black argues in favor of the longer text, while Macdonald Daly's piece, initially written as the introduction to a modern edition of the 1913 version, favors the earlier published novel. Readers wishing to assess the nature of Garnett's editing for themselves are advised that the final pages of the Penguin edition contain a full listing of the words and passages that he cut from the novel.

Readers should note that the second version of the novel edited by Helen Baron and published as *Paul Morel* by Cambridge University Press in 2003 also contains the surviving fragments of the 1912 version of the text, including Jessie Chambers's annotations on chapter 9, plus the early, unfinished piece entitled 'Matilda'.

Early Responses to the Novel and Reception on Publication

Responses to the Novel Prior to Publication

The form and content of *Sons and Lovers* were hotly contested long before the novel was published. Jessie Chambers and Frieda Weekley read and contributed to debates around the plot and structure of the novel as it was written; Heinemann read and rejected the third version; and, of course, Edward Garnett advised Lawrence and acted as his editor. Two of these early engagements with the novel are accessible to modern readers: Heinemann's letter of rejection is reproduced in a footnote in the first volume of Lawrence's letters (see endnote 11 below), and Garnett's editing of the novel can now be fully assessed. But Jessie Chambers's involvement with the novel is more complex than I have so far suggested. Attempting to alter Lawrence's attitude to the past, in 1911 Chambers wrote a short story recalling an occasion on which Lawrence had told her that he could not love her as a husband should love his wife. The event subsequently found its way into the second version of Lawrence's novel in the form of an important exchange between Paul and Miriam, and the scene was retained through to the final text (264). In late 1911, Chambers developed the short story into a novel entitled 'The Rathe Primrose'; in the winter of 1912–13 this novel was rewritten, on the recommendation of Edward Garnett. Chambers sent Garnett the finished book in March 1913, at a time when Lawrence was making final proof corrections to *Sons and Lovers.* Garnett forwarded the novel to Lawrence in May. It arrived too late to influence Lawrence's work, though when he read it he claimed he felt 'so miserable [he] had hardly the energy to walk out of the house for two days.'[16] Jessie Chambers felt even greater pains on perusing the edited proofs of *Sons and Lovers,* which Lawrence had forwarded to her two months earlier: exposure to them meant that she could 'neither eat nor sleep, and I sit in front of the fire and shiver as if I had ague fits'.[17] The finalized, conflicting accounts of their shared pasts brought to light accumulated feelings of betrayal, resentment, guilt and sorrow. In fact, we know very little about Chambers's book because she later destroyed it, along with all of Lawrence's letters. However, we do know that the main character's name was Eunice Temple (a fictional self-portrait and an alternative version of Lawrence's Miriam): when Chambers published her *Personal Record* of Lawrence in 1935, she did so under the pseudonym 'E.T.'

The content of *Sons and Lovers,* then, and more specifically its use of biographical detail and perspective, was clearly challenged in rather specific ways by people around Lawrence who had financial or emotional investments in the novel. Faced by these competing voices, Lawrence listened and took advice, but he also defended his right to see and transform events according to his own artistic needs. He told Jessie Chambers in May 1912 that she would have to 'go on forgiving [him]';[18] he was keen to claim for the novel a structure and significance that transcended any merely emotional or personal involvement he might have in his materials. In January 1913 he wrote a foreword to the novel, which he sent on to Garnett.[19] He was eager to write one, though it was not his intention to have it actually printed in the book. This foreword, which is permeated by a dense biblical language, represents an attempt on Lawrence's part to understand the broader significance of the family drama he had written. Subverting the words of John the Baptist in the New Testament, Lawrence argues that the Flesh of the woman is made Word by the work of man: 'every woman . . . demands that a man shall come home to her with joy and weariness of the work he has done during the day: that he shall then while he is with her, be re-born of her; that in the morning he shall go forth with his new strength' (472). If the man does not fulfil this role, then the woman will either reject him, or turn to her son, whose life will be ruined in turn. Lawrence told Garnett that the foreword would amuse him, and he later claimed that he would "die of shame" if it were printed,[20] but its content was apparently hotly debated with Frieda, and one suspects that it also served the purpose of re-stating his defence and justification of his novel's structure and development to the man who had cut it so extensively. Whatever the degree of importance we attach to it, Lawrence's desire to write the foreword is significant. It demonstrates his conviction that the message of *Sons and Lovers* deserved to be taken seriously by his English readership: he was 'so sure that only through a re-adjustment between men and women, and a making free and healthy of the sex' would England 'get out of her present atrophy'.[21]

Publication and Reception

The publication of the book in England by Duckworth on 29 May 1913 (it appeared in America, published by Mitchell Kennerley, on 17 September) put an end to the complex negotiations with Garnett, Frieda, and Jessie Chambers, and initiated a new phase in its reception. It was generally well received by reviewers on both sides of the Atlantic.[22] In England, it was praised for its power and realism, though some found cause to criticize in it the brutality that Frieda had earlier celebrated.[23] The most significant review of it in America came from Alfred Kuttner, who saw in it a presentation of psychosexual interactions comparable to those described by Freud. His review in *New Republic* for 10 April 1915 was later expanded into an article published in the *Psychoanalytic Review* in July 1916. The longer article is reproduced in an appendix to this volume on the grounds that it is an historically important response to *Sons and Lovers.* In a letter of 16 September 1916, Lawrence told a friend that he had read and hated this article: he bemoaned its critical treatment of his 'poor book: it was, as art, a fairly complete truth: so they carve a half lie out of it, and say 'Voilà'. Swine!'[24] The strength of Lawrence's response to the article reflects his argument with Freud over the nature of the unconscious, which Lawrence came to associate with the pristine body, rather than with the Id as the origin of repressions and complexes.[25]

Subsequent Critical Reputation and Approaches to the Novel

Critical Reputation

One contemporary review that appeared in the London *Standard* in May 1913 suggested that *Sons and Lovers* was the book in which D. H. Lawrence had come to full maturity as a writer. In 1927, T. S. Eliot, mistakenly believing *Sons and Lovers* to have been Lawrence's first published novel, referred to it as his first and best.[26] Fifteen years later, in 1942, the poet Philip Larkin wrote in a letter that, on the basis of *Sons and Lovers* alone, Lawrence could still be called England's greatest novelist.[27] Nevertheless, academic opinion on the merits of Lawrence's third novel in relation to his later works was settled rather early: Lawrence criticism since the 1950s has acknowledged the many fine qualities of the novel but generally viewed the next two novels, *The Rainbow* and *Women in Love*, as his finest. In *D. H. Lawrence: Novelist* (1955), F. R. Leavis, the most influential of twentieth-century Lawrence critics, called *Sons and Lovers* "a work of striking original genius" but discovered in it no signs of greatness.[28] The response should be understood in its true context as reflecting Leavis's sense that by the mid-1950s *Sons and Lovers* had received much popular praise while the later novels had been overlooked; in recent years academic opinion has swung back somewhat in favor of the earlier novel. As Michael Bell notes in the opening essay of this collection, debate still rages as to whether *Sons and Lovers* is the final work of Lawrence's youth or the first work of his maturity. In some respects it is a Janus-faced novel, still exhibiting signs of an Edwardian scheme of construction, but also anticipating Lawrence's later incursions into experimental modernist explorations of consciousness. Lawrence frequently breaks away from convention to give us direct access to the main protagonist's thoughts and feelings. For instance, we hear Paul's reflections on Clara Dawes as she walks on the beach near Theddlethorpe, and some remarkable expressionist passages at the very end of the novel invoke Paul's grief, his detachment from his surroundings, and his altered sense of time and space.

Narrative Technique

Discussions of narrative technique in *Sons and Lovers* (beginning with a perceptive anonymous review in the *Athenaeum* in 1913)[29] have almost invariably concentrated on the (questionable) centrality of Paul's perspective. Jessie Chambers's 1935 memoir of Lawrence concluded with a final chapter on the novel in which Lawrence's commitment to Paul's view of things is charged with distorting the truth of the account.[30] In an important essay in 1948, Mark Schorer criticized Lawrence for lacking the kind of detachment necessary to acts of fictional self-analysis, citing Chambers's book to support his thesis.[31] Lawrence's unsure handling of his art is held accountable for a perceived contrast between what we are told about the characters and how we see the characters behaving. According to Schorer, Paul's perspective stays close to Mrs Morel, demonizing the father, yet in action (he argues) Mrs Morel's stern and jealous love for Paul is shown to be destructive while the father is revealed to be passionate and sociable, his violence a response to his alienation within the home rather than to any inherent flaw in his nature.

The conflict between telling and showing, which Schorer views as a failure of technique and understanding, has, however, been seized upon by later critics as a positive virtue in the novel. In an essay published in 1968, Louis L. Martz focused on the portrayal of Miriam, showing how our sense of her as excessively spiritual and possessive is conditioned by Paul's partial vision.[32] In places the action of the novel allows us to see her as a positive foil to Mrs Morel: Miriam remains defiantly open to experience in spite of her constrictive upbringing. It is paradoxical to diagnose Paul as a psychologically damaged individual whilst uncritically endorsing his view of things. According to this reading, *Sons and Lovers* exists outside the realist tradition (with its reliance on an omniscient position of narration), generating meaning through the constant clash of different subjective responses to situations.[33]

Other criticism has tended to negotiate a path between viewing the novel as a one-sided act of self-analysis and seeing it as a radically subjective, even ironic, depiction of psychological imbalance. Neither Mark Spilka nor Dorothy Van Ghent agreed that *Sons and Lovers* manages consistently to reflect Paul's distorted consciousness: the narrator's perspective is said to become almost indistinguishable from Paul's perspective in part 2.[34] In a more recent book on Lawrence, however, Diane S. Bonds has examined the relation between narrative commentary, action and speech in *Sons and Lovers,* and she argues that the transitions in the novel frequently invite, but then elude meaning, rather than building up a convincing set of hypotheses and proofs.[35] Her deconstructive approach uncovers a consistent shifting of perspective in the narration, which frustrates any attempt to uncover an omniscient position or to adopt a stable critical stance vis-à-vis Paul.

This argument may appear to have brought us to the fruitful

impasse of poststructuralist indeterminacy, but two of the essays in this volume illustrate recent approaches that, by attempting to account for the shifts—even shiftiness—in the text, put equivocation back in the service of meaning. Rick Rylance's historicizing approach sees the novel as epitomizing an uncertainty in the young Lawrence between different modes of belief and systems of thought. If actions invite multiple interpretations and positions of certainty are no sooner invoked than brought into question, then the resulting ambiguity reflects Lawrence's own position as a writer struggling to accommodate a commitment to individual experience within a fictional form rooted in convention and moral consensus. Helen Baron takes a different angle on the question of indeterminacy. Comparing the final draft of the novel to the second version, she shows that Lawrence enhanced the degree of narrative intrusion in the later drafts of the novel; the second version was more inclined to let actions hint at the unsaid, or indeed at the inarticulable. This comparative textual approach enables us to glimpse through the equivocation the complexities of a narrative method grappling with the shifting significances of gesture, symbolism and body language in a medium where development and understanding are privileged terms.

History and Ideology

Early in his writing career, Lawrence was persuaded by Ford Madox Hueffer to draw on his working-class background to provide a rare insider's view of working-class life in the English Midlands. A number of his early plays and short stories pay testament to his ability as a recorder of working-class domestic life.[36] Of all Lawrence's novels, *Sons and Lovers* comes closest to providing the rich social panorama that Hueffer envisioned. Yet even here, and in spite of the extraordinary attention to historical detail in the novel, we should be careful to avoid assuming that Lawrence operates unequivocally as the working-class novelist his early mentors hoped he might become. Lawrence's relation to the mining community in which he grew up was extremely complex and the complexity is felt most keenly in the novels. While Lawrence would go on drawing on this community for the rest of his career, re-imagining it in novels as dissimilar as *The Rainbow, The Lost Girl* and *Lady Chatterley's Lover,* his writing was also the very thing that set him apart from active participation in it. His first two works, *The White Peacock* (1911) and *The Trespasser* (1912), concern themselves primarily with the cultured middle classes; glimpses of working-class life in *The White Peacock* are severely abbreviated. *Sons and Lovers* includes scenes whose power clearly derives from experience: we might recall Paul's sharp embarrassment on collecting his father's wages, or his watching the lights from the miners' lamps sprawling over the ceiling of his bedroom as they walk past his window to their nine o'clock night shift. Yet critics have also noted in the novel what they see as Lawrence's failure to portray the harsh realities of working-class life, and in particular Walter Morel's working life down the pit. Walter's violent bad temper is seen in action on several occasions, and his drunkenness is stressed throughout the early chapters, but we arguably get no real sense of the conditions of his working life which might help to account for his behavior above ground. Lawrence himself later came to regret his treatment of his father in the novel, and in several late autobiographical writings he celebrated the sense of masculine togetherness experienced by the miners of his father's generation.[37] There is, however, a way in which this process of redressing the balance in favor of his father entails another kind of idealization on the one side akin to the blindness of his earlier criticism. Both responses reveal an author caught up in the paradox encountered by other modernist exiles like James Joyce, Katherine Mansfield, and Franz Kafka: writing about a specific society from a position of partial alienation.

Criticism of the novel's engagement with history has moved from outright praise to an examination of the nature of its underlying social sympathies and of Lawrence's ideological investments. Julian Moynahan, writing on *Sons and Lovers* in 1963, knew of no novel except *Middlemarch* in which 'people are so rooted in concrete social history, and in a region so concretely rendered'.[38] Ten years later, Scott Sanders focused on Lawrence's depiction of Walter Morel as a failure in life, arguing that this unanimous verdict in the novel is largely a consequence of Lawrence having uncritically adopted Mrs Morel's bourgeois ideology of self-improvement.[39] According to this reading of the novel, Lawrence fails to examine the nature of social conditioning in Walter's case because of his fundamental belief in individual autonomy. Education and relationships are seen as vehicles of social change. Where Mrs Morel is dragged into the mire of working-class life through a marriage based largely on passion, William's class mobility is underscored by his relationship with a woman who presents herself as of higher social status; likewise, Paul's refusal to settle for the compromises of married life with Miriam Leivers reflects a social advantage gained through education and the exercising of his artistic sensibility. Lawrence is said to have escaped from historical reality into a psychological drama that locates power in the self, not in the class system. Graham Holderness, in 1982, saw the novel as a tragic exploration of the consequences of an Edwardian ideology that, in proposing education as a means to self-improvement, produced a whole generation of displaced, alienated and deeply troubled social climbers.[40] William dies in an indifferent London, while Paul is left with a feeling of separation as he turns with defiant optimism to the lights of Nottingham's factories and streets. Macdonald Daly's essay on relationship and class in the novel, reproduced in the present volume, acknowledges its evasive approach to the realities of working-class life but notes how subtly class conflict nevertheless makes itself felt in the novel's language (or languages) and in its treatment of sexuality. Daly argues that the unceasing conflict between different types of language (Mrs Morel's, Walter's, the narrator's) signals a broader uncertainty about the value of Mrs Morel's ideas of social success. Here, Lawrence is not a blind adherent to Gertrude's belief in social mobility, nor is he mounting a critique of that ideology's damaging effects: he is instead using the novel to explore the limits of autonomy.

In addition to examining Lawrence's treatment of the working class in *Sons and Lovers,* critics have been keen to examine his depiction of women, not least because the novel was written at a historical moment when various women's movements were actively seeking political enfranchisement. Within eighteen months of the novel's publication Britain was at war and women were required to enter the workplace to aid the war effort: gender politics would be permanently affected by the experience. A number of Lawrence's closest female friends in 1910–13 were involved with groups lobbying for female emancipation, and most of them shared his route out of working-class life through education and teaching. After Lawrence wrote *Sons and Lovers*, he turned his attention to female experience, writing to a friend 'I shall do my work for women, better than the suffrage'.[41] His next novel, *The Rainbow*, has as its central protagonist a young woman (Ursula Brangwen) who trains to teach, takes a job, and then leaves the job to pursue a university degree course. Yet, in spite of these details, *Sons and Lovers* was the main target of the feminist attacks that dented Lawrence's reputation in the 1970s. In *Sexual Politics*, Kate Millett was interested in uncovering an implicit subtext of male supremacy in the novel: she saw Paul as the benighted son, using the women in his life to support his ego and satisfy his sexual needs, then getting rid of them once they had served their purpose.[42] Millett's reading of the novel correctly identified attitudes inscribed in early twentieth-century British society, but in addressing the plot from within the changed perspective of her times she could not hope to address Lawrence's response to the 'Woman Question' from a properly historical angle. The novel is full of historical detail: Mrs Morel is a member of the Women's Guild; Clara is a suffragette who attends a gathering addressed by Margaret Bonford, a fictional character based on the radical suffragist Margaret Bondfield (1873–1953); mention is made of the W. S. P. U. (The Women's Social and Political Union), the suffragette pressure group founded in 1903 by Emmeline Pankhurst; and Lawrence reveals not only Paul's response to the fight for women's rights (he views it on the whole with a humorous petulance) but also the response of an older generation of women (Mrs Radford, Clara's mother, views her daughter's political activities as a symptom of her immediate marital problems). One approach would be to see the dismissive attitudes expressed in the novel towards the suffrage as signs of a chauvinist failure of sympathy in Lawrence; a more historically grounded approach would recognize Lawrence's readiness to address the issue with a frankness that accurately represents contemporary responses. Though Millett's attack has influenced subsequent gender-based accounts of the novel (an influence felt most sharply in a 1978 essay by Faith Pullin),[43] more recent feminist criticism has tried to understand the novel in its historical context. In *D. H. Lawrence and Feminism,* Hilary Simpson argues that the novel is peculiarly sensitive to the economic basis of women's oppression, but, since it is not concerned to examine in any detail the workings of the industrial or political worlds, its view of political movements is kept at the level of superficial recognition.[44] The essay by Margaret Storch, reprinted in this volume, considers Lawrence's representation of women in the context of female emancipation and an historical situation in which young men both felt threatened by shows of female power and recognized the control women have over men's emotional lives. Adopting a modern psychoanalytic methodology, Storch argues that the underlying emotional subtext of the novel is Paul's aggressive hatred of matriarchal power: his occasionally cruel responses to women in the novel should be seen as symptoms of his powerlessness, not as signs of an abusive chauvinism.

Psychoanalytic Perspectives

Storch's essay contributes to a modern trend in psychoanalytic approaches to the novel set out in books by Judith Ruderman, Barbara Ann Schapiro, and James C. Cowan.[45] These critics depart from the earlier Freudian approaches to the novel by adopting the 'object relations' theories of Melanie Klein, D. W. Winnicott, Heinz Kohut, and others. As my discussion of the novel's composition has made clear, the final drafts of the novel were informed in part by Frieda Weekley's awareness of Freud's theories, as well as her attitudes to women, children and sexuality. During their first meeting in March 1912, Frieda and Lawrence apparently talked about Oedipus, and (according to Frieda's account) 'understanding leaped through [their] words'.[46] The exchange may

have specifically contributed to Lawrence's revision of the scene
from the previous draft in which Paul fervently kisses his mother;
in the new version, he and Gertrude are interrupted in their
embrace by the arrival of Walter Morel, and, following an argument, Paul pleads with his mother not to sleep with her husband.[47] Frieda may well have been able to give a Freudian gloss
to this mother-father-son interaction, enabling Lawrence to grasp
the underlying emotional structure of his developing novel, but
this does not mean that the novel resolves itself into a simple
demonstration of Freud's Oedipal theory. As we have noted,
Lawrence took offence at Alfred Kuttner's 1916 Freudian article
because he thought it carved 'a half lie' out of 'a fairly complete
truth', reducing art to theory. Later, he would take issue with
Freud's idea of the unconscious in two books, *Psychoanalysis and the
Unconscious* (1921) and *Fantasia of the Unconscious* (1922). However, a
Freudian approach to the novel persisted through to the 1980s,
with some accounts not only discussing the Oedipus complex but
also reading the novel alongside Freud's almost contemporaneous
1912 paper 'On the Universal Tendency to Debasement in the
Sphere of Love', which diagnoses an affective tendency in the
male psyche (originating in the maternal bond) to dissociate sexual and spiritual modes of love. Paul's relationships with Miriam
and Clara appear to bear out Freud's point: with Miriam he has an
intellectual kinship that militates against sexual fulfilment, whilst
with Clara the sexual fulfilment masks emotional detachment.

A Freudian approach to Lawrence necessarily centred on *Sons
and Lovers* because the novel seemed so conducive to analysis. Recent criticism, drawing on more modern psychoanalytic theories,
moves the emphasis from Oedipal conflict to pre-Oedipal narcissistic deficits. Here, Paul's (and Lawrence's) psychological traits are
traced back to his failed relationship with maternal and paternal
images in his early years. Paul overidealizes his mother whilst
failing to idealize his father. He is left attempting to give structure
to his life through fantasies that express his hatred of his mother's
power over him and that display his yearning for a close relationship with a powerful male. Two moments in the novel seem
worthy of comment here. The first is the scene in chapter 4 in

which the young Paul burns his sister Annie's doll in an act whose symbolism is noted by Margaret Storch; the second is Paul's feeling of connectedness with Baxter Dawes in the aftermath of their fight (Baxter, as critics have noted, shares many traits in common with Walter Morel). The bond between Paul and Baxter is replicated in slightly different forms in later novels by Lawrence (most notably in the relations between Rupert Birkin and Gerald Crich in *Women in Love*), suggesting to some that a fantasized father figure lies at the unconscious heart of Lawrence's imagination. Barbara Ann Schapiro's essay in this volume demonstrates the modern psychoanalytic approach to the novel.

The essays by Jack Stewart and Louis K. Greiff do not so readily fit into the three broad critical categories outlined above, though they do contribute significantly to new lines of critical approach to Lawrence. Stewart's essay focuses on the novel's concern with forms of expression, examining Paul Morel's role as a painter striving to express a vision of life in a novel which to some extent replicates his attempts to give expression to a sense of the intangible. Stewart examines the novel's relation to literary realism and suggests that it reveals the maturity of an author who had assimilated the methods of the nineteenth-century literary tradition and begun to transform these methods through his application of techniques adapted from the visual arts, and particularly from Impressionism and Expressionism. Louis K. Greiff is also concerned with visual elements in the novel in his analysis of its adaptation to the screen in the famous 1960 film version, directed by Jack Cardiff. Through a detailed discussion of several scenes from the film, Greiff shows how adaptation entails interpretation, and in many cases it calls for directors to eschew the authority of the text to translate words into images.

In a sense, what Greiff identifies as a creative process of re-writing and fresh assimilation applies equally across the whole range of critical response to *Sons and Lovers*. The essays collected here frequently examine the same episodes and discuss similar topics, but the diversity of the approaches serves to emphasize the text's richness and openness to interpretation. The contributors demonstrate how completely the agenda for studying the novel has shifted in recent years. Rather than upbraiding Lawrence for his cruel treatment of Jessie Chambers, or using the novel to access the author's struggle against industrialism or his entrapment in a kind of Oedipal cul-de-sac, these critics stress the complex and puzzling nature of the text, tracing its many different voices and registers. What has so clearly happened to the psychoanalytic approaches to the book—getting away from reductive Freudianism—has also happened with regard to the gender issues and the historical ones: there has been a richening and a deepening of interest, and as a result there is now far less concern to apply excessive praise to it or to condemn its perceived weaknesses. The old battles are no longer being fought: the passage of time (together with the new text) has allowed us to see the whole novel differently. A work whose composition was shaped by dialogues between the past and the present goes on talking to us in different ways across the historical divide, unsettling and challenging and moving us.

Notes

1. *The Letters of D. H. Lawrence*, Volume I, ed. James T. Boulton (Cambridge: Cambridge University Press, 1979), 551.

2. *The Letters of D. H. Lawrence*, Volume II, eds. George J. Zytaruk and James T. Boulton (Cambridge: Cambridge University Press, 1981), 90.

3. The early draft outline of the novel, first reproduced in John Worthen, *D. H. Lawrence: The Early Years, 1885–1912* (Cambridge: Cambridge University Press, 1991), 278–79, has been tentatively dated to September 1910 in the Introduction to the Cambridge edition of *Sons and Lovers*, eds. Helen Baron and Carl Baron (Cambridge: Cambridge University Press, 1992), xxvi, though it may have been written slightly earlier. Lawrence wrote to Sydney Pawling on 18 October 1910 that the novel was one-eighth written. See *Letters*, I, 184.

4. *The White Peacock* (1911), *The Trespasser* (1912), and *Love Poems and Others* (1913).

5. *Letters*, I, 190.

6. 'Matilda' is included in D. H. Lawrence, *Paul Morel*, ed. Helen Baron (Cambridge: Cambridge University Press, 2003), 143–60.

7. This cancelled passage was published for the first time in D. H. Lawrence, *The White Peacock*, ed. Andrew Robertson (Cambridge: Cambridge University Press, 1982), 369–71.

8. See the Cambridge edition of *Sons and Lovers*, xxvi, where Helen and Carl Baron note that the following plotlines appear both in *Paul Morel* and in the 1913 version of *Sons and Lovers*: 'he pushes her out of the house before the birth of their son', 'tears without cause', 'move from Breach', 'Father hospital', 'filling straws', and 'W[illia]m. [original name of Paul] begins at Haywoods'.

9. See Jessie Chambers, *D. H. Lawrence: A Personal Record by 'E.T.'* (London: Jonathan Cape, 1935), 190.

10. Lawrence wrote a number of poems expressing his grief on the death of his mother. On a manuscript copy of one of these poems, entitled 'My Love, My Mother', Frieda wrote (probably some time between May and July 1912) marginal and end comments deploring the nature of Lawrence's reverence for his mother and emphasizing the damage done to him by the maternal bond. See John Worthen, *D. H. Lawrence: The Early Years, 1885–1912*, 411–12 (and Illustration 42).

11. Heinemann's letter to Lawrence (dated 1 July 1912) is reproduced in *Letters*, I, 421, n. 4.

12. Ibid., 449.

13. Ibid., 477.

14. See Helen Baron, 'Lawrence's *Sons and Lovers* versus Garnett's', *Essays in Criticism*, Vol. 42, No. 4 (October 1992), 265–78.

15. See *'Sons and Lovers': A Facsimile of the Manuscript*, ed. Mark Schorer (Berkeley: University of California Press, 1977), 9.

16. *Letters*, I, 551.

17. *The Collected Letters of Jessie Chambers*, ed. George J. Zytaruk, in a special edition of the *D. H. Lawrence Review*, Vol. 12, Nos. 1–2 (spring–summer 1979), 27.

18. *Letters*, I, 408.

19. For the full text of the foreword, see the Cambridge edition of *Sons and Lovers*, 467–73; it is also reproduced with the same pagination in the Penguin edition of the novel taken from the Cambridge text, eds. Helen Baron and Carl Baron (Harmondsworth: Penguin, 1994).

20. *Letters*, I, 507, 510.

21. Ibid., 544.

22. A selection of contemporary reviews can be found in R. P. Draper ed., *D. H. Lawrence: The Critical Heritage* (London: Routledge and Kegan Paul, 1970), 58–80.

23. See *Letters*, I, 550.

24. *Letters*, II, 655.

25. For a discussion of Lawrence's relation to Freud, see Fiona Becket's essay 'Lawrence and Psychoanalysis', in *The Cambridge Companion to D. H. Lawrence*, ed. Anne Fernihough (Cambridge: Cambridge University Press, 2001), 217–33.

26. See T. S. Eliot, 'Le Roman Anglais Contemporain', *La Nouvelle Revue Français*, 28 (May 1927), 671: 'Le premier que je crois le meilleur, *Sons and Lovers*'.

27. The letter to J. B. Sutton is in *Selected Letters of Philip Larkin 1940–1985* (London and Boston: Faber and Faber, 1992), 32.

28. F. R. Leavis, *D. H. Lawrence: Novelist* (London: Chatto and Windus, 1955), 18–19.

29. The review appeared in the *Athenaeum* of 21 June 1913. Parts are quoted in a review of *D. H. Lawrence: The Critical Heritage*, ed. R. P. Draper, in *The Cambridge Quarterly*, Vol. 5, No. 1 (spring–summer 1970), 107–8.

30. Jessie Chambers, *D. H. Lawrence: A Personal Record by 'E.T.'*, 179–223.

31. Mark Schorer, 'Technique as Discovery', *Hudson Review*, Vol. 1 (spring 1948), 67–87.

32. Louis L. Martz, 'Portrait of Miriam: A Study in the Design of *Sons and Lovers*', in *Imagined Worlds: Essays on Some English Novels and Novelists in Honour of John Butt*, eds. Maynard Mack and Ian Gregor (London: Methuen, 1968), 342–68.

33. See John Worthen, 'Lawrence as Dramatist', *The Cambridge Companion to D. H. Lawrence*, 137–53, especially 150–52.

34. Mark Spilka, *The Love Ethic of D. H. Lawrence* (London: Dennis Dobson, 1958), and Dorothy Van Ghent, 'On *Sons and Lovers*', in her *The English Novel: Form and Function* (New York: Harper and Row, 1961), 245–61.

35. Diane S. Bonds, *Language and the Self in D. H. Lawrence* (Ann Arbor, MI: UMI Research Press, 1987), 29–52 (chapter 2, '*Sons and Lovers*: A Metaphysical Unsettling').

36. See, for example, the plays *A Collier's Friday Night* and *The Widowing of Mrs. Holroyd*, and the short stories 'Odour of Chrysanthemums', 'Daughters of the Vicar' and 'The Miner at Home'.

37. See the essays '[Return to Bestwood]', 'Getting On', 'Which Class I Belong To' and 'Nottingham and the Mining Countryside', now col-

lected in D. H. Lawrence, *Late Essays and Articles*, ed. James T. Boulton (Cambridge: Cambridge University Press, 2004).

38. Julian Moynahan, *The Deed of Life: The Novels and Tales of D. H. Lawrence* (Princeton, NJ: Princeton University Press, 1963), 20.

39. Scott Sanders, *D. H. Lawrence: The World of the Major Novels* (London: Vision, 1973), 32–42.

40. Graham Holderness, *D. H. Lawrence: History, Ideology and Fiction* (Dublin: Gill and Macmillan, 1982), 134–58.

41. *Letters*, I, 490.

42. Kate Millett, *Sexual Politics* (London: Rupert Hart-Davis, 1971), 237–93, especially 245–57.

43. See Faith Pullin, 'Lawrence's Treatment of Women in *Sons and Lovers*', in *Lawrence and Women*, ed. Anne Smith (London: Vision, 1978), 49–74.

44. Hilary Simpson, *D. H. Lawrence and Feminism* (London and Canberra: Croom Helm, 1982), 26–37.

45. Judith Ruderman, *D. H. Lawrence and the Devouring Mother: The Search for a Patriarchal Ideal of Leadership* (Durham, NC: Duke University Press, 1984); Barbara Ann Schapiro, *D. H. Lawrence and the Paradoxes of Psychic Life* (Albany: State University of New York Press, 1999); and James C. Cowan, *D. H. Lawrence: Self and Sexuality* (Columbus: Ohio State University Press, 2002).

46. See Frieda Lawrence, '*Not I, But the Wind . . .*' (Santa Fe, NM: Rydal Press, 1934), 22.

47. Compare *Paul Morel*, 102–3, and *Sons and Lovers*, 252–54. We are grateful to John Turner for drawing our attention to the coincidence of Lawrence's revision of this scene and his meeting with Frieda on 3 March 1912.

Excerpts from Lawrence's Letters

I WILL GIVE YOU—with no intermediary this time—my third novel, 'Paul Morel', which is plotted out very interestingly (to me), and about one eighth of which is written. 'Paul Morel' will be a novel—not a florid prose poem, or a decorated idyll running to seed in realism: but a restrained, *somewhat* impersonal novel. It interests me very much.
(To Sydney Pawling, 18 October 1910)

I think L[awrence] quite missed the point in 'Paul Morel'. He really loved his mother more than any body, even with his other women, real love, sort of Oedipus, his mother must have been adorable—he is writing P.M. again, reads bits to me and we fight like blazes over it, he is so often beside the point 'but "I'll learn him to be a toad" as the boy said as he stamped on the toad'.
(Frieda Weekley, to Edward Garnett, 7 September 1912)

I hasten to tell you I sent the MS. of the Paul Morel novel to Duckworth, registered, yesterday. And I want to defend it, quick.

I wrote it again, pruning it and shaping it and filling it in. I tell you it has got form—*form:* haven't I made it patiently, out of sweat as well as blood. It follows this idea: a woman of character and refinement goes into the lower class, and has no satisfaction in her own life. She has had a passion for her husband, so the children are born of passion, and have heaps of vitality. But as her sons grow up she selects them as lovers—first the eldest, then the second. These sons are *urged* into life by their reciprocal love of their mother—urged on and on. But when they come to manhood, they can't love, because their mother is the strongest power in their lives, and holds them.—It's rather like Goethe and his mother and Frau von Stein and Christiana—. As soon as the young men come into contact with women, there's a split. William gives his sex to a fribble, and his mother holds his soul. But the split kills him, because he doesn't know where he is. The next son gets a woman who fights for his soul—fights his mother. The son loves the mother—all the sons hate and are jealous of the father. The battle goes on between the mother and the girl, with the son as object. The mother gradually proves stronger, because of the tie of blood. The son decides to leave his soul in his mother's hands, and, like his elder brother, go for passion. He gets passion. Then the split begins to tell again. But, almost unconsciously, the mother realises what is the matter, and begins to die. The son casts off his mistress, attends to his mother dying. He is left in the end naked of everything, with the drift towards death.

It is a great tragedy, and I tell you I've written a great book. It's the tragedy of thousands of young men in England . . . Now tell me if I haven't worked out my theme, like life, but always my theme. Read my novel—it's a great novel. If *you* can't see the development—which is slow like growth—I can.
(To Edward Garnett, 19 November 1912)

I also feel as if I ought to say something about L.s formlessness. I dont think he has 'no form'; I used to. But now I think anybody must see in Paul Morel the hang of it. The mother is really the

thread, the domineering note, I think the honesty, the vividness of a book suffers if you subject it to 'form'.
(Frieda Weekley, to Edward Garnett, 19 November 1912)

Pray to your Gods for me that *Sons and Lovers* shall succeed. People *should* begin to take me seriously now. And I do so break my heart over England, when I read the *New Machiavelli* [a novel by H. G. Wells]. And I am so sure that only through a re-adjustment between men and women, and a making free and healthy of the sex, will she get out of her present atrophy. Oh Lord, and if I don't 'subdue my art to a metaphysic', as somebody very beautifully said of Hardy, I do write because I want folk—English folk—to alter, and have more sense.
(To Arthur McLeod, 23 April 1913)

You must continue to believe in me—I don't mean in my talent only—because I depend on you a bit. One doesn't know, till one is a bit at odds with the world, how much one's friends who believe in one rather generously, mean to one.—I felt you had gone off from me a bit, because of *Sons and Lovers.* But one sheds ones sicknesses in books—repeats and presents again ones emotions, to be master of them.
(To Arthur McLeod, 26 October 1913)

In a few days time I shall send you the first half of the Sisters— which I should rather call The Wedding Ring [an early version of a project which produced *The Rainbow* and *Women in Love*]—to Duckworths. It is *very* different from *Sons and Lovers.* written in another language almost. I shall be sorry if you don't like it, but am prepared.—I shan't write in the same manner as *Sons and Lovers* again, I think: in that hard, violent style full of sensation and presentation. You must see what you think of the new style.
(To Edward Garnett, 30 December 1913)

"A Restrained, *Somewhat* Impersonal Novel"

MICHAEL BELL

◆　◆　◆

THE RECURRENT PROBLEM raised by *Sons and Lovers* is whether it should be seen as the last novel of Lawrence's apprenticeship or the first of his maturity. I put it in this way to suggest that disagreements on this novel will frequently involve differing perceptions of 'mature' Lawrence as much as differing judgements of the work itself. It is not my intention to rehearse the history of criticism with respect to *Sons and Lovers*, but its peculiar critical elusiveness and the related difficulty of placing it within Lawrence's *œuvre*, are in themselves a significant clue to the reading of Lawrence more generally. It is principally in this light that I wish to reconsider what it is about *Sons and Lovers* that has made it such a difficult case.

The White Peacock and *The Trespasser* kept their biographical implications at arm's length. Their respective techniques of first person narration and flashback are to a significant extent distancing devices whereby biographical concerns are expressed without becoming the central and direct focus. *Sons and Lovers* was the first of Lawrence's novels in which a motive of self-understanding became paramount. In this book Lawrence gave fictional expression to the intense relationship with his own mother which had, in its possessiveness, checked his capacity in early manhood, or before meeting Frieda Weekley, to give himself fully to another woman. As is well known, the figure of Miriam Leivers is closely based on his own girlfriend of adolescence, Jessie Chambers. The invented figure of Clara Dawes broadens the implications by showing Paul Morel's 'failure' with two quite different women. The broadening of implication is crucial. Lawrence is seeking to understand the emotional impasse of his early life partly by seeing it in a representative light as is signalled particularly by the last-minute change of title from *Paul Morel* to *Sons and Lovers.* The highly personal material of the work necessitated, as Lawrence recognised, a correspondingly impersonal treatment. Hence his remark that it would be 'a restrained, *somewhat* impersonal novel'.[1] The critical difficulty with *Sons and Lovers* concerns how, and how effectively, it has achieved that aim: in particular, the extent to which the book makes Miriam the scapegoat for what is really Paul's emotional block. But the further importance of this question for the present argument is that it bears upon Lawrence's growing recognition of an impersonal dimension in the life of feeling; a recognition which is crucial to his mature metaphysic.

It should be said at once that a significant difficulty for all readers trying to come to terms with this book lies in the vivid success of so much of it. There is no doubt of its local quality. And there is as usual some consciousness within the novel of the question of representation and one of Paul's remarks on his painting is often rightly quoted as indicating an important quality of Lawrence's best writing at all times.

> "the shimmering protoplasm in the leaves and everywhere, and not the stiffness of the shape. That seems dead to me. Only this shimmeriness is the real living. The shape is a dead crust. The shimmer is inside, really." (183)

This points to the quality in Lawrence's narrative prose which has been variously compared to the impressionists and to van

Gogh. He seems to respond not so much to the 'thing' as to the movement of life in the thing. *Sons and Lovers* is already full of writing which magnificently answers to this description. Yet it may be significant that Paul's remarks here relate to the spatial medium of painting rather than to the temporal medium of narrative. For the critical argument over *Sons and Lovers* concerns not the existence of this ability but the larger use to which it is put. If there is some tendentiousness about the work as a whole this is manifest at the level of strategic narrative control rather than of moment by moment description. This is not a novel in which we hear two voices; but that, many have alleged, is precisely its problem. Is there not a suppressed Miriam voice whose story represents a crucial part of the truth about Paul?

In that respect, the more pertinent instances of self-consciousness about representation in the book are those which bear upon questions of story-telling. Paul's father, Mr Morel, loves to tell stories to his children:

> "Tell us about down-pit, Daddy."
> This Morel loved to do.
> "Well, there's one little 'oss, we call 'im Taffy," he would begin. "An' he's a fawce un!"
> Morel had a warm way of telling a story. He made one feel Taffy's cunning. (89)

It is no bad epitome of the inextricable truth and tendentiousness of *Sons and Lovers* that the usually inarticulate Morel, who comes so badly out of the novel as a whole despite sympathetic moments such as this, should be its best story-teller. He 'made one feel Taffy's cunning' would be a good summary of the quality most to be prized in the best of Lawrence's own writing of all kinds. It is a capacity to intuit and transmit the life in other things without possession or interference. Morel has no idea or purpose in his story other than to convey a quality of being and relationship. The 'happy evenings' when he was able to enjoy this present relationship with his children occurred only when he 'had some job to do'. Morel's story-telling, that is to say, depends upon his present absorption in an activity as well as implying an earlier responsiveness to the experience being narrated. And, of course, his almost complete inarticulacy with regard to the intellectual and introspective realms effectively protects him from being anything other than a warm medium for the narration. Lawrence has more complex purposes in his story-telling but these purposes are ultimately underwritten by his capacity for a comparable absorption, his freedom from self, in the face of other beings. Precisely because he is not an articulate man generally, Morel points us to a value often obscured by the complex ambitions of Lawrence's mature fiction. *Sons and Lovers,* especially in its first half, provides abundant examples of this essential Lawrentian quality: experience re-created with an emotional participation so full as to seem simply to yield the object itself. His writing has shed the literariness of his two previous novels and has become capable of what Jessie Chambers called 'his seemingly effortless translation of life'. As she says, 'He did not distinguish between small and great happenings; the common round was full of mystery awaiting interpretation.'[2]

This is a rather different way of looking at the feckless lack of will that Mrs Morel, and Paul, see in Morel. Although Paul finally begins to come to terms with the rough masculinity of his father as displaced on to Baxter Dawes, the estranged husband of his lover, Clara, there are other things he might still have learned from Morel. For the book contains another important story-teller in the figure of Paul himself and when this is presented dramatically at one point it contrasts sharply with Morel's warmth and truth. In the chapter 'Defeat of Miriam' Paul entertains the Leivers family with his imitation of local Methodist preachers.

> He sat at the head of the table, his mobile face, with the eyes that could be so beautiful, shining with tenderness or dancing with laughter, now taking on one expression and then another, in imitation of various people he was mocking. His mockery always hurt her—it was too near the reality. He was too clever and cruel. She felt that when his eyes were like this, hard with mocking hate, he would spare neither himself nor anybody

else. But . . . Mr Leivers, just awake from his Sunday nap, was rubbing his head in amusement. (256)

This incident occurs just after an episode in which, unbeknown to the rest of the family, Paul has been harsh to Miriam. Although the perception here is through Miriam's mixture of love and hurt, the negative comment on Paul is not unfair. Paul is using a genuine ability to get inside the figures in question but he is indeed 'using' it. And Miriam is aware, as the others are not, that he is entertaining her family at this moment primarily as a way of excluding her and covering his own awkwardness. His act of narration, like his relation to the subjects of it, is a subtle 'using' of them rather than a disinterested or loving participation. Paul's story-telling here is some way from the Lawrentian principle that 'even satire is a form of sympathy'.[3] It is not the making of fun, even to the point of satire, that is in question so much as the underlying relationship with the subject and the design on the audience.

But if Paul is an important story-teller in the book at large, it is not because of an occasional incident such as this. It is because the Paul perceived by Miriam here as sparing 'neither himself nor anybody else' is effectively entrusted with a considerable part of the narrative viewpoint in *Sons and Lovers*. In this sense the book does indeed have, if not two competing voices, then a divided voice within its formally single narration. Much of the book, particularly in the first part, comes from the voice that can make you 'feel Taffy's cunning' while the latter part uses Paul's viewpoint in a way that has seemed to many readers to give it a tendentious undertow of self-vindication. From this point of view the very power of the narrative, as with Paul's accurate mimicry, makes it more, rather than less, disturbing.

The critical difficulty to which this gives rise is well illustrated in the episode just quoted, for it actually allows us to analyse what is wrong with Paul even while it exemplifies the effective working of his viewpoint in the narrative. For Miriam rightly puts her finger on the way his 'cruelty' is directed at himself as much as at others. If the book is distorted it is not by any simple self-vindicatory projection of Paul's problems on to others. It is hard on him too. But this is part of the problem, for equality of hardness is not the same as a steady, disinterested vision. On the contrary, it can disguise more essential distortions beneath an apparent even-handedness. And so, in the present passage, our awareness of Miriam's hurt partially encourages us to relativise and discount the true force of her perception of him. It has a ventriloquial effect ultimately reinforcing the governing perspective of Paul/Lawrence. Hence the critique has been made but its final effect, for some readers, is equivocally pre-emptive and defensive.

The characteristic elusiveness of *Sons and Lovers,* as exemplified in this episode, has been the subject of much published discussion in which the two most sophisticated readings are tantalisingly close while remaining crucially opposed. Both readings invoke Lawrence's mature fiction as a way of assessing *Sons and Lovers* and come up with opposite judgements. The positive case has been put by Louis Martz. He indicates how all the evidence we need for understanding Paul is put into the novel so that we can in effect trust the tale if not the teller. Lawrence was struggling towards an understanding, was 'shedding his sickness' in a creative way, so that much of the maturer understanding has got into the book dramatically if not as a clear personal perception of the author at the time. The opposite case has been put most strongly by J. C. F. Littlewood.[4] For Littlewood, the crucial value in Lawrence is precisely his capacity for an unobstructed, enhancing responsiveness to all forms of life. Hence, while seeing the local power and truth of the narrative, and the existence of the contrary evidence within the book, Littlewood is concerned with the governing spirit of the whole. By the standards of what he values in the mature Lawrence, Littlewood finds *Sons and Lovers* still too trammelled by personal motive. The outcome includes an idealising of the mother figure which actually obscures her real strength and her corresponding significance for the development of her son. And likewise, he argues, although Jessie Chambers's memoir may not always have distinguished the interests of art from those of biography, her objections have more critical substance than has often been allowed. In fact, Littlewood insists, her objections with respect to the treatment of Miriam were not just to personal 'betrayal', which would indeed be irrelevant artistically, but to Lawrence's artistic betrayal of himself. The problems are not just between the book and the life; they are actually in the book.

Littlewood makes his case with some vehemence partly because he sees the more positive reading as a lazy readiness to be beguiled by the book; a readiness which signals a failure to appreciate the true value of Lawrence's mature genius. His account is vulnerable in detail partly because it was based on the then available published version of the novel, from which Garnett had removed substantial and highly relevant episodes, rather than the manuscript version which was subsequently published.[5] None the less, Littlewood's critique seems to me essentially right. One should not confuse Lawrence's still partial struggle towards an impersonal understanding with his later achievements in that regard. But my reason for rehearsing the arguments here is to indicate how the dramatised struggle in *Sons and Lovers* is such a fatally close simulation of the mature narrative method. It is so close that these two readings of the novel can occupy almost the same space while standing on opposite sides of their mutual watershed so that the argument takes on at times a quasi-theological fineness.

We can see the mature Lawrentian method forming itself in *Sons and Lovers.* In order to dramatise a long-term and deep-lying emotional process, he exploits its moments of intensity or crisis, which are often locally reactive, and therefore misleading if taken in isolation. The significance of such moments is to be found in their transience and subjectivity rather than through some average or generalised meaning. He has to embody the emotional material dramatically while avoiding a fixed point of view. Hence his method of third-person omniscience at the service of the character's emotional subjectivity. In the work for which he is important, Lawrence's need to relativise the point of view has equal priority with his doctrinal and prophetic absoluteness. For his relativity is not just between characters but between moments and impulses within the same character. With hindsight we can

appreciate how the highly 'subjective' local use of Paul's perception in *Sons and Lovers* was to provide the method for an impersonal
dramatisation of long-term emotional processes in his later fiction. But the novel itself does not consistently generate that sec-
ondary understanding of its immediate action. The novel records,
often in a penetrating and impressive way, the emotional process
as experienced *by* Paul but does not quite communicate the process itself.

I take it that the underlying reason for this, even apart from
Lawrence's biographical involvement, is that the nature of the
emotional process in question was still not fully clear to him.
Most importantly, the struggle for an impersonal understanding
of feeling was inextricable from an understanding of feeling as
impersonal. The book hovers on the brink in this respect too. It
contains passages which seem to answer to Lawrence's mature
'metaphysic' of impersonal feeling yet, as with the disinterested-
ness of the narrative handling, there is an uncertainty as to the
overall vision to which they belong.

One such memorable episode is the pregnant Mrs Morel's
night scene in the garden after being shut out by her husband.

The moon was high and magnificent in the August night. Mrs
Morel, seared with passion, shivered to find herself out there
in a great, white light, that fell cold on her, and gave a shock
to her inflamed soul. She stood for a few moments helplessly
staring at the glistening great rhubarb leaves near the door.
Then she got the air into her breast. She walked down the
garden path, trembling in every limb, while the child boiled
within her. For a while, she could not control her consciousness; mechanically she went over the last scene, then over it
again, certain phrases, certain moments coming each time like
a brand red hot, down on her soul: and each time she enacted
again the past hour, each time the brand came down at the
same points, till the mark was burnt in, and the pain burnt
out, and at last she came to herself. She must have been half
an hour in this delirious condition. Then the presence of the
night came again to her. She glanced round in fear. She had

wandered to the side garden, where she was walking up and down the path beside the currant bushes under the long wall. The garden was a narrow strip, bounded from the road that cut transversely between the blocks, by a thick thorn hedge.

She hurried out of the side garden to the front, where she could stand as if in an immense gulf of white light, the moon streaming high in face of her, the moonlight standing up from the hills in front, and filling the valley where the Bottoms crouched, almost blindingly. There, panting and half weeping in reaction from the stress, she murmured to herself over and again: "The nuisance!—the nuisance!"

She became aware of something about her. With an effort, she roused herself, to see what it was that penetrated her consciousness. The tall white lilies were reeling in the moonlight, and the air was charged with their perfume, as with a presence. Mrs Morel gasped slightly in fear. She touched the big, pallid flowers on their petals, then shivered. They seemed to be stretching in the moonlight. She put her hand into one white bin: the gold scarcely showed on her fingers by moonlight. She bent down, to look at the bin-ful of yellow pollen: but it only appeared dusky. Then she drank a deep draught of the scent. It almost made her dizzy.

She looked round her. The privet hedge had a faint glitter among its blackness. Various white flowers were out. In front, the hill rose into indistinctness, barred by high black hedges, and nervous with cattle moving in the dim moonlight. Here and there the moonlight seemed to stir and ripple.

Mrs Morel leaned on the garden gate, looking out, and she lost herself awhile. She did not know what she thought. Except for a slight feeling of sickness, and her consciousness in the child, her self melted out like scent into the shiny, pale air. After a time, the child too melted with her in the mixing-pot of moonlight, and she rested with the hills and lilies and houses, all swum together in a kind of swoon.

When she came to herself, she was tired for sleep. Languidly, she looked about her; the clumps of white phlox seemed like bushes spread with linen; a moth ricochetted over them, and

right across the garden. Following it with her eye roused her.
A few whiffs of the raw strong scent of phlox invigorated her.
She passed along the path hesitating at the white rose-bush. It
smelled sweet and simple. She touched the white ruffles of the
roses. Their fresh scent and cool, soft leaves reminded her of
the morning-time and sunshine. She was very fond of them.
But she was tired and wanted to sleep. In the mysterious out-
of-doors she felt forlorn.

There was no noise anywhere. Evidently the children had
not been wakened, or had gone to sleep again. A train, three
miles away, roared across the valley. The night was very large,
and very strange, stretching its hoary distances infinitely. And
out of the silver-grey fog of darkness came sounds vague and
hoarse: a corncrake not far off, sound of a train like a sigh,
and distant shouts of men. (33–35)

This passage must be a common stand-by for introducing students to Lawrence. The prose puts itself at the disposal of Mrs
Morel's experience here with poetic precision and fullness. But
the exemplary value of this passage is of a more specific kind, for
the emotional process undergone by Mrs Morel enacts a paradigmatic Lawrentian structure in her loss and recovery of wholeness.
The characteristic starting point of Lawrence's fiction is a passional
crisis. It is not just that there is something wrong in the character's life, but that the character feels this to be so. And Lawrence
will then follow the repetitions, reactions and blind alleys in the
resulting emotional struggle. It is not surprising, therefore, that
such extended crises are often highly complex both in themselves
and in their circumstantial forms. The value of the present passage in this respect lies in its condensed completeness as a paradigm for more complex, and hence potentially misreadable, experiences elsewhere. The features I have in mind are briefly the
following.

At the beginning of the passage Mrs Morel is unable to cope
either with her external circumstances or, more importantly, with
her own feelings. Specifically, it is her mind, her conscious will,

that cannot cope and which is reduced to a mechanism spinning out of control. The subsequent paragraphs then trace a rhythmic series, or a cyclic repetition, whereby the same elements acquire a constantly modified value in her response. In broad terms she moves from helpless passivity to a controlled poise but in such a way as to dissolve the distinction between active and passive. Recovery of self is through a loss of self.

When she is first really conscious of the outside world at all it is only as a 'presence' invoking a vague fear and focused in the dazzling light of the moon. When she eventually becomes 'aware of something about her' it is because it has now actively 'penetrated her consciousness' as the lilies appear to be 'stretching in the moonlight'. The world first comes to her rather than she to it. At this point there is still something automatic and reactive about her response, although it has an increasing inwardness as her sensory attention moves in turn through sight, touch and smell until she merges oceanically with the night environment; a moment in which it would be hard to distinguish a despairing abnegation of self from positive pleasure in floating with the whole. When she comes round from this 'swoon' her mood, and her capacity, are very different. The same senses of sight, touch and smell govern her response but in a different order and to a contrary effect. Smell, rather than being the point of merging with the whole, is now the stimulus to a distinctive attention. Her newly active and discriminating responsiveness is caught through the use of simile. The phlox 'seemed like bushes spread with linen'. It is not just the homely and appropriate nature of the simile here, although that does bear upon the way she eventually returns to the house and her domestic chores by the end of the episode. It is rather that the use of simile at all, as attributed to Mrs Morel's consciousness at this point, catches her newly recovered poise. The simple declarative sentences of the final brief paragraph catch the escape from self. The largeness of the world is experienced here with a new sense of wonder as she is freed not only from emotional pain but from its attendant self-preoccupation. The final note is one of return to social, as well as natural, relatedness. This moment anticipates the ending of the novel, in which Paul also turns in the night of his despair towards the 'faintly humming, glowing town'.

I have suggested that the usefulness of this episode as an introduction to Lawrence lies in its paradigmatic completeness. Depictions of passional struggle in his fiction have often misled readers by their concentration upon a single momentary phase such as rejection, swooning or submission which is then taken to be a Lawrentian emotional ideal. Here, by contrast, it is abundantly evident that Mrs Morel's moment of oceanic swooning, for example, is not a value in itself nor in any way the culmination of the emotional process. It is a necessary phase in her final recovery of herself and therefore stands in significant contrast to the romantic merging with the world seen in *The Trespasser.* She regains her personal poise because she is able to open herself to something other than her immediately conscious will.

To what extent that something is outside her, or is 'really' inside her but symbolically embodied in the environment, and if so whether by her or by Lawrence, is impossible to say; these distinctions have all been elided. Not only is she opened to something beyond her conscious will, it is not even a decision of the will to do so. This controlled elision is crucial to Lawrence's mature dramatisation of feeling. In the present case he offers a psychological equivalent to the traditional religious truth that it is sometimes necessary to lose your soul in order to gain it or to die in order to live. This is very different from the simple rejection of 'mind' that is still amazingly attributed to him by readers invoking against him the very dualism he of all people has radically exposed as in itself an alienated, mental projection. The Cartesian categories dissolve as he renders the inextricability of inner and outer in the life of feeling.

Hence, the first step towards understanding 'impersonality' in the domain of feeling is to recognise the questionable nature of the personal ego to which it stands in implicit contrast. Both Heidegger and Lawrence would claim that the inextricable experience of 'being in a world' has been reified by culture and language into the conventional dualism of self as distinct from the world. If the reification of aspects—seeing an aspect as a self-standing whole—is the complementary error to failing to see them at all, then this is a case of what Wittgenstein called 'aspect blindness' on a massive scale.[6] What is at stake in emotional 'impersonality', then, is a dissolution of this dualism; for the dualism has in itself enormous emotional consequences. Only under extreme shock has Mrs Morel been driven to the eventually healing loss of her mental grip on her 'self' so that the life of feeling can assert its own, more sophisticated, ontology.

But the very fact that the episode has such an exemplary, and conveniently isolable, value may give us pause from another point of view. How precisely does it fit into the larger context of *Sons and Lovers*? Some critics have seen in *Sons and Lovers* intimations of a later metaphysic of feeling which transcend, perhaps even contradict, their context in this novel. If this is such a passage the question is a delicate one. For there is no question as to its narrative and thematic pertinence. What is at stake is how far this episode is consistent with the range and depth of Mrs Morel's emotional nature as seen more generally in the book. Of course, this is a younger figure than the embittered woman of Paul's adolescence; and the young Mrs Morel has a well-established responsiveness to flowers and the natural world. Hence, if she evinces an unusual depth of response while under a special pressure and while she is turned away from her husband, that makes good psychological sense as an indication of the potential self that is repressed within the marriage. Yet, at the same time, it is as if the momentary shaking-off of the husband figure were releasing something in Lawrence's imagination too; partly on Mrs Morel's behalf and partly triggered by her. Indeed, the vivid opening of this passage suggests something of Lawrence's own peculiar sensitivity to the moon as recorded by Jessie Chambers in her memoir, and as shown in the later episode on the Lincolnshire coast, whereas what we otherwise see of Mrs Morel suggests someone whose personal will-power makes her more radically repressive than is suggested by this episode.[7]

In its way of standing slightly outside the general drift of the characterisation, this passage is comparable to the description of

Mr Morel's story-telling. In contrast with the diminishing or displacement of this question in *The White Peacock,* Lawrence is now engaging with the emotional significance of his own parents. But his vision of this is not yet steady and whole, so that their true meaning comes through in *Sons and Lovers* rather fitfully and against the conscious grain of the book. Perhaps one reason for this unsteady perception is that the true strengths of his parents are beginning to be internalised as elements of Lawrence's own metaphysic and are then being attributed back on to the parents in a slightly piecemeal way. In other words, a traditional way of looking at the uncertain focus with which the rounded evidence of the narrative is presented, is to see an authorial *parti pris* qualified by a richer, and perhaps less conscious, responsiveness. But part of the reason for resisting this interpretation has always been the sense that the qualifying presentation, as in the Mr Morel passage, seems anything but unconscious. It may be more useful to understand the uncertain focus as arising from the way the parental figures themselves are now being seen in the light of an ontological vision which is beginning to transcend them but is not yet fully independent of them. The son's deepest response to his parents is to assimilate their truly positive qualities into himself. As he does so he becomes less Paul Morel and more D. H. Lawrence. On this reading, the equivocal relation between Paul and the author has two aspects. While the author undoubtedly has some self-vindicatory interest in Paul, Paul is at the same time the figure through whom Lawrence is struggling towards a more impersonal metaphysic of feeling and of narration.

In the latter part of the book there is a more crucial incident which has long attracted comment along the same lines as I have suggested in the Mrs Morel episode. This is the sexual consummation of Paul and Clara out in the open field. It ends as follows:

> He lifted his head and looked into her eyes. They were dark and shining and strange, life wild at the source staring into his life, stranger to him, yet meeting him. And he put his face down on her throat, afraid. What was she. A strong, strange,

wild life, that breathed with his in the darkness through this hour. It was all so much bigger than themselves, that he was hushed. They had met, and included in their meeting the thrust of the manifold grass stems, the cry of the peewit, the wheel of the stars. (398)

Littlewood has commented on the inconsistency of this episode in the Clara relationship; an inconsistency which is commonly obscured, he suggests, by the reader's unconsciously anticipating the concerns of, and recognitions of, *The Rainbow*.[8] The passional transcendence of self experienced here by Paul, and possibly Clara, is fundamental to the later novel, as is the image of the 'stranger' focusing the otherness to which the relationship gives access. Yet the moment is hard to place satisfactorily in relation to the generally 'derelict' drift of Paul's life in the latter part of the novel. Now, once again, the book does offer an explanation of the relationship which accommodates both aspects. As a young man with a passionate but frustrated nature Paul might well have genuine intimations of such passional transcendence with a woman to whom he is ultimately not suited. Ursula Brangwen has such moments with Anton Skrebensky and Lawrence is certainly at pains to show the gradual recognition on the part of Paul and Clara that the experience they each want cannot truly be found in the other. Indeed the immediate aftermath of the present encounter is a narrative elaboration of this radical flaw in their relationship. None the less, it seems to me that Littlewood was essentially right to see the episode as in some measure transcending its narrative context. In view of Paul's later reaction to the experience, we may wonder whether the touch of cliché in 'It was all so much bigger than themselves' is a deliberately dramatised emptiness underlying Paul's desire or an authorial straining after an authentic experience not quite justified by the relationship. It is indicative, at least, that this phrase occurs at the moment of transition between Paul's viewpoint, which would support the first reading, and an apparent attribution to both of them which would support the second. Another way of putting the point in relation to the present theme would be to say that, however we read it in detail, the 'impersonal' dimension of this experience is ambivalently perceived.

For indeed, the word 'impersonal' occurs centrally in the subsequent account of Paul's reaction to this moment.

> After that, the fire slowly went down. He felt more and more that his experience had been impersonal, and not Clara. He loved her. There was a big tenderness, as after a strong emotion they had known together. But it was not she who could keep his soul steady. He had wanted her to be something she could not be. (399)

Here Lawrence uses the term in its normal market-place sense, with a negative implication and in opposition to the 'personal' in Clara. This properly reflects the mismatch between Paul's sexual need, which is not fundamentally related to Clara, and her personal love for him by which she generously gives herself despite her recognition of his ultimate unavailability. But this is not the way Lawrence would later come to use the word 'impersonal'. And his later use would see an essential value in precisely that intuition of strangeness which is now being dismissed as 'impersonal'. In its later implication it transfigures the personal. It dissolves the ego and gives the resulting openness to the other an annealment by passion. In that view, the 'impersonal' represents precisely the one quality that 'could keep his soul steady'. In his present analysis, by contrast, Lawrence seems to be defining Paul's feeling within a view of passional possibilities pretty much identical with Paul's own. Hence, if there is indeed some authorial equivocation, as well as a properly dramatised ambivalence, with regard to the authenticity of Paul's passional experience with Clara, it is reflected in an uncertainty about the significance of such passional experience generally and is specifically focused in the term 'impersonal'.

In this connection it is indicative that their earlier relationship has been developed in a chapter entitled 'Passion', for the analysis of the relationship rests, as has just been seen, upon a separation of the impersonality of his passionate experience from the kind of personal love felt, and sought, by Clara. It is, of course, Paul's misfortune that his mother will allow him to give only his sexuality, and not his self, to another woman. The division is imposed on him, and the vivid, chilling presentation of this psychic predicament is the central, great achievement of the novel. But Lawrence's language seems also to imply at times an authorial endorsement of this dualising of self and sexuality.

In his later, very telling, critique of John Galsworthy, Lawrence derided the idea of 'passion' in Galsworthy for its naively generalised opposition to 'social' existence in his characters.[9] In effect, Galsworthy's hand-me-down romanticism amounts to the now familiar middle-brow reduction of Lawrence, and the vigour with which the later Lawrence attacked this hypostatisation of 'passion' may partly derive from his having once been tempted to his own equivalent of it. For when it is conceived in this way as too simply oppositional to the personal and the social, 'passion' becomes an undifferentiated *Ding an sich*. It is then like the social or psychological generalisations already referred to in *The White Peacock*, and still residually present in *Sons and Lovers*, which appear to explain while really obfuscating. The mature Lawrence was to devote much of his career precisely to discriminations within this difficult domain, but at this point the appeal to 'passion' suggests some uncertainty about the metaphysic within which the emotional complex is being seen. In the light of Lawrence's later usage, his positive use of the word 'passion', and his negative use of 'impersonality', both suggest the uncertainty of his present understanding in this domain.

In both these passages the characters have an emotional experience in which their immediately personal self-concern is dissolved in a restorative impersonality. For the later Lawrence such experiences, while not necessarily normative in the sense of being frequent occurrences, are importantly so in the sense of their potentially continuing effect on the everyday self. They establish the order of significances within which the common business of living is conducted. In *Sons and Lovers* these moments do not seem to have this continued working in the psyche nor do they seem to constitute an ultimate frame of reference. And when the question of 'impersonality' is made explicit in the Clara episode, it is precisely for the purpose of denying it such a significance. But the slightly ambiguous or occasional value accorded to such moments in *Sons and Lovers* allows us to focus another aspect of impersonality. For Lawrence's sense of impersonality as an implicit ontological standpoint has implications for the author as well as for the characters.

In the episode with Mrs Morel, for example, there is a remarkable consonance between the recovery of self attained by her capacity to let herself go and the escape from authorial will by which this experience is created for us. Indeed, curiously enough, it is the recurrent authorial idealising that most reinforces our sense of Mrs Morel's emotional repression in the novel at large whereas the episode in the garden releases her by its impersonality. The husband is naturally a factor in her situation and feeling but there is no *narrative* animus against him. Neither in personal nor in narrative terms is she being defined merely in opposition to him. Indeed, the impressiveness of the passage lies in the way she re-establishes herself cosmically rather than in terms of the relationship.

This points to an important further dimension of the question to which Lawrence is still partly feeling his way in *Sons and Lovers.* Artistic impersonality in Lawrence is not an authorial posture that can be consciously applied, as it were on principle, or as a willed technique, to a given body of material. It is rather an ontological sustaining of otherness, albeit within an imaginary arena, which cannot be a neutral or indifferent act although it results in the maximum freedom of the created life. The model for this conception of authorship would be the traditional Christian God rather than the Flaubertian atheist's god invoked by Joyce's Stephen Dedalus as 'indifferent, paring his fingernails'.[10] The Christian mystery, leaving aside Calvinism, is that God sustains in being creatures who have free will. As Lawrence developed his impersonal ontology of feeling it involved, whether by parallel understanding or by some more profound identity in the creative process, a corresponding narrative quality. This is what Lawrence meant by speaking of the impersonality of Giovanni Verga as different from, and incomparably more important than, the Flaubertian preoccupation.[11] Indeed, the Flaubertian emphasis in much modern literature on impersonality as achieved through 'technique' is often precisely the symptom of an anxiety, or inadequacy, with regard to a genuinely impersonal relation to the subject.[12]

In *Sons and Lovers* Lawrence has not quite sorted out what impersonality means to him, although he seems on the verge of doing so, and this is reflected in the swervings from impersonality in his handling of the narrative itself. By the same token, his uncertainties and swervings in this regard lead us to meditate on the inextricability of emotional impersonality and artistic handling. There is indeed another parenthetic use of the same term which suggests Lawrence's groping recognition of its implication from the specifically artistic point of view. Paul's manner constantly exacerbates the antagonism between himself and Baxter Dawes. At one point we are told of Baxter how

Finding the lad's impersonal, deliberate gaze of an artist on his face, he got into a fury. (224)

As with the Miriam passage quoted above, this is a telling reflection on the less attractive side of Paul. Of course, he is a different kind of artist to the novelist and his impersonality is not necessarily Lawrence's. Yet we cannot but sense in the phrasing, 'gaze of an artist', a generic claim that reaches out, in some sense, to encompass the writer. Lawrence is clearly thinking of impersonality here in its aspect of necessary detachment rather than as a sustaining fullness of feeling *vis à vis* the other. This, indeed, echoes his remark quoted at the head of this essay: 'a restrained, *somewhat* impersonal novel'. He sees that the impersonal quality of the novel is vital, yet presents it in its negative dimension as a near-synonym for 'restraint'; something closer to the Flaubertian conception of withdrawal. The ambivalence here parallels that of the Clara episode. In that case the experience seemed good at the time but the word was then used retrospectively to dismiss it, whereas in the letter Lawrence uses the term honorifically while glossing it negatively. He seems to have intuited a crucial significance, emotionally and artistically, in the term 'impersonality', and this concern is creeping into the book as a thematically conscious one; but at this point its full meaning in either realm, and therefore in the mutuality of these realms, still escapes him.

Hence, the problems and strengths of *Sons and Lovers* can be viewed either in terms of Lawrence's struggle for self-knowledge or as part of an implicit search for his metaphysic both emotionally and artistically. The object is the same but the implications are different. The latter formulation points more clearly into the future and gives a more positive value to the local shifts and uncertainties of the book. For these, far from being simple weaknesses of the novel, were to prove the basis for Lawrence's mature artistic method. Hence the critical elusiveness of *Sons and Lovers* and the special temptations it presents for readers with an appreciation of the later Lawrence. The fictional principle to which we can now see Lawrence to have been feeling his way in *Sons and Lovers* was an ambitious and vulnerable one. It is hardly surprising that he was not fully and immediately successful in this attempt, but considered in this light the novel puts us in the position to appreciate more inwardly the achievement of the mature works which were to follow.

Notes

1. *The Letters of D. H. Lawrence*, Volume I, ed. James T. Boulton (Cambridge: Cambridge University Press, 1979), 184.

2. Jessie Chambers, *D. H. Lawrence: A Personal Record by 'E.T.'* (London: Jonathan Cape, 1935), 198.

3. D. H. Lawrence, *Lady Chatterley's Lover*, ed. Michael Squires (Cambridge: Cambridge University Press, 1993), 101.

4. Louis L. Martz, 'Portrait of Miriam: A Study in the Design of *Sons and Lovers*', in *Imagined Worlds: Essays on Some English Novels and Novelists in Honour of John Butt*, eds. Maynard Mack and Ian Gregor (London: Methuen,

1968), 343–69; J. C. F. Littlewood, 'Son and Lover', *The Cambridge Quarterly* (autumn–winter 1969–70), 323–61.

5. *'Sons and Lovers': A Facsimile of the Manuscript*, ed. Mark Schorer (Berkeley: University of California Press, 1977). See particularly the episodes of literary and intellectual discussion between Paul and Miriam, 227–30, 277, 292.

6. L. Wittgenstein, *Philosophical Investigations*, trans. G. E. M. Anscombe (Oxford: Basil Blackwell, 1958), 213–14.

7. *D. H. Lawrence: A Personal Record by 'E.T.'*, 127–28. See also Lawrence's comments on the moon in *Apocalypse*, in *Apocalypse and the Writings on Revelation*, ed. Mara Kalnins (Cambridge: Cambridge University Press, 1980), 77.

8. Littlewood, 'Son and Lover', 344.

9. 'What was there *besides* Forsytes in all the wide human world? Mr Galsworthy looked, and found nothing. Strictly and truly, after his frightened search, he had found nothing. But he came back with Irene and Bosinney, and offered us that. Here! He seems to say. Here is the anti-Forsyte! Here! Here you have it! Love! Passion! PASSION.' D. H. Lawrence, 'John Galsworthy', in *Study of Thomas Hardy and Other Essays*, ed. Bruce Steele (Cambridge: Cambridge University Press, 1985), 214. Lawrence's changing conception of passion can be seen in his letter to Frieda of 15 May 1912: 'It's a funny thing, to feel one's passion—sex desire—no longer a sort of wandering thing, but steady, and calm. I think, when one loves, one's very sex passion becomes calm, a steady sort of force, instead of a storm. Passion, that nearly drives one mad, is far away from real love. I am realising things I never thought to realise.' *Letters*, I, 403.

10. James Joyce, *A Portrait of the Artist as a Young Man*, ed. Richard Ellman (New York: Viking, 1964), 215.

11. 'But Verga was caught up by the grand idea of self-effacement in art. Anything more confused, more silly, really, than the pages prefacing the excellent story *Gramigna's Lover*, would be hard to find, from the pen of a great writer. The moment Verga starts talking theories, our interest wilts immediately. The theories were none of his own: just borrowed from the literary smarties of Paris. And poor Verga looks a sad sight in Paris ready-mades. And when he starts putting his theories into practice, and effacing himself, one is far more aware of his interference than when he just goes ahead. Naturally! Because self-effacement is of course self-conscious, and any form of emotional self-consciousness hinders a

first-rate artist: though it may help the second-rate.' *'Cavalleria Rusticana by Giovanni Verga'*, in D. H. Lawrence, *Introductions and Reviews*, eds. N. H. Reeve and John Worthen (Cambridge: Cambridge University Press, 2005), 171.

   12. Since this fundamental, but still commonly misunderstood, point was a primary preoccupation of F. R. Leavis, I have developed the present implication in *F. R. Leavis* (London: Routledge, 1988), 62–69.

Form: Narrative Structure

MICHAEL BLACK

◆ ◆ ◆

ASKED WHY THEY ENJOYED *Sons and Lovers* and remember
it with pleasure, many readers would answer that they found
it vivid, or 'realistic'. This lifelikeness starts with the evocation of
the countryside and the town, the mining community and its
people, and the Morel parents themselves, who are portrayed so
carefully, so much in the round that most people find that good
balances bad. We find fresh and arresting the scene where Morel
gets up, breakfasts and goes off to the pit: this is how it once
was, and it both renders a way of life, now lost, in a given place
at a certain time, and gives us a sympathetic sense of him as a
man comfortably rooted in his way of life and his work. What
he is feeling at this moment, or as he picks mushrooms on the
way to the pit (cut by Garnett) is the joy that is often unconscious. This is not wage slavery or industrial oppression; Morel
lives in a way that he loves. What he does, where he lives, give
him his identity. It is his emotional life which threatens it: just
the opposite of the conventional notion of industrial life. Similarly the later scenes in which he does little cobbling or tinkering

jobs about the house, makes fuses, or tells the children about 'down pit' show a man at ease with himself and his children, happy for the moment just to be, so that one is bound to ponder what has gone wrong.

A parallel with Morel's life at the pit is young Paul's introduction to work at Jordan's: the whole long day, from the train journey in to the return at night. The people at the little factory are realised in all their strange individuality; the organisation, the work, give the sense of a microcosm full of living energies. Day-to-day clerical work, writing letters, keeping accounts, sending out goods to customers, is what hundreds of millions still do, but it does not get much of a showing in art. I doubt if there is a more vivid rendering in literature of that world of daily work, seen in its fullness by someone who has done it.

Two brief quotations sum up this capacity to see ordinary things freshly. They show that 'realism' is an inadequate word. Paul goes to Jordan's for his interview with his mother: it is a strange new world: 'On the table was a pile of trusses, yellow wash-leather hoops tangled together. They looked new and living' (119). Some pages later, again with her, he looks down on his own world, and finds the same sense in it:

> On the fallow land the young wheat shone silkily. Minton pit waved its plumes of white steam, coughed and rattled hoarsely . . .
>
> "The world is a wonderful place," she said, "and wonderfully beautiful."
>
> "And so's the pit," he said. "Look how it heaps together, like something alive, almost—a big creature that you don't know." (152)

One remembers also Mrs Morel at the market, allowing herself to buy a pretty dish with cornflowers on it, and softening to the man she has got a bargain from; or standing, seeming to listen to her iron, or the noise her needle makes, sewing. These scenes balance the others in which Morel comes home late and drunk, and they quarrel.

Much of the writing seems to have this effortless lucid veracity, like Tolstoy's, so that scenes and people come up off the page like life. There are elements which are pure realism, creating the circumstances: little episodes like the yeast-seller 'Barm-O' (cut by Garnett), or 'Hose', the middleman who gets the miners' wives to seam stockings at twopence-halfpenny the dozen, or the way the wives, when the baby is coming, summon help from the woman next door: about 'raking' the fire at night and putting out the miner's pit-clothes to warm—the reader will reel off other examples once this game is started. There is too the serious social or industrial history; one learns what a butty is, how the mining teams work, what was paid and how it was divided up (the scene in which Paul collects his father's wages), how the wives managed in good weeks and bad including accidents and sickness, the hierarchy of streets to live in, and how the ashpits spoiled them all.

There is also the dialect, transcribed carefully and uncondescendingly, not quite for the first time in literature, since Jefferies's *Amaryllis at the Fair* had rendered a Southern dialect with equal care. But it is still a new note: this is dialect rendered by a speaker, not an observer; and while it is full of wit, savour and character it is not a way of demoting the speakers to a lower class in the drama, a kind of chorus with a tone of automatic comedy, as in Dickens, or even in Hardy. It is structural: Morel cannot speak any other way, except in parody, and his wife will not speak that way; it is an emblem of the rift between them. Paul can move in and out of dialect: with his mother and Miriam he speaks the language of consciousness: dialect is the language of instinctive tenderness in which he addresses Clara after they have made love for the first time. Genteel readers in 1913 might also have been shocked to read Baxter Dawes's bad language—presumably the first uses of 'bugger' and 'sod' in modern literature.

Then one thinks, these pleasures of fresh outward-looking are nearly all in Part I. This is not the eye of childhood, exactly, but childhood memories recovered with their persistent power and vividness. Or it is like being happily in love: the whole world comes alive in the same way. Part II is different; the presiding mood is bafflement, struggle, failure to get things clear, as in a frustration-dream. Something here is less impersonal: not more involved in what is related, but less able to stand outside and just see all round it. That something is the presiding consciousness. So far as it is Paul Morel's, it is in the nature of the case that it cannot be outside itself and objective. So far as it is Lawrence's, it cannot afford to be outside Paul's consciousness, giving the reader an undermining comment on what happens. It is Lawrence's intention that we should feel with his alter ego, enter into his state. How can he and we do this, and still remain free? It is the question.

Nearly all discussion of *Sons and Lovers* is conditioned by this knowledge that the book is based on Lawrence's own experience. The unsophisticated but sensible question, what is the novel about? is thus foreclosed: it is about his problems, and the argument goes off into other questions such as, was Lawrence fair to his parents or to Jessie Chambers? Even the afterthought 'But this is a novel, not an autobiography' can be diverted in the same direction by asking: does the narrative voice seem too much Lawrence's, and is it too favourable to Paul? The assumption is that we are dealing with fiction as catharsis, as self-therapy. From early days, some readers recognised an archetypal situation: here was Freud's Oedipal conflict dramatised, in the longest and most vivid of all case-histories, recorded by a self-analyst of genius. The implication is the one reached long ago by Jessie: once Lawrence had had this settling of accounts with himself and his family situation he could go on to write what he really wanted to write; and *Sons and Lovers* is therefore set aside from the rest of the work. This begs the question, did he settle the account, *could* he?

Lawrence himself seemed to foster this argument by making remarks like the ones in the letter to McLeod about 'shedding' his 'sicknesses'. A later reflection introduces a slight shift of stance, but encourages us to stay within the biographical frame: 'I would write a different "Sons and Lovers" now; my mother was wrong, and I thought she was absolutely right.'[1] Similarly, in 'Women Are So Cocksure' he wrote: 'My mother spoilt her life with her moral frenzy against John Barleycorn... And at fifty, when the best part of life was gone, she realised it. And then what would she not have given to have her life again, her young children, her tipsy husband, and a proper natural insouciance, to get the best out of it all.'[2] The reader who bears in mind Lawrence's own dictum 'Never trust the artist. Trust the tale' might reply that the tale tells us that it is not in the Mrs Morel he has given us to have that reaction. But in any case the novel does both of the parent-figures far more justice than he suggests.[3]

THE GENERAL INSTINCT that this is importantly Lawrence's story is not mistaken, provided that we see how much he has shaped it in order to give it representative force, such that it ceases to be merely personal; and how by doing so he has convincingly become impersonal without providing undermining comment.

This could not simply be a matter of doing what any writer might do in order to disguise the real people who are the originals of certain characters, or just to make a shapely plot. So, for instance, Paul is an artist, not a writer. It is the brother Arthur who goes to Nottingham High School and on to college, not Paul; indeed Paul's brothers and sisters are unlike Lawrence's in many ways, including their actual number. Lawrence only worked at Haywood's, the medical appliance manufacturers, for four months, whereas Paul works at Jordan's for years and becomes an overseer. Miriam is less of an intellectual than Jessie was; but then Paul is less of an intellectual than Lawrence. The whole affair with Clara Dawes, and the relationship of rivalry with her husband, is imagined, though it may borrow elements of Lawrence's affairs with Alice Dax and Frieda. And so on; one could specify smaller departures, and there must be thousands that we simply do not know about.

In one sense this *is* mere detail; the central story remains Lawrence's, and above all the conflict between his roles as son and as lover. Yet cumulatively, the differences begin to translate the story of Lawrence's childhood and youth into something wider. They should be seen as the detail of a larger change, where Lawrence's rewritings finally translated his material into 'form', to use the contentious term. This form does create an imaginative but dispassionate element in the writing, in the first place by creating noticeable parallels, symmetries and recurrences. These suggest that the central experience which is Paul's is part of a wider pattern, first within the family itself, then in the vividly created mining community, where it is a recognisable element of social morality, and finally in the whole universe which the closing paragraphs confront in all seriousness.

At two points especially all the themes coalesce: at the end of each Part. It is striking that the division into two Parts survives from the earliest 'plotting out'. The proportions are important; Part I has six chapters or some 160 pages, Part II eight or 280; the one is like a first movement preluding the other in which things are substantially developed and worked out. At the end of the first, the elder brother William, who is the central childish consciousness in the first three chapters, and whose experiences importantly prefigure Paul's, dies. Paul has now to move forward to claim his mother's attention. The little touch which the reader is most likely to notice as a link with the end of Part II is that as the father Morel and his mates struggle to bring the great coffin into the house the living child makes a claim, breaking into the Biblical note of the mother's grief:

> "Oh my son—my son—my son!"
> "Mother!" Paul whimpered, his hand round her waist. "Mother!"
> She did not hear.
> "Oh my son, my son!" she repeated. (169)

Two pages later, Paul is mortally ill, and the mother is forced to turn her attention to the living son, for fear that he too may die:

> "I s'll die, mother!" he cried, heaving for breath on the pillow.
> She lifted him up, crying in a small voice:
> "Oh, my son, my son!"
> That brought him to. He realised her. (171)

The transference has been made, for good and ill ('Mrs Morel's life now rooted itself in Paul'). At the end of Part II, in an enormous climax to the whole book, the son's first desperate claim, the one made as the coffin comes in, is repeated in exactly the same words, but he cannot now receive the later confirming answer. 'He realised her' had been, we have learned, a doubtful way of finding his own identity. Now he has to realise himself:

> "Mother!" he whimpered, "mother!"
> She was the only thing that held him up, himself, amid all this. And she was gone, intermingled herself! He wanted her to touch him, have him alongside with her.
> But no, he would not give in. (464)

The first edition and most subsequent printings misread 'whimpered' as 'whispered', thus eliminating a main clue to the parallel. It is like a musical motif recurring at important moments: here, at the end of each of the two large movements or acts. The reader is made to think of the parallels, but also of the differences in the situations: especially that the mother is now dead and the living son must either die or live as his own centre of life. The question is, has she enabled him, or has she incapacitated him? Can he become himself? The strange but powerful realism of 'He wanted her to touch him, have him alongside with her' starts as evocation of their being in bed together all those years ago. But it is equivocal now; a grown man can't want to be in bed with his mother. In any case, her bed is the grave. Does he want that? He realises that he does not.

Once that deft symmetry between the parts is recognised, other symmetries multiply. They become what Garnett called form or we now call structure; but they are not fully separable from what is also called style, the language. So, for instance, in that extraordinary scene of William's homecoming, dead, the reader may feel the resonance of certain phrases which are also waiting, as it were, to become fully, orchestrally, deployed at the end of the book. I analyse that great finale below. Meanwhile, the waiting phrases are: 'The ash-tree stood monstrous and black, in front of the wide darkness'; 'the front door, which opened straight from the night into the room'; and 'by the open door, against the night, Annie stood leaning forward . . . ' (168–9). The ash-tree, resonating in the wind, has been established as a kind of link between the parents' discord and the night outside. The other phrases imply that as the huge coffin ('the great, dark weight') bursts in, 'night' and 'darkness' threaten to invade the home. They hint at more than death. These forces have been invoked earlier in the narrative, and are the elements which link what is personal with what is familial and what is universal, what is enormously out there. They are, here as elsewhere, dreads; and they raise the question, are they Paul's childish dreads, or Lawrence's, or is he, through Paul, putting us in touch with something universal to which the child-mind is open, and which we need to recover and respect?

Some of the recurrences are all-pervasive, a matter of the texture of the writing, which is usually metaphorical even when it seems to be realistic: I touch on these below: the ash-tree, the sense of night, of darkness, of a space waiting to burst in are examples. The structural ones may be duple, as between the two Parts: we have just seen the final one. Some are triple, reflecting the other structural principle that Paul has three women—his mother, Miriam and Clara—and Lawrence needs to inflect his motifs to represent the differing nature of the three relationships. Some of these recurrences are slight, almost unnoticeable: for instance Paul pins flowers, or berries, on to the breast of each of his three women (210, 281, 364); or he helps each of them over a stile (153, 184–5, 352). Each little incident is symptomatic, and expresses the nature of the woman and the relationship. So, for instance, Paul doesn't want his mother to know that he has pinned the flowers so carefully for Miriam, and breaks off, hearing her approach. Mrs Morel finds stiles a nuisance but doggedly goes over, refusing his help. Miriam is afraid to jump into his waiting arms (we think of the episodes with the pecking hen, and the swing, where she is also afraid to let herself go). Clara jumps wholeheartedly, laughing, and is caught and covered with kisses.

As for the duple pattern, that of the two sons, it is the simplest and most explicit—more so now that Garnett's cuts have been restored. In chapter I the baby which Gertrude Morel is carrying is Paul, but the child in whom she invests her hope is William ('The world seemed a dreary place . . . at least until William grew up'–13). She has turned from the father; a crucial moment in the process is the hair-cutting episode (23–4; it is easy to think that Paul is the victim, but it is William). By the time Paul is born, 'Already William was a lover to her' and 'did not like the new baby' (44; cut by Garnett). William is antagonistic to the father long before Paul can be; 'all his young soul was his mother's' (49). The antagonism, the rivalry, shows itself most clearly in the scene when father and son nearly fight in the presence of the mother (83); there is a precise parallel in Part II where Paul also nearly fights with Morel (253). This follows a virtual love-scene between mother and son, which Morel interrupts; after the near-fight Paul begs his mother not to share the husband's bed. So the parallel is also a development, an intensification; once William is dead the mother turns to the chosen son, and he to her, with tragic force.

As William grows up, he shows himself clever and ambitious; in a long passage also cut by Garnett, he teaches other boys his skills, but is so much quicker than they are that he has no patience, and abuses them verbally (71). His mother has to remonstrate, in exactly the same way as, later, Mrs Leivers has to tell Paul to be more patient with Miriam (188–9). In the first passage, with William, there is a long quasi courtship scene of loving play between mother and son, ending 'They left each other glowing warm: he made her feel warm inside, and she him' (73; cut). This is paralleled in Part II by more than one scene between Paul and his mother. There are well-imagined complexities here: for instance, in the scene where William puts on his Highlander's kit to go to a fancy-dress ball, 'all his pride was built on *her* seeing him' (76; also cut); but she refuses to look. It is conveyed to the reader that William has now displaced his father in a specific way, as skilful dancer. It was important in his courtship that Morel had had this gift (which Lawrence valued). It was part of the vitality which first won the mother's love, a matter in which he was a more favoured nature; so now the mother fears the boy will become like his father, while the father, remembering his own past skill and his pleasure in it, is obscurely jealous. These are scenes of some subtlety, but Garnett presumably failed to see the points being implied.

William's charm and grace mean that he is a favourite with the girls, and this makes his mother jealous; she turns the girls away at the door. 'And tell your girls, my son, that when they're running after you, they're not to come and ask your mother for you' she says (75). There are several implications here: the charm foreshadows Paul's gift with the girls at Jordan's, but the jealousy foreshadows the triangle with Paul and Miriam. But Mrs Morel's emotions are not merely negative:

> the carelessness went out of his eyes.
>
> His mother . . . felt a little chill at her heart. Was he going to 'come off'? . . . Perhaps she only wanted him to be himself, to develop and bring to fruit all that she had put into him. In him, she wanted to see her life's fruition . . . And with all the strength of her soul she tried to keep him strong and balanced and moving straight forwards. But he was baffling, without clarity of purpose. Sometimes he lapsed and was purely like his father . . .
>
> . . . She did not mind flirtations . . . But she dreaded lest he should come a cropper over some shallow hussy. (77–8; cut by Garnett)

He says that the flirtations are nothing serious; and 'I shan't get married till I meet a woman like you' (74; cut). This is a painful irony; but it also foreshadows the several occasions when Paul makes exactly the same promise: Paul's later formulation, and the irony is now a savage one, is: 'I'll never marry while I've got you' (286). And of course he does not; the question at the end is, can he ever? In all these cases until the final one, both son-lovers indulge a little fantasy; the assumption is that Morel is dead, and mother and son are going to live together in a nice little house with a servant, and be happy ever after.

Her dread is fulfilled; William does 'come a cropper over some shallow hussy'. Here is one of the points where the duple pattern modulates into the triple one. William falls for his 'Gipsy', and brings her home, as Paul later brings Clara home: the symmetry is marked by Morel's being charming, indeed courtly, to both his sons' young women. Gipsy is pathetically inadequate beneath the glamour. Yet Paul too is captivated; and in a strange scene threads flowers in her hair, calling her a 'young witch-woman' (158); this parallels the later scene when he drops flowers over Clara's hair, saying 'Ashes to ashes and dust to dust/If the Lord won't have you the devil must' (279). Between the two incidents he has said to Miriam 'If you put red berries in your hair . . . why would you look like some witch or priestess, and never like a reveller' (226). These are small examples of the peculiarly Lawrentian way of opening up the story towards another realm beyond social or psychological realism. Making sense of them here, one might point to the pervasive sense of a strange realm of 'night': here it is the place where witches, priestesses and revellers have their being. For a child, certainly; but for an adult?

Gipsy's photograph, in evening dress with naked shoulders, shocks Mrs Morel (126). Here is a reveller, a night-person, who has bewitched her son: 'when I'm with her in the evenings, I am awfully fond of her', he says (148), as if this explained something. (This note recurs with Paul and Clara.) In the day, she is trivial and useless, no companion. Mrs Morel has a specific fear, that William will be trapped into marriage; so she will not go to bed before the two young people have gone up separately ('Can't you trust us, mother?' he says, twice–148). This is exactly like Paul and Clara later, after the theatre, fencing with her mother, but Paul eludes her watchfulness, to enter into the paradisal scene of love-making in the little Nottingham house when the old woman has gone up to bed (382ff). Mrs Morel's foreboding ('they'll hang on to each other till they kill each other'–164; cut) comes partly true; William's own prophecy wholly true ('He hated her . . . "if I died, she'd have forgotten me in three months" '–163).

William dies of erysipelas, made fatal by overwork. Or that is the ordinary explanation of his death in Part I. In Part II Paul gives the death its deeper significance within the scheme of the whole novel. From a cosmic or Darwinian point of view it was mere 'waste'; his own insight is that it followed a tragic failure to follow the right path. In a long conversation with Miriam, cut by Garnett, he says 'I reckon we've got a proper way to go—and if we go it, we're all right . . . But if we go wrong, we die. I'm sure our William went wrong somewhere . . . What we are inside makes us so that we ought to go one particular way, and no other.' It does not occur to him that William 'went wrong' partly because of the relationship with his mother, so that there is a lesson for him; and this unconsciousness is dangerous. At this moment he has a sublime confidence that he himself is following his true course: 'Yes—I'm certain' (193). He has no sense yet that he is under the same spell, or in the same difficulty, as his brother. That hubris is profoundly questioned at the end of the book, where he, like William, is left with the 'drift . . . towards death' (451).

William's 'going wrong' is what his mother fears, though she puts it in a way which Lawrence implicitly questions: in the social-moral terms of her class. Here is one point where the personal becomes the familial and the social in an external way, and Lawrence builds it up in order to break it down. Mrs Morel has 'gone wrong' herself through a mistaken marriage. The fear that her sons will do the same leads her into a double bind. Her jealousy, her fear of losing the two sons in whom she has placed all her love, is reinforced by her sense that she has invested her own fulfilment in them, and does not want them to fail in life. That wish reinforces the prudent vigilance of the parent who has to enforce the morality of the tribe—if only to stop the children making the mistake she made. William says of his first girls, 'I only want a bit of fun with them'; she replies, 'But they don't merely want a bit of fun with *you*' (74). She produces a startling dog-analogy, saying that he presses up against girls wanting to be petted. He thinks he can turn the figure against her: 'When they've done, I trot away.' She replies, 'But one day you'll find a string round your neck' (80). Dogs mate, but don't get married;

they trot away. William thinks they are free, but she reminds him that they are domesticated, like it or not. She speaks as one who is not free.

One book which Lawrence pondered on this topic was Hardy's *Jude the Obscure*. Jude finds a string round his neck when he is tricked into marriage by a girl who falsely tells him she is pregnant. He does the right thing, by the standards of the tribe, and the marriage is a disaster. William several times insists to his mother that although he is clear that his Gipsy is a 'fribble' (Lawrence's word in the letter to Garnett about form) he has 'gone too far' to abandon her now; more than once he says 'it' or 'he' has gone too far (161, 162), and adds: 'For *some* things, I couldn't do without her——.' What could they be? 'I can't give her up *now*' (162). It is a shock to realise that these coded messages may be the language of sexuality, which was not allowed other language then. We infer that he may have been seduced by her flagrant sexual display, and the code will not let him abandon a woman he has 'ruined'. It is a fatal weakness which Paul later refuses to emulate; twice he transgresses the tribal sexual rule; nonetheless it is clear to him when he breaks with Miriam, after she has given herself to him at his own insistence, that he has by the standards of their class, or indeed by any standards, done her a wrong. 'He knew he had landed her in a nasty hole, and was leaving her in the lurch' (340). He is returning her to her people, 'ruined' in the terms of the old morality which he can neither accept nor ignore:

> As she went home, solitary, in her new frock, having her people to face at the other end, he stood still with shame and pain in the highroad, thinking of the suffering he caused her. (343)

Within his own family he has also had the example of his other brother Arthur. Leaving the army, he gets a girl pregnant, has to marry her, and the baby is born six months after the wedding:

He was caught now. It did not matter how he kicked and struggled, he was fast. For a time he chafed . . . He grumbled for hours to his mother. She only said "Well, my lad, you did it yourself, now you must make the best of it." And then the grit came out in him. He . . . acknowledged that he belonged to his wife and child, and did make a good best of it. (300–1)

That last phrase recurs a few pages later. Sue, the overseer at Jordan's, is leaving to get married, and says to Paul that she wishes she wasn't. Their little exchange shows how deeply the social-linguistic code is internalised.

"Nay Susan, you won't make me believe that."
"Shan't I? You *can* believe it though. I'd rather stop here a thousand times."
Paul was perturbed.
"Why, Susan?"
The girl's colour was high, and her eyes flashed.
"That's why!"
"And must you?"
For answer, she looked at him . . . He understood.
"Ah, I'm sorry," he said. Tears came to her eyes.
"But you'll see it'll turn out all right. You'll make the best of it," he continued, rather wistfully.
"There's nothing else for it."
"Yea, there's making the worst of it. Try and make it all right." (304–5)

'Making the best', or worst, of the shotgun wedding sounds like a very stoical attitude; the usual completion of the phrase is 'of a bad job'. Paul is determined that he is not going to give in to that pressure: 'It seemed to him that to sacrifice himself in a marriage he did not want would be degrading, and would undo all his life, make it a nullity' (322). The word 'sacrifice' proves to be thematic, though here it seems literal. When Paul is having his affair with Clara he is consciously going against the code, though paradoxically his mother feels he is safe with a married woman. He talks bluntly both to his mother and to Miriam. His mother says—'you know what folk are, and if once she gets talked about—' and he replies 'Then she must pay, we both must pay. Folk are so frightened of paying' (358–9). Miriam makes the point that under the double standard the woman pays more: 'The man does as he likes—' When he replies, 'Then let the woman also', she says, 'You don't understand what a woman forfeits—' He counters '. . . if a woman's got nothing but her fair fame to feed on—why, it's thin tack, and a donkey would die of it' (361). This is brave talk, but is all taken at the level of what Lawrence called idea and will: what one thinks. It is not so easy when one is dealing at the deeper level of what one mysteriously is.

It is becoming clear that another answer to the question 'What is the novel about?' is, love and marriage at the turn of the century, when the fierce traditional morality was first being questioned. What the old tribal rules controlled was sexuality: if young people got caught, they had to marry. If they married, they had to stay married, like it or not. This background of rule-governed behaviour is in the first half of the novel very guarded about sexuality, as one of the things that is not discussed, not even mentioned: hence the coded messages from William and Sue. In the second Part, Paul has sexual experiences which are actually described, and it is difficult for the reader born after 1945 to grasp how upsetting this was in 1913. Not only that: Lawrence also conveys that sexual acts, which still to many writers seem mechanical and repetitive, are actually different in their meanings, according to the feeling they express.

Paul's experience with Miriam is in the first place willed, by him. He has told her that he thinks it ought now to be the next thing they do, he is of an age, and they both think, don't they, that it ought to be a wonderful thing. He ignores for the moment, and she suppresses, the inborn virginity which is the shared consequence of their parentage, and she enters into it in a spirit of conscious self-sacrifice. What he feels afterwards is a revulsion— a sense of deathliness—which he cannot understand.

When he turns to Clara he is more free of his psychic burden simply because he does not have the affinity with her which he has with Miriam (she is not so like his mother). The sexuality is liberating. The great scene downstairs in Clara's house after her mother has gone up to bed is by a long way the most explicit in English literature up to this point, especially now that Garnett's small but crucial cuts are restored: for instance, the curious little observation that in Clara's bedroom Paul sees a pair of her stockings, on an impulse puts them on, and knows that he must have her. In 1913, this seemed obscene; now, it combines insight with neat symbolism. I say 'explicit', but might have said 'poetic', for the imagery of the cut passages suggests a literary debt, to Baudelaire. The other great scene of love-making, outdoors in the field with the peewits screaming, also has a literary cast: it is as if Lawrence is trying to imagine what this great experience might be like, and succeeding pretty well. The failure with Miriam, on the other hand, is painfully real.

PAUL MOREL'S PROBLEMS are symptomatic of the difficulties many people face in arriving at a good relationship. Perhaps they always have, but now there is a greater consciousness of their nature. And that is another part of the theme: the 'dynastic' nature of the novel, the fact that it follows two generations, implies that a social, almost a tribal unselfconsciousness in an older generation has to be followed by a personal self-consciousness in the next one if the problems are to be understood, even more if they are to be overcome. This raises the question, do you overcome things by understanding them (the premiss of psychoanalysis)?

The merely tribal marriage which is the background and a recurrent observed event is evidently rejected at a conscious level by Paul; and he presses this advanced or liberated view on his mother, who listens as a sceptical former participant now an observer, or on Miriam and Clara, who both have feminist leanings which give them another perspective. What he also presses on them is a need for a love which is frank about sexual need, and acts out that frankness. He talks Miriam, against her deeper inclination, into a sexual relationship, and is then dismayed to find how much he is himself unsatisfied by her sacrifice. With Clara he feels it is more 'impersonal'; but it is still his demand on her, and at the end she too rejects him for wanting it rather than her. What he does not know is the extent to which his demand on them is denatured by his own psychic deformation. All his ideas are only that, ideas: good in themselves as counters in a discussion, but not actually the deep springs of his actions.

A marriage which was not tribally enforced, seems to have been a love-match, can still turn out wrong. The great example is the marriage of Gertrude Coppard and Walter Morel, which begins with the glamorous night of a Christmas dance and becomes a lifelong conflict. This is the central structural element of the novel in the sense that it determines both the duple pattern, of the two sons, their fates worked out in the two Parts, and the triple pattern of Paul's relationships with his three women. The parental conflict dominates Part I; it has counterparts in Part II in the marriages of Miriam's parents, the Leiverses, and of Clara and Baxter Dawes. The events themselves are the main thread of Part I; in Part II Paul's blind actions are a consequence and a comment; we sense him groping towards, but never quite reaching, a conscious view of the effect on him of his parents' relationship.

We have seen that when he talks to Miriam about the sense he has made of William's death, he cannot go on to see that the parents' failure and the mother's dominance are factors. He comes to this very slowly, perhaps never perceives it squarely, perhaps cannot afford to. It is, rather, refracted by other elements of his experience, and primarily by the marriage of Baxter and Clara Dawes, which is seen, but slowly, to follow the pattern of the Morels.

The episode with Clara, being mostly Lawrence's imagining, is written off by many readers as less important than his other experiences, which are 'real'. In the terms of Lawrence's letter to Garnett, here is the other son 'going for passion'; it makes sense as the next move in his story, but feels a bit made-up. Here too the common instinct is basically right; the episode is not convincing in the same painful way as the rest of the book. Nonetheless Lawrence uses it very subtly in so far as he shows it to be on the surface a form of unconscious escape for Paul, or a false way out of his problem; while below the surface it gives him a parable or model which takes him closer, almost all the way, to a true picture of his parents.

Here the duple rhythm operates. Certain judgements in Part I are qualified in Part II. Think for instance of the categorical statements where the narrative simply gives Mrs Morel's point of view, and then issues in statements such as: 'At last Mrs Morel despised her husband' (22); 'she destroyed him' (25). A little more even-handedly, it also points out that 'She could not be content with the little he might be' (25). As for him, feeling himself displaced by the children, 'he half acquiesced' (62). So far as he is given an inner life at all, it is a sad one: 'His soul would reach out in its blind way to her, and find her gone. He felt a sort of emptiness, almost like a vacuum in his soul' (63). (The notation quietly planted but not developed there, the sense of emptiness, a void, is crucially developed later.)

Paul's first attempt really to reflect on the Morel's marriage is triggered by trying to make sense of that of the Daweses. As he talks to Clara about it, trying to understand what happened, an opinion crystallises, and surprisingly, it is hostile to her. She explains that she had thought she loved Dawes, and 'he wanted me'. 'And you sort of walked into it without thinking?' Paul asks. The marriage went wrong, she says, because Dawes never waked her, 'never got there'. She redefines this mysterious formula as 'He wanted to bully me, because he hadn't got me. And then I felt as if I wanted to run . . . he seemed as if he couldn't get *at* me, really. And then he got brutal.' Paul pursues her: did she ever give Dawes a chance to 'come near to you . . . I suppose he couldn't *make* himself mean everything to you?' (317–18). They feel they are out of their depth, and the conversation lapses. Later, he renews the attack (for so it has become): 'Were you horrid with Baxter Dawes? . . . weren't you horrid with him? Didn't you do something that knocked him to pieces? . . . I feel you did something to him—sort of broke him—broke his manliness . . . I believe you did him as much damage, more than he did you, by sort of cutting him underneath, and making him feel ashamed

... Making him feel as if he were nothing—*I* know' (319–20; cut). It is as if he is speaking for his father, without realising it. If *he* now knows, it is because his own family background provides the parallel case, and he can speak out of it instinctively without reflecting on what he is saying.

In a later conversation with Miriam, it is she who makes the comparison. Developing the 'sleeping beauty' fairy-tale analogy, Paul says 'With him, she [Clara] was only half alive, the rest was dormant . . . And she *had* to be awakened.' That seems to justify his own role, as useful prince. It is Miriam who says 'It was something like your mother and father.' He half agrees, but fends off total identification by making the remarkable distinction that his mother 'got *real* joy and satisfaction out of my father at first. I believe she had a passion for him . . . That's what one *must have* . . . the real, real flame of feeling through another person . . . See, my mother looks as if she'd *had* everything that was necessary for her living and developing . . . she had the real thing. She knows—she has been there' (361–2). 'There' is Clara's word, and its recurrences in the novel give it a strange force, to do with really existing, being oneself, and being oneself for another person. He may be implying: that's what I'm now doing for Clara; but, for the moment he is speaking for his mother. He knows that; but not what he is implying about his father, still less that he is making it possible for a listener to reflect that his failure with Clara is exactly described by her own earlier words about Dawes.

There is also something romantic and limited about this description of the Morels; it leaves out of account their struggle, the deadlock, and especially how any blame for it might be apportioned. If the accusation levelled at Clara, that it was more her fault, and she had been 'horrid' to Dawes, strikes the reader as a deflected criticism of his mother for her part in all that, a not unjust one, it is crucial that he does not see it.

One might indulge the paradox that the Paul who can reach this point of near-detachment and near-insight could, if he were a writer, *almost* go on to write a book like *Sons and Lovers*. To do so he would indeed have to imagine something like this whole strand of the novel, the part which is 'not real' precisely because it goes beyond his own experience; and this in order to reach a point of true detachment, of self-knowledge and self-criticism by showing the hidden pattern in his own behaviour. And Lawrence himself *has* done that: the episode with Clara shows it. We can see that Paul's 'going for passion' is only half the point. He could get passion anywhere: enlightenment is quite another thing. He does not quite get it; it is in the nature of the case that he can't; but we do, and it is the author who gives it to us in this profoundly indirect way.

The formal symmetries start to do this for us, especially the duple one: not as mere pattern, but as significance. In Part I it has been very carefully established that the two sons, first William, and then Paul, are jealous of their father, are his rivals, resent the father's bond with the mother; both of them respond to his provocations with an approach to violence. Paul nearly fights his father because he interrupts what is to all intents a love-scene with the mother. As a child Paul even wishes his father dead, prays that he may be killed 'at pit' (85). Now in Part II he is in love with a strong-minded married woman with a defeated husband; he feels a conscious rivalry with the other man. Dawes is a working man, like Morel: manly, unselfconscious, falling into drunkenness because undermined by the failure of the marriage. He and Paul frankly hate each other, and yet the jealousy is a mysterious bond between them. There is a murderous fight; Paul nearly throttles Dawes, who gives Paul a brutal kicking and leaves him for dead. But Paul makes contact with him later, is reconciled and as it were formally returns his wife to him: she is really his, in a way that he can never allow that his mother is his father's, and should be returned to *him.*

Because of his partial vision, Paul is startled when at the end of their affair Clara accuses him of just the inadequacies she had found in Dawes, and in just the same mysterious terms: she says to him, as if Gipsy had suddenly been given a consciousness and had turned on William, it is as if 'you only loved me at night'. 'The night is free to you', he replies (403), but she won't be fobbed off with a split-off part of him: 'You've never come near to me. You can't come out of yourself, you can't' (406–7). With Miriam too he thinks he is ending their affair as a matter of conscious choice, and is taken aback when he is accused of being himself an unsatisfactory partner in the relationship: irritated, she says he is like a child of four, producing the telling response: 'All right, if I'm a child of four, what do you want me for. *I* don't want another mother' (340). There is the problem; in important ways Miriam is like his mother, which is why there is an inner resistance in him, which she divines: ' "It has been one long battle between us—you fighting away from me . . . It has always been you fighting me off." . . . He sat aghast . . . Then it had been monstrous' (341). The word is his.

At last, at the conscious level, he attempts to grasp these failures. There is a touching moment when he says to his mother: 'You know mother, I think there must be something the matter with me, that I *can't* love . . . I feel sometimes as if I wronged my women, mother . . . to *give* myself to them in marriage—I couldn't. I couldn't belong to them.' She says he hasn't met the right woman. He says, and he may now really know the truth of it, 'And I never shall meet the right woman while you live.' As for her reaction, Lawrence only says:

> His mother turned away her face, sat looking across the room, very quiet, grave, with something of renunciation . . . Now she began to feel again tired, as if she were done. (395)

The implications delicately hinted at in 'grave', 'renunciation' and 'done' are silently fulfilled in the plot; she begins to die, as if something in her knows she must.

OTHER CONNECTIONS BEGIN to be made in the mind. At a merely verbal level, the fight with Dawes may remind the reader who knows Lawrence's own reading, of Scott's 'Lady of the Lake' and George Eliot's *Romola* (Lawrence was fascinated by the idea of one man strangling another). But where is it that Paul and Dawes meet and fight at night? Not perhaps at a place where three roads cross, where Oedipus, unknowing, killed his father? No; actually outside Nottingham, between one stile and the next. Nonetheless,

the scene is carefully set, in the quasi-mythopoeic terms which
the novel deploys:

> The town ceases almost abruptly on the edge of a steep hollow.
> There the houses with their yellow lights stand up against the
> darkness. He went over the and dropped quickly into the hol-
> low of the fields . . . Behind, the houses stood on the brim of
> the dip, black against the sky, like wild beasts glaring curiously
> with yellow eyes down into the darkness. It was the town that
> seemed savage and uncouth, glaring on the clouds at the back
> of him. (409)

In the Dawes affair Lawrence *is* very subtly rewriting the Oedipus legend. The novel has Paul fall in love with women in
whom we can see something of his mother, and he half-wants
to kill, but importantly is reconciled with, a man in whom he
can almost see his father. It is a kind of deflection: he can sym-
pathise with Dawes, instead of his actual father; and the relationship with Clara has no point when his mother is dead. That with
his mother is severed, but not resolved, by her death, which is
the equivalent of Jocasta's suicide. He can return Clara to her
husband as a sad substitute for returning his mother to his father.

Once one has seen one such link, other memories stir: what
was Hamlet's mother called? Gertrude, like Mrs Morel. So that
when Paul says, just after he has nearly fought his father: 'Sleep
with Annie, mother, not with him . . . Don't sleep with him,
mother' (254), we are surely meant to think of Hamlet saying,
just after he has killed Polonius, thinking it was the hated uncle
who has usurped his own as well as his father's love for his
mother:

> Goodnight—but go not to my uncle's bed:
> Assume a virtue if you have it not.

We know too that Lawrence saw Ibsen's *Ghosts* in Munich in
the summer of 1912. (By an extraordinary coincidence, he saw
both *Ghosts* and *Hamlet* in rapid succession in Gargnano in Decem-

ber 1912 and January 1913, and this triggered a whole theme in *Twilight in Italy*.) But he knew Ibsen well; *Hedda Gabler* gives him his reveller with leaves and berries in her hair. In *Ghosts* the son Oswald is also a painter, we remember; and the mother looks back on a bad marriage to a drunk, but comes to feel that what had really animated him as a young man was 'the joy of living' which she has repressed in him. The son's heredity manifests itself as syphilis: he knows that this will degenerate into dementia, and hopes for a moment that the girl he discovers to be his bastard half sister will have the strength to give him the fatal dose of morphia he has acquired for the time when it is needed; but now the mother must do this for him in his total dependence: strong curtain. Lawrence inverts this situation and takes the melodrama out of it. His painter and the sister give the morphia to the dying mother. It is possible that Lawrence really did this; but I think it is imagined, and that it is Lawrence's subtle reversal of Ibsen's situation. The duple rhythm is seen here too. William dies of erysipelas, Gertrude Morel of cancer. Those are the real immediate medical conditions, like Oswald's syphilis in *Ghosts*. Paul is able to divine the symbolism, the deeper life-threat, in the case of William, but not for his mother (Lawrence does this explicitly in the letter to Garnett). And of course Paul cannot diagnose his own trouble, though he becomes aware that he has one.

The old Greek myth puts things in stark and absolute terms: the son does kill his father, marries the mother, has children by her and must be punished by self-mutilation and exile if the curse on the city-state is to be removed. Freud's psychoanalytical appropriation of the myth is a little less stark; the son does want to kill the father and marry the mother, but this is metaphorised into a fantasy indulged by the infant. Ibsen's metaphorisation turns the hereditary effect of marital conflict into a positivist upshot, syphilis, and makes the son literally dependent on the mother for life-support and euthanasia. Lawrence on the other hand sees the heredity, the result of conflict in the previous generation, as what we daily see it to be. The son's attempt to place his love elsewhere than in the mother and his rivalry other than in his father is frustrated; he is as if condemned to repeat their mistakes, in subtly disguised forms: finds that the other women he tries to love embody aspects of his mother, which is both why he chooses them and why in the end he rejects them; what is more, the loved women find aspects of his parents, including his father, in him: his heredity is his failure to be 'there', to come out of himself.

So the repetitions in the plot are not merely formal: they convey what Lawrence in the letter to Garnett called his 'theme': it is a specifically modern tragic principle. The classic dynastic curse is replaced by the psychological truth that family relationships, without which we do not become persons with identities, also inflict damage, which we may see repeated in generation after generation. It is in the nature of the case that the protagonists are both agents and victims: above all that they do not have full consciousness of what they are and do. The answer to critics who say that the narrator is too identified with Paul's point of view must be that to have that voice acting as analyst as we go along would undermine the essential principle that these things are difficult, for most people impossible, to discover. Half the problem is the unconsciousness of it. To have an unconscious protagonist is, in Henry James's terms, correctly to dramatise. It is for the reader to discover, with the necessary degree of difficulty, what the characters cannot see, and the way to do this is to follow the implications of the careful structure, shaped with an art which Lawrence is not usually credited with.

Notes

1. Frieda Lawrence, '*Not I, But The Wind . . .*' (London: Heinemann, 1935), 52.
2. D. H. Lawrence, *Late Essays and Articles,* ed. James T. Boulton (Cambridge: Cambridge University Press, 2004), 117.
3. The dictum appears in the essay 'The Spirit of Place' in D. H. Lawrence, *Studies in Classic American Literature,* eds. Ezra Greenspan, Lindeth Vasey and John Worthen (Cambridge: Cambridge University Press, 2003), 14.

Relationship and Class in *Sons and Lovers*

MACDONALD DALY

◆ ◆ ◆

N O R E A D I N G O F *Sons and Lovers* can neglect the explanation Lawrence himself offered for it in a letter to Edward Garnett, his literary mentor, on 19 November 1912, the day after he had sent the completed manuscript of the novel to the London publisher Duckworth, for whom Garnett was a reader. This was the fourth manuscript version of the novel (Lawrence was still referring to it as 'Paul Morel', after its hero, although he had first suggested 'Sons and Lovers' in October), and Lawrence, writing from Italy, wanted to ensure in advance of his responding to the manuscript that Garnett understood what he was trying to achieve. He also needed to reassure Garnett that the latest version addressed the older man's criticisms of earlier drafts: 'I want to defend it, quick. I wrote it again, pruning it and shaping it and filling it in. I tell you it has got form—*form*.' Lawrence went on to give his well-known précis of the narrative flow and thematic shape of the book:

> It follows this idea: a woman of character and refinement goes into the lower class, and has no satisfaction in her own life.

She has had a passion for her husband, so the children are born of passion, and have heaps of vitality. But as her sons grow up she selects them as lovers—first the eldest, then the second. These sons are *urged* into life by their reciprocal love of their mother—urged on and on. But when they come to manhood, they can't love, because their mother is the strongest power in their lives, and holds them . . . As soon as the young men come into contact with women, there's a split. William gives his sex to a fribble, and his mother holds his soul. But the split kills him, because he doesn't know where he is. The next son gets a woman who fights for his soul— fights his mother. The son loves the mother—all the sons hate and are jealous of the father. The battle goes on between the mother and the girl, with the son as object. The mother gradually proves stronger, because of the tie of blood. The son decides to leave his soul in his mother's hands, and, like his elder brother, go for passion. He gets passion. Then the split begins to tell again. But, almost unconsciously, the mother realises what is the matter, and begins to die. The son casts off his mistress, attends to his mother dying. He is left in the end naked of everything, with the drift towards death.

It is a great tragedy, and I tell you I've written a great book. It's the tragedy of thousands of young men in England . . . [1]

This description makes the novel sound more tightly organised than many of its readers believe: but here Lawrence was attempting to describe it in terms which would be found persuasive by a well-respected literary figure whose taste in fiction was a good deal more conventional than his own. Lawrence's repeated emphases on 'form' and pattern (note how both sons are said to repeat the same cycle of emotion, culminating in 'splitting') are an attempt to insert his novel into a tradition of exquisitely crafted and shaped fiction, in the manner of Flaubert, which Garnett deeply admired. Moreover, the manuscript Lawrence is eulogising was not identical to the text finally published in 1913. Garnett was far from persuaded by Lawrence's comments, and proceeded, with the consent of the author (who needed the money, among other things), to excise a number of passages from the manuscript. His reasons for doing so were partly economic—the novel was, in commercial terms, too long—but also aesthetic: in particular Garnett cast a sceptical eye over Lawrence's dialogue, which was a major recipient of his editorial scalpel. Garnett's method in itself reveals that Lawrence's text was not the seamless, well-formed structure he seems to be describing in the passage above, for he was often able to identify and remove substantial passages without any apparent slippage in sense or need to write linking passages. In all, about one tenth of the manuscript was omitted from the novel published by Duckworth on 29 May 1913.

Although Lawrence's slightly exaggerated description of the novel's structure is modulated by these personal and financial circumstances, its substance deserves serious consideration. The most peculiar thing about his description is how Freudian it is. His announcement of the main themes of *Sons and Lovers* would have struck early readers of the novel as surprising, possibly outrageous: the novel, he says, explores the sexual tensions within families, depicts familial relationships as thwarted and thwarting sexual ones, and in so doing, Lawrence goes on to claim, diagnoses this as a general social problem and not just a singular aberration in the fictional Morel family. Freudian ideas are nowadays fairly familiar, particularly the notion of the male infant developing an 'Oedipus complex', in which he realises that his parents have a sexual relationship and consequently becomes jealous of the father. It is doubtful that Lawrence had read Freud at this time—when eventually he did he did not like Freud's thinking or its implications—and so what looks like a grasp of certain psychoanalytic ideas here is probably indebted to the little Lawrence had learned about the subject from his German partner, Frieda. Freudian ideas were by no means as acceptable then as they were later to become, and Lawrence's apparently intuitive shadowing of some of them is remarkable.

Consider two short quotations from Freud. The first is from his essay 'Family Romances', first published in 1908. Attempting to explain the hostility shown by developing children to their parents, Freud remarks, 'the influence of sex is already in evidence, for a boy is far more inclined to feel hostile impulses towards his father than towards his mother and has a far more intense desire to get free from *him* than from *her*'.[2] In this sense, the 'tragedy' (Lawrence's word) for Paul Morel and 'thousands of young men in England' is that this is not just a childhood phase, but a condition which seems to carry on into later years, partly because their mothers, dissatisfied with their own sexual relationships in marriage, have actively transferred their sexual desires onto their sons. These desires cannot be expressed or acted upon because they are incestuous, and incest is a major taboo. The mothers react by sublimating their feelings into other forms of desire: possessiveness towards, or claims to power over the son.

This is a persuasive description of what happens in *Sons and Lovers*. Paul Morel comes to despise his father and have an intense relationship, which is often extremely intimate, both verbally and physically, with his mother. His role towards her is dual: he is both her son and her 'lover'. But the price of being a 'lover' to his mother is that it adversely influences his relationships with the other women in his life, the more 'legitimate' objects of his sexual desires, Miriam and Clara. Most of the second half of the novel shows him becoming more and more entangled in a sexual web, with his desires tugging in several ways at once. Consider Freud again, in his essay 'On the Universal Tendency to Debasement in the Sphere of Love', published in 1912, the year *Sons and Lovers* was completed. Explaining how certain individuals who are 'divided in two directions' about sex develop a kind of 'psychical impotence' in relationships, Freud summarises: 'Where they love they do not desire and where they desire they cannot love. They seek objects which they do not need to love, in order to keep their sensuality away from the objects they love.'[3] 'Love' here means sexual love as opposed to mere affection, and Freud's description holds for Paul Morel. Where he loves (for example, his sexual relationship with Miriam) he does not desire; where he desires (i.e., his mother) he cannot love. He seeks women whom he does not need to love (Miriam, Clara) in order to keep his sensuality away from the woman he does love (his mother). It is hardly surprising, then, that psychoanalytic readings of *Sons and*

Lovers have been extremely popular in the history of criticism of the novel.

Lawrence was among the first to protest, however, at the inadequacy of psychoanalytic interpretations of *Sons and Lovers* which, he remarked in a letter (16 September 1916), 'carve a half lie out of it'.[4] What he possibly meant was that an *isolated* attention to the familial and sexual dynamics of the novel—one which ignores the much wider social context determining the ways in which the Morels behave, feel, and act towards one another and others outside the family—is likely to produce a very truncated understanding of the novel and its complexities. It is Lawrence, after all, who strikes the note of 'class' in his précis, and one of the reasons for the considerable critical stature of *Sons and Lovers* is that it is one of the first dramatisations of class conflict produced in England in the period in which Lawrence was writing, as well as one of only a handful written by authors who were themselves working class.

IT IS VIRTUALLY IMPOSSIBLE for a reader (although not for the characters) to consider sexuality separately from class in the novel. Not surprisingly, however, the unity of the two is most evidently stressed at the beginning, where it provides an origin for everything that follows. The key circumstances here are those surrounding the marriage of Gertrude Coppard and Walter Morel in Chapter I. She is twenty-three and he is twenty-seven. Walter is a miner, 'full of colour and animation', his grandparents a French refugee and an English barmaid (17); Gertrude hails from a 'good old burgher family' that has gone bankrupt (15). Each sees the other, across this class division, as an embodiment of the exotic, as the possessor of desired qualities which he or she does not have: 'He came and bowed above her. A warmth radiated through her as if she had drunk wine' (18); 'she was to the miner that thing of mystery and fascination, a lady' (17). Their initial meeting is a seeming testament to the ability of erotic power to overthrow class barriers: Gertrude and Walter liaising on the classless ground of their mutual sexual attraction. But Lawrence's account of the meeting is consistent with the way he deals with the marriage throughout the novel. It is essentially told from Gertrude's, not Walter's, point of view, and it is in Gertrude's perceptions of Walter that the notion of a 'classless' sexuality is exploded. Watching him, Gertrude registers Walter as 'well-set-up, erect and very smart' (17), a description which is primarily a sexualised reference to his physical bearing. But 'well-set-up' carries other colloquial insinuations: Walter gives the impression of being a man who has good material prospects. If he affects her like intoxicating liquor, this does not prevent her noticing (nor he from showily displaying) that he 'wore the blue ribbon of the teetotaller' (19): an outward sign of a sober mind and, in all likelihood, equally sober finances. A year later, on Gertrude's mistaken assumptions about Walter's misleading public image, they openly pronounce their sexual and economic compatibility in a sexual and economic contract: marriage.

It is from the failure of this marriage that the enormous conflict and heartache at the centre of *Sons and Lovers* unspool. The failure is not, primarily, sexual: by all accounts there is a great deal of passion early in the marriage. 'There were many, many stages in the ebbing of her love for him', we are told (62), 'but it was always ebbing'. What ruins it decisively is Walter Morel's inability to deliver to Gertrude the bourgeois material standards she has been led to expect their marriage to secure. A fundamental feature of this lifestyle is the ownership of property. Gertrude's first disappointment is the discovery that Morel, far from owning two houses as he claimed, in fact pays rent to his mother for the one in which they are living. A generous disposable income is another mark of bourgeois living, but the Morels are, in their early married life, far from having one. They are in arrears with their furniture and Morel's habitual drinking drains whatever small sums are left over. His anti-authoritarian attitude at work irritates Mrs Morel because, in her view, it ensures that he is allotted difficult and unprofitable seams of coal to mine. It should be said that this does not seem always to remain the case, and there is some evidence that telling the story largely from Mrs Morel's point of view leads to an exaggeration of Morel's irresponsibility: for all his drinking Morel is a steady worker, and in

the course of the novel the family becomes gradually more pros-
perous. But Mrs Morel's bitterness starts to entrench itself in the
initial stages of her coming to understand what her husband is
really like: 'At last Mrs Morel despised her husband. She turned
to the child, she turned from the father . . . There began a battle
between the husband and wife, a fearful, bloody battle that ended
only with the death of one. She fought to make him undertake
his own responsibilities, to make him fulfil his obligations' (22).

   This is the first of many instances in which it is made clear
that one of Mrs Morel's most frequently chosen weapons is a
certain language. The bourgeois vocabulary of contract ('responsibilities', 'obligations') is prevalent in the discourse which attaches
to her to the extent that it seems so natural that we are often
in danger of failing to notice it. The effect of this language is to
make her unhappiness seem a result exclusively of Walter Morel's
financial libertinism rather than the wasting and dehumanising
long-term pressure of poverty in the working-class community
into which she is seen as having 'descended', and of which Walter
Morel is himself a victim. Morel's personal behaviour—mainly
his frequent withholding of money for household necessities so
that he can buy drink—is depicted as the sole source of economic
deprivation within the family. This deprivation causes severe disaffection, including sexual disaffection, between husband and wife.
Exchange of intimacy and exchange of cash become fairly closely
related in the Morel household. It is no surprise that the young
Paul hands over his entire wage packet to his mother once he
starts working.

   One of the shortcomings of the novel is its failure to deal
adequately with the consequences of the discovery that Walter
Morel is much poorer than he originally makes out, and to place
readers in a position where they might understand both his motivation for deceit and the damaging result of exploding his personal mythology. Mrs Morel simply sees her husband as selfish,
perhaps malicious: it is certainly with this view that she indoc-
trinates her children. More importantly, there is no point in the
novel where we are invited to see things in a larger perspective
than the rather confined view of Mrs Morel and the children. In

particular, Morel's sub-literacy and inarticulacy conveniently prevent his own voice from being heard. In this respect, the novel puts readers in the curious position of being asked to ignore the tragedy of Walter Morel as a disadvantaged and impoverished worker (if one is to adopt the terms of Lawrence's précis, this was the tragedy of millions, rather than thousands, of people in the England of his time) in favour of the tragedy of Paul's and other young men's Oedipus complexes.

However, for all its ambiguous and evasive dealings with the emotional and material realities of working-class life, *Sons and Lovers* offers a fascinatingly 'social' reading of sexuality. Nowhere is this more profound than in the microcosmic class struggle between man and wife, which leads to an even greater polarisation than that which engendered it. We learn that it 'drove [Morel] out of his mind' and 'caused him, knowingly or unknowingly, grossly to offend her where he would not have done' (23):

> The pity was, she was too much his opposite. She could not be content with the little he might be, she would have him the much that he ought to be. So, in seeking to make him nobler than he could be, she destroyed him. She injured and hurt and scarred herself, but she lost none of her worth. She also had the children. (25)

For all that later commentators have found the narrator's loyalties unduly skewed in Mrs Morel's favour, there is extraordinary narrational insight into the nature of class deadlock in these early pages. Linguistically, the paragraph quoted above reveals a complex manoeuvring of perspective. For instance, 'the little he might be' can hardly be the phrase Walter Morel would use to describe his own potential: it is the narrator's, and it tells us a great deal about the narrator's own far from charitable view of the miner. With 'the much that he ought to be' and 'nobler' we pass to the vocabulary of Mrs Morel's own moral judgements. But then the narrator resumes control to describe the effects of her psychologically terroristic onslaught on Morel.

This shuttling to and fro in the narrative point of view goes on throughout *Sons and Lovers,* and such a constant shifting argues against the impression that Lawrence is crudely taking sides. From the paragraph quoted we learn that the narrator is caught between Walter and Gertrude Morel, is able to differentiate his own perceptions of conflict from theirs, but regularly *tends* towards sympathy with the woman. In other words, the narrator is very much in the position of one of the Morels' children, and indeed the case has often been made that, with the exception of the earliest scenes, *Sons and Lovers* reads like a first-person narrative of Paul Morel rewritten in the third person. But one of the main points of the novel is to demonstrate the great dangers of the kind of relationship which Paul and his mother have, and this in part explains the curious narrative vacillation. To live independently, in sexual and emotional and even economic terms, Paul must progressively grow apart from his mother in a way that Mrs Morel, because of her own described transference of affections, constantly inhibits. It is thus hardly surprising that the narrator of the novel is self-divided between obvious loyalty to Mrs Morel and a critical attitude towards her. In that sense the narrative formally takes us through the very process it is describing. In its final form it does not achieve anything like omniscience or objectivity; but the narrator does attain a sufficient degree of separation and detachment from the relationships he describes to distinguish him from the hero.

Mrs Morel takes possession of her sons by directing the course of their futures: ' "He is *not* going in the pit",' she says authoritatively of William, her first son (70). William's rise to the lower middle class, aged twenty, is marred by the equation of financial reward with emotional attachment (' "And I can give you twenty pounds a year, Mater—we s'll all be rolling in money" '–78), a confusion which Mrs Morel, too late, recognises keenly ('It never occurred to him that she might be more hurt at his going away, than glad of his success'–78-79). This should be a moment of great triumph for Mrs Morel, since William is crossing a class boundary; but the price of doing so, she realises, is painful separation from her. The beginning of his 'upward' journey into the bourgeoisie is also the beginning of a 'downward' spiral, a moral and physical decline. In London, he squanders his extra money on the consumerist luxuries of the bourgeois world (for his girl-friend, 'Gyp', more than himself) instead of sending it home as promised. It is implied that, in his final illness, geographical distance is the fatal factor: in the time taken for Mrs Morel to reach him, 'No one had been with him' (165). William's death is a clear sign of the contradictory consequences of the class mobility Mrs Morel continues to advocate. It brings greater material security, but with it come the new dangers of isolation and distance: individualised self-sufficiency can easily become a form of exposure.

PART TWO OF THE NOVEL is generally held to be weaker than Part One, largely on account of the narrator's perceived failure to distinguish himself from his hero (Garnett's cutting, incidentally, became less frequent as he progressed). It is worth pointing out, however, that, at first reading certainly, there is a fascinatingly exploited tension over the eventual fate of Paul Morel within the second half of the book, and indeed some final indecision as to what that fate actually is. The last two chapters are entitled 'The Release' and 'Derelict', and whether we should read the Paul Morel of the closing pages as a man who has been released from constraints in a way that will finally permit him to mature, or as a man so thoroughly released that he no longer has a fixed purpose at all, remains an open question. We know that he does not choose death, and are told, in the final sentence, that 'He walked towards the faintly humming, glowing town, quickly' (464). But this might easily be a gesture of resignation, of basic existential persistence, or of a will for unthinking immersion in the distractions of urban life, rather than the definite, purposeful, constructive decision which many critics have taken it to be. There is no authoritative reading of this conclusion. Such openness, indeed, was a Lawrentian trademark: it is there precisely so that the possibilities can be debated.

One can, nonetheless, question the contention that the narrator is insufficiently distanced from Paul Morel. There are numerous appropriate passages to consider, but one which conveniently relates to the general theme of class which I have been examining is the conversation between Paul and his mother in chapter 10:

> "You know," he said to his mother, "I don't want to belong to the well-to-do middle class. I like my common people best. I belong to the common people."
>
> "But if anyone else said so, my son, wouldn't you be in a tear. *You* know that you consider yourself equal to any gentleman."
>
> "In myself," he answered, "not in my class or my education or my manners. But in myself, I am."
>
> "Very well then—then why talk about the common people."
>
> "Because—the difference between people isn't in their class, but in themselves.—Only from the middle classes, one gets ideas, and from the common people—life itself, warmth. You feel their hates and loves—"
>
> "It's all very well, my boy—but then why don't you go and talk to your father's pals?"
>
> "But they're rather different."
>
> "Not at all. They're the common people. After all, whom do you mix with now, among the common people? Those that exchange ideas, like the middle classes. The rest don't interest you."
>
> "But—there's the life—"
>
> "I don't believe there's a jot more life from Miriam than you could get from any educated girl—say Miss Moreton. It is *you* who are snobbish about class."
>
> She frankly *wanted* him to climb into the middle classes, a thing not very difficult, she knew. And she wanted him in the end to marry a lady. (298–99)

The last paragraph, of course, is often read as the narrator's put-down of Mrs Morel, an authorial intrusion which sides with Paul in a heavy-handed attempt to manipulate the reader's responses. It guides us to see Mrs Morel's ambitions for Paul as really, in the end, rather petty. But one might legitimately ask, who really comes off best in the preceding conversation? We do not need to agree with Mrs Morel's views about class to notice how effectively she explodes Paul's somewhat romantic notion of 'the common people' (hardly a phrase favoured by those who genuinely identify with the working class). Paul's attempts to say that 'class', 'education' and 'manners' are separate from his actual self get short shrift from Mrs Morel. Their conversation itself is carried on in impeccable Standard English, and if Walter Morel were to walk in on it and ask for his dinner it would soon be obvious how much self had to do with class, education and manners. Perhaps it is this consideration which makes Mrs Morel pose that devastating question:

> "It's all very well, my boy—but then why don't you go and talk to your father's pals?"
> "But they're rather different."

The implication is that the miners are not included in Paul's notion of 'the common people': for Paul, they are beyond the pale, presumably failing to show 'life itself, warmth' or not in possession of 'hates and loves'. When Paul talks about 'common people', it becomes clear, he means someone like Miriam, who happens to work on a farm, but who most readers probably consider a very *uncommon* person indeed. I am suggesting, in other words, that it is possible to read that last paragraph ironically. It is a reflection of Paul's, but the inverted superiority inherent in it is something the narrator has deconstructed in advance.

It is possible to relate Paul's feelings about the common people to Freud's remarks about love quoted earlier: 'Where they love they do not desire and where they desire they cannot love.' Forgetting for the moment that this refers to individual personal relationships, and thinking about it in terms of Paul's expressed preference for 'the common people' rather than 'the middle classes', it becomes apparent that where he loves (i.e., the life, warmth, hates, loves of 'the common people') he does not desire (because 'the common people' have no 'ideas'); where he desires (i.e., the converse of ideas he finds in 'the middle classes') he cannot love (because they lack life, warmth, hates, loves and so on). This makes it possible intimately to relate Paul's sexual difficulties to his problem in finding a social identity with which he can feel comfortable. Rather than depicting sexuality as something which is merely individualised and private, the novel by this means shows how it may be related to much wider social experiences affected by class and class mobility. The tensions in Paul's relationship with Miriam, for example, are not simply bound up with his emotional tie to his mother, but also with Miriam's coming from a class from which he is being encouraged to escape. Love is not merely associated with personal matters of physical attraction and emotional compatibility, but has a much wider social dimension rooted in precisely those things which Paul sees as having nothing to do with the self—class, education and manners—all of which are ultimately dependent on economics. One of the achievements of *Sons and Lovers* is that it encourages us to look through romantic notions of love to see the material basis, the economic roots of sexual life.

There are reasons to be less impressed with *Sons and Lovers*. If this is what the novel is doing, it may not be doing it clearly enough. There is confusion, perhaps plain dishonesty, about working-class life in its pages. Mrs Morel's question—'It's all very well, my boy—but then why don't you go and talk to your father's pals?'—is ironic because it can also be fired at the novel. *Sons and Lovers* itself never really goes and talks to Walter Morel's pals. The novel remains almost totally within a domestic environment regulated by Mrs Morel's ideological views. The novel's narrator, if not tied to, almost always remains with his hero, Paul Morel: the occasions when he follows Walter Morel to the pub or to the coal face are so infrequent and fleeting that they hardly make an impact. Its understanding of Walter Morel and the industrial working class he represents can legitimately be said to be external and lacking in both sympathy and empathy: an inability to identify imaginatively with the life of the class in which he had his origins was the price Lawrence paid, it might be argued, for the social mobility he had himself experienced by 1912.

THESE CONTRADICTIONS AND AMBIGUITIES in *Sons and Lovers* make it, I think, more rather than less interesting: they turn the novel into a field for open debate rather than an occasion for conclusive judgement. The questions it asks about the relationship between sexuality and class are as important today as they were when the novel was published. To be sure, the particular family and class structures represented in the novel are no longer so common (which is not the same as saying that the 'traditional' family is an irrelevant concept, or that we live in a 'classless' society). When people are inserted, largely through parentage, at particular points on the spectrum of class, any movement they make can have repercussions in seemingly separate areas of experience: political, sexual, aesthetic. *Sons and Lovers* was D. H. Lawrence's own attempt, based on his own early life but not wholly determined by it, to map the confluences of these seemingly distinct regions of social experience. Each of us, in reading it, is challenged to do the same for ourselves.

Notes

1. *The Letters of D. H. Lawrence,* Volume I, ed. James T. Boulton (Cambridge: Cambridge University Press, 1979), 476–77.
2. Sigmund Freud, *On Sexuality: Three Essays on the Theory of Sexuality and Other Works,* trans. Angela Richards (Harmondsworth: Penguin, 1977), 222.
3. Ibid., 251.
4. *The Letters of D. H. Lawrence,* Volume II, eds. George J. Zytaruk and James T. Boulton (Cambridge: Cambridge University Press, 1981), 655.

A Modern Psychoanalytic Approach
to *Sons and Lovers*

BARBARA ANN SCHAPIRO

◆　◆　◆

Gertrude and Paul: The Depressed Mother
and the Dependent Child

Critics have generally recognized *Sons and Lovers,* Lawrence's third
novel, as one of the author's most finely observed and moving
works. It has nevertheless provoked controversy over the question
of aesthetic control: does the novel lose command of tone and
point of view? Many readers have noticed the contradictions between the dramatic presentation of the characters and the inter-
pretive commentary on them. As H. M. Daleski observes, "The
weight of hostile comment which Lawrence directs against Morel
is balanced by the unconscious sympathy with which he is presented dramatically, while the overt celebration of Mrs Morel is
challenged by the harshness of the character in action."[1] Mark
Schorer indeed proclaims the novel a technical failure because of
such contradictions; the "psychological tension," he believes, "dis-
rupts the form" of the novel.[2]

Conversely, more recent critics commmend the novel expressly for its manipulation of narrative point of view. Helen and Carl Baron, in their introduction to the Cambridge University Press edition of the novel, stress the deliberate "ambiguity" in the narrative perspective, a "blending of the way people perceive each other," such that the reader is invited to "notice how feelings are silently passed between people so that they are unconsciously affected by each other's emotions" (xxx–xxxi). Other critics emphasize that Paul's perspective should not be confused with that of the author or the omniscient narrator. Geoffrey Harvey, for instance, argues that "Paul's point of view is by no means the only one . . . His version of the truth of his story is centrally important and a crucial means of gaining sympathy for him, but it is endlessly qualified by other competing perspectives, and in control of these viewpoints is the implied author, who is concerned throughout to testify to the complexity of the truth."[3] Harvey's position is similar to Cynthia Lewiecki-Wilson's claim that the "narration combines both omniscient point of view and subjectivity, resulting in a textual voice that authorizes each character's experiences as equally legitimate, presenting competing centers of 'authenticity.' "[4]

The authorization of each character's subjective authenticity— the affirmation of the character's compelling inner life, of his or her needs and desires even as they conflict with the needs and desires of the character most ostensibly identified with the author—reflects, in the language of my critical framework, an intersubjective consciousness. Such intersubjective consciousness functions simultaneously with the projection of unconscious narcissistic fantasies—fantasies most associated with the authorial alter ego character—onto all of the characters. The result is a conflictual, sometimes contradictory character portrayal that is nevertheless true to the complex dialectic of projection and awareness—projection of one's own inner world and empathic awareness of the inner world of the other—that distinguishes real human relationships. The tension between intersubjective consciousness and narcissistic projection is especially apparent in the characterization of Mrs Morel.

Judith Arcana has traced what she sees as a tradition of "whole-sale mother-blaming" in *Sons and Lovers* criticism. She ties this phenomenon to an "oedipalized mother-blaming" in our culture at large.[5] The view of Gertrude Morel as the destroyer of her husband and the devourer of her sons, she argues, "ignores one basic conflict the novel presents: the intensity and power of Gertrude Morel thwarted by the utter impotence of her situation."[6] She quotes Lydia Blanchard's description of Gertrude as "a woman trapped in a marriage she does not want, hemmed in by a world that allows her no positive outlets for her talents and energies, who must live a vicarious existence through her sons."[7]

This is indeed the perspective that the novel's first three chapters in particular present. The mother is depicted not merely as an object of anger or desire for her husband and children but as a suffering subject in her own right. The compassionate rendering of Mrs Morel's inner pain is a predominant feature of the early chapters. Granted this focus is not sustained throughout the novel—Paul's subjectivity becomes the reigning perspective of part 2—but to ignore the sensitive portrayal of the mother's distress in part 1, as Arcana asserts, is to neglect a vital aspect of the novel.

While I disagree with Arcana that the fantasy of the mother as destroyer and devourer is only projected onto the novel by critics brain-washed by Oedipal theory (the fantasy is there in the text, too), I do believe that *Sons and Lovers* demonstrates how that fantasy is grounded in the mother's thwarted subjectivity. The first chapter emphatically establishes the mother's lack of "I-ness," her sense that she has no self, no individual agency or authentic being in her own right:

And looking ahead, the prospect of her life made her feel as if she were buried alive.

... She seemed so far away from her girlhood, she wondered if it were the same person walking heavily up the back garden at the Bottoms, as had run so lightly on the breakwater at Sheerness, ten years before.

"What have *I* to do with it!" she said to herself. "What have
I to do with all this. Even the child I am going to have! It
doesn't seem as if *I* were taken into account."

Sometimes life takes hold of one, carries the body along,
accomplishes one's history, and yet is not real, but leaves one's
self as it were slurred over. (14)

Because the mother does not feel herself "real," the discovery of
reality for the child she carries will prove to be exceedingly difficult. Lack of faith in the mother's independent reality and the
comcomitant sense of one's own insubstantiality or hollowness
constitute the core problem for Paul; it is indeed the fundamental
problem that Lawrence's fiction repeatedly, and so creatively, addresses.

Lawrence is astutely aware of the social and economic circumstances contributing to the mother's narcissistically impaired state.
Gertrude's economic dependency in a loveless marriage keeps her
powerless, angry, and resentful. As a woman, her options for self-
realization and expression are limited to her role as mother and,
as Blanchard notes, to a vicarious experience of achievement
through the lives of her sons:

The world seemed a dreary place, where nothing else would
happen for her—at least until William grew up. But for herself, nothing but this dreary endurance—till the children grew
up. And the children! She could not afford to have this third.
She did not want it. The father was serving beer in a public
house, swilling himself drunk. She despised him, and was tied
to him. This coming child was too much for her. If it were
not for William and Annie, she was sick of it, the struggle with
poverty and ugliness and meanness. (13)

By presenting Mrs Morel's perspective, the narrative displays
an empathic understanding of the mother's resentment of her
fetus, Paul. This is rather remarkable given the autobiographical
nature of the novel and the authorial identification with Paul.
The fact that Mrs Morel "did not want," indeed "dreaded this

baby" (13,50) is repeated several times in the opening chapters. We are also told of her great shame and guilt over feeling such antipathy toward her baby, and we will certainly see Paul suffer the consequences. As Jeffrey Berman points out, Gertrude is an "alternately overloving and underloving" mother.[8] The narrative identification with the mother's anguish in this first part of the book, however, resists a simplistic interpretation of the novel that "blames" Gertrude Morel for her failures as a mother.

Sons and Lovers dramatizes Mrs Morel's rigidity and lack of sensuality, but it also allows the reader to see the mother herself as the beleaguered child of a cold, harsh parent—her overbearing father, George Coppard: he is described as "proud in his bearing, handsome, and rather bitter; who preferred theology in reading, and who drew near in sympathy only to one man, the Apostle Paul; who was harsh in government, and in familiarity ironic; who ignored all sensuous pleasure" (18). Though we are told Gertrude preferred her mother and "hated her father's overbearing manner towards her gentle, humorous, kindly-souled mother" (15–16), it is her father's emotional legacy that she bears: "She was a puritan, like her father, high-minded, and really stern" (18). If one is assigning blame, in other words, one must look to Lawrence's explicit representation of the repressive, patriarchal culture of which Gertrude is a product.

The narrator also informs us that before meeting Walter Morel, Gertrude had loved a young man, John Field, whom she was prevented from marrying by economic constraints and by Field's own rigid, autocratic father. When Field tells her he would like to go into the ministry, Gertrude responds, "Then why don't you—why don't you ... If *I* were a man, nothing would stop me" (16). Field replies, "But my father's so stiff necked. He means to put me into the business, and I know he'll do it" (16). Field's father loses the business, but Field pursues neither the ministry nor Gertrude: he becomes a teacher and marries an elderly woman with property. "And still," the narrator asserts, "Mrs Morel preserved John Field's bible ... [She] kept his memory intact in her heart, for her own sake. To her dying day, for thirty-five years, she did not speak of him" (17).

The portrait of Gertrude that emerges in this first chapter allows the reader to understand her brittleness. The hard, affectless surface or shell protects against deep disappointment and personal diminishment, against the emotional rejection she suffered as a daughter and a woman in a father's world. After marrying Walter, she again experiences humiliation and betrayal when she learns that the house she believed was her husband's does not actually belong to him: "Gertrude sat white and silent. She was her father now . . . She said very little to her husband, but her manner had changed towards him. Something in her proud, honorable soul had crystallised out hard as rock" (21).

Lawrence's fiction regularly portrays characters whose souls have hardened and "crystallised" as a result of severe narcissistic injury. A shameful feeling of rejection—rejection of her feeling, desiring self—underlies Mrs Morel's proud, impenetrable surface. The condition infuses much of Lawrence's fiction. It fits Harry Guntrip's description of schizoid phenomena in which the self, by warding off its intolerable, painful feelings, becomes insulated from all emotion, indeed from the affective core of its being.[9] The predominant subjective experience for the schizoid individual, and for so many Lawrence characters, is consequently one of emptiness or inner void.

Gertrude was originally attracted to Walter because he promised to fill the void by representing precisely what she (and her father) lacked—spontaneous, emotional and physical expressiveness: "the dusky, golden softness of this man's sensuous flame of life, that flowed from off his flesh like the flame from a candle, not baffled and gripped into incandescence by thought and spirit as her life was, seemed to her something wonderful, beyond her" (18). As Lawrence came to recognize so clearly, however, another person can never complete or fill the void in the self. Selves can only balance and complement one another. The empty or fractured self may typically seek to absorb or devour the other in an attempt to compensate for the deficiency, but Lawrence shows again and again how that sort of relationship is doomed.

Because Gertrude "had no life of her own," the narrator explains, "she had to put her own living aside, put it in the bank, as it were, of her children. She thought and waited for them, dreamed what they would do, with herself behind them as motor force, when they grew up. Already William was a lover to her" (44). *Sons and Lovers* is indeed the quintessential Oedipal novel; it demonstrates exactly how the Oedipal fantasy becomes bloated and inflamed by the mother's wounded narcissism or impaired subjectivity. The early scenes in the novel consistently spotlight Mrs Morel's subjective experiences of loss, exclusion, and betrayal. In the scene in which Morel chops off William's baby curls, for instance, the narrator focuses on Mrs Morel's emotional devastation:

> It was her first baby. She went very white, and was unable to speak . . . "Oh—my boy!—" she faltered. Her lip trembled, her face broke, and, snatching up the child, she buried her face in his shoulder and cried painfully. She was one of those women who cannot cry: whom it hurts as it hurts a man. It was like ripping something out of her, her sobbing . . . [S]he knew, and Morel knew, that that act had caused something momentous to take place in her soul. She remembered the scene all her life, as one in which she had suffered the most intensely. (24)

Her reaction may in fact be irrational and excessive, but her pain, as the narrative enforces, is nonetheless real. Prior to the incident we are told of Gertrude's loneliness and isolation "miles away from her own people"; her passionate bond and identification with her male child provide the only sense of meaningful connection and value in her life: "He came just when her own bitterness of disillusion was hardest to bear; when her faith in life was shaken, and her soul felt dreary and lonely. She made much of the child, and the father was jealous" (22). The narrator, however, does not blame Morel—cutting the child's hair was not a malicious act. The reader may even feel, like the critic Harvey, that Morel "has as much right as she has to decide when the baby's hair will be cut; that his desire to observe social convention is not unreasonable; and that his wife's overreaction is made to seem tragically absurd by his stunned silence."[10] Nevertheless, the narrative choice to describe the event primarily from Mrs Morel's point of view is significant and reflects empathy with the mother's profound sense of loss, however irrational that feeling may be.[11]

The other scene that vividly depicts the mother's desolation, one of the most famous in all of Lawrence's fiction, is that of Mrs Morel and the white lilies. Once again the emotional context for the scene is rejection and betrayal: Mrs Morel has been locked out of the house by her drunken husband. Outside, she is struck by the brutal light of the moon just as she had been struck by her husband's brutal treatment: "Mrs Morel, seared with passion, shivered to find herself out there in a great, white light, that fell cold on her, and gave a shock to her inflamed soul" (33). She wanders around in a "delirious condition," mentally reenacting the painful scene until, as usual, she has successfully numbed the pain through defensive, "mechanical" mental effort: "mechanically she went over the last scene, then over it again, certain phrases, certain moments coming each time like a brand red hot, down on her soul: and each time . . . the brand came down at the same points, till the mark was burnt in, and the pain burnt out" (33–34). Finally,

> She hurried out of the side garden to the front, where she could stand as if in an immense gulf of white light, the moon streaming high in face of her, the moonlight standing up from the hills in front, and filling the valley where the Bottoms crouched, almost blindlingly . . .
>
> She became aware of something about her. With an effort, she roused herself, to see what it was that penetrated her consciousness. The tall white lilies were reeling in the moonlight, and the air was charged with their perfume, as with a presence. Mrs Morel gasped slightly in fear. She touched the big, pallid flowers on their petals, then shivered. They seemed to be stretching in the moonlight. She put her hand into one white bin: the gold scarcely showed on her fingers by moonlight. She bent down, to look at the bin-ful of yellow pollen: but it only appeared dusky. Then she drank a deep draught of the scent. It almost made her dizzy.

She looked round her. The privet hedge had a faint glitter among its blackness. Various white flowers were out. In front, the hill rose into indistinctness, barred by high black hedges, and nervous with cattle moving in the dim moonlight. Here and there the moonlight seemed to stir and ripple.

Mrs Morel leaned on the garden gate, looking out, and she lost herself awhile. She did not know what she thought. Except for a slight feeling of sickness, and her consciousness in the child, her self melted out like scent into the shiny, pale air. After a time, the child too melted with her in the mixing-pot of moonlight, and she rested with the hills and lilies and houses, all swum together in a kind of swoon. (34)

Critics all agree that the imagistic rendering of Mrs Morel's interior state here is extraordinary; they disagree, however, over the exact meaning or interpretation of the images.[12] I would like to emphasize two major points. First, the mother's initial subjective state—her forlorn, outcast position and her sense of violation and helpless fury—echoes that of a narcissistically injured child. Throughout Lawrence's work, the mother is repeatedly cast as the object of the child's narcissistic rage; in this scene the mother is *both* the suffering subject and the hated object—represented by the archetypally maternal moon, here figured as a cold, aggressive, and blinding force.[13] The mother's internal suffering is foregrounded even as the scene symbolically projects the external image of a remorseless and overpowering mother. Second, the merging fantasy with which the scene culminates is directly related to the condition of narcissistic injury with which the scene begins. The prevailing psychoanalytic view of merging fantasies today is that they represent less a regression to an actual prior symbiotic state than a reaction to early failures of attunement and recognition. If the infant's assertion of its spontaneous, physical and emotional being is not recognized by the attuned response of the other, the baby experiences narcissistic rejection, a denial of its affective vitality or being. The child, moreover, may feel that its experience of bodily feelings and desires is shameful and must be kept hidden and rigidly in check. The result is a loss of the sense of subjective reality or authenticity. Such a state can trigger the opposite fantasy: the fantasy of letting go and abolishing all barriers and boundaries as one seeks the bodily, affective affirmation of self that was experienced as denied or withheld.

The lily scene paradoxically casts the mother herself in the role of the maternally rebuffed and bereft child. The imagery of the first part of the scene also enacts a basic assertion-recognition dynamic. The tall white lilies reeling and stretching in the moonlight suggest a passionate (indeed phallic) self-assertion that both mirrors and balances the powerful assertiveness of the white moon. Beneath the exterior whiteness of the lilies, associated like the moon with coldness and chastity, is an interior of yellow pollen and perfumed scent, connoting a "dusky" sensuality (and echoing the sensuous "dusky, golden softness" of Mr Morel, quoted earlier). Mrs Morel's reaching in to touch and then deeply inhaling the scent represent an attempt to access a hidden, repressed sensuality or bodily vitality. The explicitly oral metaphor—"she drank a deep draught of the scent"—also ties the scene psychologically to the primary mother-child relationship and its initial oral mode of connection.

The act of imbibing the pollen leaves Mrs Morel in a dizzy, disoriented state, and the two paragraphs that follow describe a blurring of boundaries and a mystical, melting fluidity. The fantasy emphasizes a profound relaxing of restraints and a surrendering of mental defenses—"she lost herself awhile. She did not know what she thought"—(recall Mrs Morel's exhausting mental efforts earlier to defend against emotional pain). The moonlight at the end is no longer aggressive but holding and containing—a "mixing-pot of moonlight" in which "she rested with the hills and lilies and houses." The regressive fantasy of merging or melting, again, does not reflect a desire to return to an actual former state of bliss or oneness with the mother; as this scene makes clear, it is a reaction, an imaginative effort to reverse an actual former state of emotional, bodily frigidity and nonattunement, and to dissolve the rigid mental barriers defending against pain and rejection.

The fantasy of idealized attunement and perfect harmony, however, cannot be sustained. When Mrs Morel finally leaves the garden she is once more feeling fatigued and desolate: "she was tired and wanted to sleep. In the mysterious out-of-doors she felt forlorn" (35). Mrs Morel's depression is key to understanding the psychological problems of her sons and the symbolic imagery of the above scene. Gertrude's lost contact with her own authentic emotional and bodily life will make it difficult for her to recognize the passional life of her sons. Paul will himself continually reenact the dynamics of the lily scene as he struggles to assert himself and be recognized by mother/moon/woman. He too will seek to recover a lost authenticity and hidden sensuality with a desire so intense it threatens boundaries and loss of self. His experience of his mother as withdrawn and withholding both excites acute narcissistic rage (most often projected in the image of a hostile, rejecting mother) and exacerbates the Oedipal desire to penetrate, merge with, and possess her.

The narrative shows Paul even as an infant as heir to his mother's stunted life, to her sadness and shame. Mrs Morel notes "the peculiar heaviness of its [the baby's] eyes, as if it were trying to understand something that was pain . . . It had blue eyes like her own, but its look was heavy, steady, as if it had realised something that had stunned some point of its soul" (50). She decides to call him Paul, "she knew not why" (51). The name, however, echoes her father's affinity with the cold, harsh Apostle Paul "who ignored all sensuous pleasure." The mother cannot help but bequeath to her son her own puritanical, affectively impoverished heritage.

Mrs Morel's depression is mirrored in her child who, the narrator tells us, trotted after her "like her shadow" and "would have fits of depression" that are particularly unsettling for his mother: "It made her feel beside herself." She plumps him in a little chair in the yard, exclaiming, "Now cry there, Misery!" (64). Because Mrs Morel has defensively warded off her own deep sadness and shame, she is unable to tolerate or empathize with her son's negative affects—his feelings of grief and anger—as well. Throughout his life Paul is unable to tell his mother about

any of his failures or disgraces: "he never told her anything disagreeable that was said to him, only the nice things, trying always
to make her believe he was happy and well-liked, and that the
world went well with him . . . He brought her everything, except
his small shames and ignominies" (135).

Unable to express himself fully in relation to his mother, Paul
never feels fully recognized or realized by her. Only his mother
holds the power to confer reality and authenticate his experience
of himself. "The children," the narrator relates, "alone with their
mother, told her all about the day's happenings, everything.
Nothing had really taken place in them, until it was told to their
mother" (87). For Paul, "There was one place in the world that
stood solid and did not melt into unreality: the place where his
mother was. Everybody else could grow shadowy, almost non-
existent to him, but she could not. It was as if the pivot and pole
of his life, from which he could not escape, was his mother"
(261). The mother's dependence on her children—particularly
her sons—to provide her own missing self-esteem makes it difficult for her children to discover their own independent selves,
and thus they remain resentfully dependent, unable to "escape"
her orbit.

The mother will assume gigantic, fearsome proportions in fantasy precisely because of the belittlement and self-suppression she
suffered in reality. Paul's crippling dependence on her is thus
paradoxically due to his sense that she is vitally dependent on
him—that he is responsible for filling her emptiness, providing her
missing self-esteem, and relieving her suffering. "It hurt the boy
keenly, this feeling about her, that she had never had her life's
fulfilment: and his own incapability to make up to her hurt him
with a sense of impotence, yet made him patiently dogged inside.
It was his childish aim" (91). This is also the obsessive aim of the
boy Paul in the story "The Rocking-Horse Winner." The scene in
part 2 of *Sons and Lovers* where Paul and his mother view Lincoln
cathedral symbolically captures the psychological dilemma of a
child's dependence on a depressed mother.

The scene imagistically parallels the mother and the cathedral:

He looked at his mother. Her blue eyes were watching the cathedral quietly. She seemed again to be beyond him. Something in the eternal repose of the uplifted cathedral, blue and noble against the sky, was reflected in her, something of the fatality. What was, *was!*—with all his young will he could not alter it. He saw her face, . . . her mouth always closed with disillusion; and there was on her the same eternal look, as if she knew fate at last. He beat against it with all the strength of his soul.

"Look mother how big she is above the town! Think, there are streets and streets below her: she looks bigger than the city altogether."

"So she does!" exclaimed his mother, breaking bright into life again. But he had seen her sitting, looking steady out of the window at the cathedral, her face and eyes fixed, reflecting the relentlessness of life. And the crow's-feet near her eyes, and her mouth shut so hard, made him feel he would go mad. (280–81)

The passage emphasizes, above all, the mother's remoteness in relation to her son. Like the cathedral, she seemed "to be beyond him," excluding him, shutting him out with her hard, "fixed" stoicism. Due to maternal depression, the child experiences the mother as affectively closed-off and hopelessly inaccessible. The experience arouses intense narcissistic fury and ignites the Oedipal desire to penetrate her barriers. The boy tries to reach the mother by praising the cathedral's grandeur and power, declaring how much "bigger than the city" it looks. He is, in essence, trying to enhance the mother's self-esteem, to make her feel important and powerful. Although she brightens briefly, Paul realizes that her other look of tight constraint and disillusion represents the hard reality he is powerless to change.

"The Rocking-Horse Winner," as mentioned, is also about a child's furious and futile attempt to access a depressed mother. The story, unlike *Sons and Lovers,* does not give much attention to the sources of the mother's calcified inner state. Only the opening paragraph offers a succinct assessment of her condition:

There was a woman who was beautiful, who started with all the advantages, yet she had no luck. She married for love, and the love turned to dust. She had bonny children, yet she felt they had been thrust upon her, and she could not love them. They looked at her coldly, as if they were finding fault with her. And hurriedly, she felt she must cover up some fault in herself. Yet what it was that she must cover up, she never knew. Nevertheless, when her children were present, she always felt the centre of her heart go hard. This troubled her, and in her manner she was all the more gentle and anxious for her children, as if she loved them very much. Only she herself knew that at the centre of her heart was a hard little place that could not feel love, no, not for anybody.[14]

Berman is correct, I believe, in pointing out the similarity between the mother in this story and Mrs Morel.[15] Arcana, on the other hand, makes a distinction between the story and the novel, claiming that the story is indeed "mother-blaming": the text of the story "never redeems her, and the mother's utter inability to respond to him [her son] turns us away from empathy with her character."[16] Though the focus of the story is on the boy's inner world, not the mother's, the narrative tone is not accusatory. In the above paragraph, the mother's condition is simply observed and reported. The narrative makes it clear, furthermore, that the mother's emptiness and inability to feel represent a loss for her as well as her children. The issue of blame seems to me more a matter of the reader's projection than an actual concern of the narrator or implied author.

Like Gertrude Morel, the mother in this story is trapped in a loveless marriage and by a maternal role she feels has "been thrust upon her." Without any sense of her own effective agency, life seems to her a matter of "luck," that is, of forces beyond her control. She feels subject to a fate that is either benevolent or withholding, with no power to affect or influence that fate herself. From a psychoanalytic perspective, such a state suggests a child's dependence on a nonattuned other, an other whom the child experiences as nonresponsive and beyond her control. The other's lack of response to the child's agentic expression ultimately has a nullifying, numbing effect. Time and again in Lawrence's fiction we see a woman forced into a childlike position of dependency in marriage and in a culture that refuses to recognize her as a subject in her own right—a situation that repeats and telescopes a narcissistically wounded infantile state. Although the story, unlike the novel, does not pursue the roots of the mother's emptiness in empathetic detail, the opening paragraph does place her condition in context. Lawrence seems aware, as usual, that the inability to feel is always a response and a defense.

"The Rocking-Horse Winner" is about the child's battle to break through the mother's defensive numbness and receive the affective recognition he craves. Paul's childlike association of "luck" with "lucre," along with his mother's anxiety about money, make him believe that he could fill his mother's affective hollowness by winning at the horse races and thus providing her with "luck." The desire to compensate the mother's emotional shortage and "fill" her himself is inevitably sexualized, evident in the orgasmic imagery of the child's feverish, back and forth riding on his wooden horse. The masturbatory, mechanistic, mentally controlling nature of the child's riding represents a state of being that Lawrence revolted against repeatedly in his writing. Paul's state also implies the sort of fusion Lawrence dreaded: the boundaries between the internal and the external have collapsed. The self's inner wishes magically affect the outside, material world. The story thus allows us to glimpse the emotional and relational origins of that state of solipsistic isolation and omnipotent control toward which Lawrence was powerfully drawn as well as repulsed.

The sexual implications of Paul's rocking-horse riding, furthermore, cannot be wholly explained by the Oedipal drive. Sexuality, as Stephen Mitchell has discussed, is a prime arena for the playing out of basic self-other boundary issues. "Sex," he explains, "is a powerful organizer of experience. Bodily sensations and sensual pleasures define one's skin, one's outline, one's boundaries."[17] The pleasurable release of tension, according to Mitchell, is not the fundamental aim of sexuality; rather, it is "the establishment and maintenance of relatedness," of emotional responsiveness and connection.[18] Thus the interpretation of Lawrence's story need not begin and end with the sexual symbolism and the Oedipal fantasy. The sexual and the Oedipal are informed by still deeper emotional and relational dynamics. The frenzied fantasy of sexualized union with the mother reflects a more profound need to fill the mother's emptiness and heal her wound, to unfreeze her affective core and secure her emotional response, her recognition.

The scene near the story's end, when the mother finally discovers her son wildly "plunging to and fro" on his horse, symbolically enacts the longed-for recognition originally impeded by the mother's emotional frigidity: "Then suddenly she switched on the light, and saw her son, in his green pyjamas, madly surging on his rocking-horse. The blaze of light suddenly lit him up, as he urged the wooden horse, and lit her up, as she stood, blonde, in her dress of pale green and crystal, in the doorway."[19] The son has finally obtained the mother's recognition. The light and color imagery conveys the basic psychological dynamic. Mother and son are at last united and in harmony, connected by the blazing light that illuminates them each together and by their matching green attire. Unlike the light, however, the green is not a "blazing," vital hue but "pale green and crystal," evoking the affectively frozen condition that provoked the son's frenzied activity in the first place. Soon after this scene the boy dies. The child cannot fill the void in the mother's self, though he was willing to sacrifice his own self in the effort.

The enraged hostility and aggression toward the mother apparent throughout Lawrence's writing emerge, therefore, less in response to the mother's real power or strength than as a reaction to her impaired state, to her emotional calcification and psychic fragility. In *Sons and Lovers* such maternally directed violence is expressed symbolically in two scenes—the broken doll and bread-burning episodes. In the first incident, after Paul accidentally breaks Annie's doll, he conducts a strangely sadistic doll-sacrifice ceremony:

> He made an altar of bricks, pulled some of the shavings out
> of Arabella's body, put the waxen fragments into the hollow

face, poured on a little paraffin, and set the whole thing alight. He watched with wicked satisfaction the drops of wax melt off the broken forehead of Arabella, and drop like sweat into the flame. So long as the stupid big doll burned, he rejoiced in silence. At the end, he poked among the embers with a stick, fished out the arms and legs, all blackened, and smashed them under stones.

"That's the sacrifice of Missis Arabella," he said. "An' I'm glad there's nothing left of her."

Which disturbed Annie inwardly, although she could say nothing. He seemed to hate the doll so intensely, because he had broken it. (82–83)

Psychoanalytic critics have generally interpreted the doll in this scene as representative of the mother and the ritual sacrifice as a reflection of Paul's enraged and destructive feelings toward her.[20] I have also discussed the episode briefly in *Literature and the Relational Self*.[21] There I stress the importance of Annie's assertion that Paul "seemed to hate the doll so intensely, because he had broken it," and I argue that Paul's sadism reflects his fear and hatred "of his own destructive rage and the fragile vulnerability of mother/self." I would like to extend that interpretation here by considering the scene in relation to D. W. Winnicott's concept of object use. Winnicott argues that the infant needs to "destroy" the object psychically and the object must survive in order for the infant to "use" or discover the real object—an object whose existence is independent of and outside the infant's mental control.

Michael Eigen offers a wonderfully evocative description of this process:

A kind of psychic explosion takes place in which one lets go as fully as possible. In the other's survival, otherness is born (or reborn) and the self quickens. In such an instance fury or rage is deeper than hate . . . The baby's wrath plays a role in exploding fantasy and reaching the realness of himself and others. An explosion clears the air. The discovery that the other continues to be alive in spite of one's fantasy of destruction creates or ratifies a joyous shock of difference. One is liberated by the other's survival and aliveness.[22]

The doll episode, I believe, displays the emotional and psychic consequences of the mother's *failure* to survive. Annie's observation that Paul hates the doll so intensely *because* he had broken it is key. Storch and Dervin conflate the original breaking of the doll with the sadistic ritual, seeing both as reflective of the son's murderous fury toward the mother. A distinction, however, needs to be made. Paul does not originally break the doll out of hate; rather, the doll gets broken in the wake of a Winnicottian destructiveness—a furious, assertive physicality, an unrestrained "letting go." The doll, hidden under a cover, indeed breaks when Paul is jumping excitedly on the sofa. The child is then horrified and enraged at the doll's failure to survive. In Winnicott's terms, the doll/mother has failed to survive the child's ruthless self-assertion. Without the mother's intact externality or otherness, there are then no limits or bounds to the child's own terrifying destructiveness. At this point, in Eigen's words, "fury turns to hate" and "the child becomes addicted to omnipotent fantasy control," of which the sadistic doll-burning ritual is a powerfully vivid example.[23]

This interpretation can help illuminate, I believe, the sadistic strains that run throughout Lawrence's fiction. Ghent has also written about sadism as a breakdown product of failed object use. "If the subjective object never becomes real . . . and externality is not discovered," Ghent explains, then the subject is "made to feel that he or she is destructive; and finally, fear and hatred of the other develops, and with them, characterological destructiveness comes into being. In short, we have the development of sadism . . . the need to aggressively control the other as a perversion of object usage."[24] Because the construction of the mother's own psychic world is so brittle, she cannot withstand the child's psychic destruction. Thus beneath the fantasy of maternal omnipotence in Lawrence's fiction is ironically just the opposite experience: an experience of the mother's acute vulnerability, of her inability to tolerate the child's furious assertion of his bodily, passionate self.

The same unconscious experience of the mother is apparent in the bread-burning episode. Paul is assigned the task of tending to his mother's loaves of bread baking in the oven. He is joined at home first by Miriam and then by the coquettish young woman Beatrice. Paul flirts with the seductive Beatrice, and Miriam angrily notices "his full, almost sensual mouth quivering. He was not himself" (244). Miriam then reminds him of the bread, which Paul discovers to his horror has charred and burned. He wraps up the most severely burnt loaf in a damp towel and hides it in the pantry. A bit later, alone with Miriam, Paul feels anxiously conflicted over his desire to kiss her: "Her dark eyes were naked with their love, afraid, and yearning . . . She lost all her self control, was exposed in fear. And he knew, before he could kiss her, he must drive something out of himself. And a touch of hate for her crept back again into his heart" (247). At this point he suddenly remembers the bread, and Miriam observes "something cruel in the swift way he pitched the bread out of the tins" (247). When his mother returns home, Paul notices that she is looking especially frail and ill, "bluish round the mouth" (249), and he fears that she may have a serious heart problem. Storch interprets the bread-burning episode as another vengeful fantasy against the powerful mother. The loaves, she says, symbolize "maternal power," and "[t]he burning of the loaves and the burial of the shrouded or swathed loaf is a reflection of the unthinkable and the unapproachable: the wish for the death of the repressive mother who curtails desire."[25] As with the doll episode, however, I believe a distinction needs to be made between the initial destructive act, the burning, and the consequent symbolic act of swathing the loaf and burying it in the pantry.

I agree that the "desiccated loaf . . . swathed up in the scullery" (248) likely reflects a sadistic death wish, but that wish follows a symbolic expression of maternal vulnerability, not maternal power. As a result of Paul losing himself, as Miriam bitterly notes, of relaxing his mental defenses—his conscious, vigilant self—and indulging his sensuality, the bread is ruined. The loaves are indeed associated with the mother, and once again, in Winnicott's terms, she has failed to survive. The burned loaves reflect an unconscious fear, not a wish: the fear that one's spontaneous passion is lethal, that the release of any erotic or aggressive impulse will destroy the other. A sadistic fantasy follows, just as the "hate" Paul feels toward Miriam and the cruelty she observes in his handling of the second batch of loaves follow his experience of Miriam as exposed, undefended, and perilously vulnerable. Finally, the mother's return is marked by her debilitated state and impaired heart, a confirmation of her terrible fragility.

This psychological dynamic can also help make sense of a curious scene in a later story by Lawrence entitled "The Fox." When Henry sees March for the first time in a dress, rather than the "hard-cloth breeches . . . strong as armour" that she is accustomed to wear, he suddenly loses his desire for her and is stricken with a "grave weight of responsibility . . . She was soft and accessible in her dress. The thought went home in him like an everlasting responsibility."[26] This sentiment is repeated throughout the next several pages: "Since he had realised that she was a woman, and vulnerable, accessible, a certain heaviness had possessed his soul . . . She was the woman, and he was responsible for the strange vulnerability he had suddenly realised in her."[27] This burdensome sense of the woman's vulnerability is exactly what inflames Henry's need to dominate and control. Without faith in the woman's otherness or ability to survive, he cannot let go himself nor can he let the woman go. In Jessica Benjamin's terms, the assertion–recognition dialectic breaks down and is reconfigured in the polarized dynamic of domination and submission.[28]

In *Sons and Lovers* Paul experiences both his mother and Miriam as repressive because he fears they cannot withstand the uninhibited expression of his passionate, bodily being, the abandonment of mental restraints or "letting go" that sexuality entails. His occasionally vicious treatment of Miriam, which I will examine in the next section, is a result of what he experiences as her infuriating frailty and is related to the sadistic symbolic fantasies discussed above. Nevertheless, the narrative also displays an empathic identification with the mother and with Miriam which functions simultaneously with the unconscious anger, resentment, and sadistic fantasies of omnipotent control. The narrative presentation of Mrs Morel is astute and emotionally honest even while we see the distortions created by Paul's unconscious fears and desires.

At times Paul's defensive misrepresentations of his mother strikingly contradict the dramatic presentation of her. At one point he characterizes her as a basically "jolly" woman (216), and another time he tells Miriam, "See, my mother looks as if she'd *had* everything that was necessary for her living and developing. There's not a tiny bit of a feeling of sterility about her" (362). The reader, at least this reader, balks at that representation. Paul needs to believe that his mother is jolly and fulfilled because the burden of the opposite reality is so intolerable to him: the mother's depression, her emptiness and emotional sterility, are precisely what the text so effectively portrays.

Paul's internal world mirrors his mother's. Gertrude Morel's narcissistically wounded condition, the lack of recognition and the consequent shame and rage she suffers are reproduced in her son. The subjective experience of emptiness and the detachment from affective, bodily life are passed down relationally from mother to child. Paul battles against his identification with his depressed mother as he seeks to assert himself and realize his own authentic life. The battle is one that Lawrence continually waged himself thoughout his life and his art. In his best work, the identification with the mother's shame and depression is relinquished without a wholesale repudiation of his maternal ties.

The conflictual relationship between Paul and Mrs Morel reflects, finally, the crucial tensions of psychic life: the "intricate and subtle dialectic," in Mitchell's words, between "spontaneous vitality and self-expression" and the need to "preserve secure and familiar connections with others."[29] Or, in Benjamin's and Winnicott's terms, the dialectical needs of recognizing and being recognized by the m/other while also asserting the self and indeed psychically "destroying" her. Paul's faith in his mother's "survival," despite her actual death, is hard-won, but the end of the novel, as well as Lawrence's very ability to write so creatively and productively, suggest that such faith ultimately prevailed.

Miriam and Paul: Self-Mistrust and the Failure of Otherness

The most common critical view of Miriam is that she represents simply one more version of the stifling and possessive mother.[30] Seeking to rescue Miriam from the prevailing negative perspective, Louis Martz argues that her character is far more complex than either Paul or most critics allow. Martz points, for instance, to the scene in which she overcomes her fear of letting the hen peck corn from her hand. The scene demonstrates, he says, Miriam's extreme sensitivity, along with her shy desire for new experience, and shows that for all her shyness and shrinking she is nevertheless capable of a strong response.[31] Martz believes that the complex view of Miriam recedes as the narrator becomes less objective and more identified with Paul in part 2 of the novel.

Tension exists throughout the novel, I believe, between an empathic rendering of Miriam's complex inner life, her dynamic subjectivity, and her status as the object of Paul's narcissistic projections. As much as Miriam is another version of the devouring mother, she is equally another version of Paul himself. In many respects her conflicted subjectivity mirrors his. Ross Murfin has observed that "the very words [Lawrence] uses to criticize Miriam are nearly identical to those Lawrence has used to characterize Paul."[32] Murfin notes such words as "tight," "intense," "hypersensitive," and "suffering." The fact that Miriam's interior life is so identified with Paul's is precisely what dooms their relationship: neither feels fully real or alive, and neither fully trusts in the other's independent reality.

Paul's contempt for Miriam's intensity and suffering reflects, above all, his own self-contempt. "Paul hated her," the narrator asserts, "because, somehow, she spoilt his ease and naturalness. And he writhed himself with a feeling of humiliation" (217). Miriam indeed holds up a mirror to his own (and his mother's) constrained emotional life and bodily shame, to his very lack of ease and naturalness. Paul complains about Miriam's heated, "overcharged" intensity—"There was no looseness or abandon about her" (184)—but he shares that hot intensity far more than he likes to admit. At one point, when reflecting on his response to the "cool" Clara, he does in fact acknowledge it: "He marvelled at her [Clara's] coldness. He had to do everything hotly. She must be something special" (307).

Miriam's anxieties are typical of those that torment so many Lawrence characters. The scene in which Paul pushes her on the swing for instance, symbolically plays out the intense fear of sexual release—of physically and emotionally "letting go" and surrendering to the other—that runs throughout Lawrence's fiction. Miriam is terrified of abandoning herself: "Down to her bowels went the hot wave of fear. She was in his hands. Again, firm and inevitable came the thrust at the right moment. She gripped the rope, almost swooning" (182). In this scene Paul is granted the looseness and abandon that are typically craved, but the narrative is concentrated on Miriam's point of view, on her interior state, not Paul's. The flood of fear and yearning that rises within her is the most characteristically Lawrentian aspect of the scene.

> There was something fascinating to her in him. For the moment he was nothing but a piece of swinging stuff, not a particle of him that did not swing. She could never lose herself so . . . It roused a warmth in her. It were almost as if he were a flame that had lit a warmth in her, whilst he swung in the middle air. (182)

This is one of the most familiar relational scenarios in Lawrence's fiction: the other possesses an unselfconscious spontaneity, warmth, and animal vitality that the self lacks. The cold, deficient self is deeply attracted, compelled by the other's radiating warmth, but also dreads being overwhelmed by the other's very potency and vitality. This dynamic propels such short stories as "The Prussian Officer," "The Blind Man," and "The Princess." The deficient self in these stories, as elsewhere in Lawrence's fiction, is sometimes male and sometimes female. In the confrontational scenes between the deficient self and the idealized other, however, the locus of authorial identification and narrative perspective is primarily with the fearful, conflicted self. In the swing scene it is Miriam, not Paul, who represents that essential subjective position.

The narrative in *Sons and Lovers* displays an empathic understanding of the roots of Miriam's inner deficiency (as it does with Mrs Morel) in her thwarted life as a female in a house ruled by males. We see her ridiculed and emotionally abused by her rough and insensitive brothers, much like Mabel in the story "The Horse-Dealer's Daughter." Miriam is also keenly aware of her inferior status in the larger world. Deprived of opportunity for self-expression and achievement, she is angry and bitter. She protests to Paul that she has been denied the chance " 'of learning—of doing anything. It's not fair, because I'm a woman' " (185). The mental, imaginative realm becomes her only recourse, her only means of compensating for the self-denigration and persistent narcissistic wounding she has suffered:

> She hated her position as swine-girl. She wanted to be considered. She wanted to learn, thinking that if she could read . . . the world would have a different face for her, and a deepened respect. She could not be princess by wealth or standing. So, she was mad to have learning whereon to pride herself. (174)

Lawrence thus shows Miriam's injured narcissism as having both familial and cultural roots. Because others did not recognize or believe in her, she "did not believe in herself, primarily" (255). Paul accuses her of not wanting to love, but of having an "abnormal craving" to be loved: "You absorb, absorb, as if you must fill yourself up with love, because you've got a shortage somewhere" (258). And Miriam herself suspects the truth of this accusation:

> Perhaps he could not love her. Perhaps she had not in herself that which he wanted. It was the deepest motive of her soul, this self-mistrust. It was so deep she dared neither realise nor

acknowledge it. Perhaps she was deficient. Like an infinitely
subtle shame, it.kept her always back. (260)

Yet Miriam also wonders if the same might not be true of Paul.
"Was *he* deficient in something? Perhaps he was" (261). Paul indeed
confesses to his mother, "I think there must be something the
matter with me, that I *can't* love" (395). Just as Paul accuses Miriam of abstracting him and of failing "to realise *him*" in their
lovemaking (227), so Clara accuses Paul of the very same things:
"About *me* you know nothing," she says bitterly—"about *me*! . . .
you've never come near to me. You can't come out of yourself,
you can't" (406–7).

If Miriam in her innermost being feels defective and ineffectual,
she also discovers a similar emotional reality at the heart of Paul.
In a quietly moving scene in the novel, Miriam silently watches
as Paul stands in the middle of the road, doggedly working on a
broken umbrella. The umbrella had significantly once belonged
to William:

> Turning a corner in the lane, she came upon Paul who stood
> bent over something, his mind fixed on it, working away stead-
> ily, patiently, a little hopelessly. She hesitated in her approach,
> to watch.
>
> He remained concentrated in the middle of the road. Be-
> yond, one rift of rich gold in that colourless grey evening
> seemed to make him stand out in dark relief. She saw him
> slender and firm, as if the setting sun had given him to her.
> A deep pain took hold of her, and she knew she must love
> him. And she had discovered him, discovered in him a rare
> potentiality, discovered his loneliness. Quivering as at some
> 'Annunciation', she went slowly forward. (201)

In this scene Miriam indeed "discovers" Paul in all his vulnerability and loneliness—his hopelessness yet persistence at repair-
ing what he cannot fix, at restoring what is irreparably damaged
or lost. His mother's love was originally focused on William, not
him, and he cannot bring William back nor secure his mother's

unconditional love in the same way, no matter how assiduously he tries. The broken umbrella, like the impaired bond with his beloved mother, is stubbornly resistant to his most determined efforts. Miriam intuitively recognizes this even before she learns that the umbrella was originally William's. She has discovered him, exposed and vulnerable, which the image of him standing out in solitary relief against the evening sky enforces. Such deep, intimate knowledge of the other can indeed be described as love. The reference to the Annunciation, however, poses a question: is it Miriam's love for Paul that is self-sacrificial and Christ-like or Paul's for his mother? Both possibilities are equally plausible, a point that further emphasizes the deep alliance and identification of these two characters.

It is little wonder that Jessie Chambers failed to recognize herself in the portrait of Miriam: though the character is based on the external facts of her life, Miriam's conflicted inner life most powerfully resembles Lawrence's own. The author indeed grants Miriam subject status by endowing her with his own inner complexity and allowing her to suffer *like* his protagonist self. Paul, however, is never able to relate to Miriam as *other* than self, as other than the object of his narcissistic projections. For the reader, though, Clara's character once again serves as a corrective, highlighting the limitations in Paul's perception of Miriam. When Paul complains about Miriam's wanting "a sort of soul union," Clara responds:

> "But how do you know what she wants?"
> "I've been with her for seven years."
> "And you haven't found out the very first thing about her."
> "What's that?"
> "That she doesn't want any of your soul communion. That's your own imagination. She wants you."
> He pondered over this. Perhaps he was wrong.
> "But she seems—" he began.
> "You've never tried," she answered. (321)

Clara's comments reflect an awareness that Paul's problems with Miriam are more likely due to his own fantasies and projections than to Miriam's actual character. Paul is oblivious, Clara suggests, of Miriam's real desires, of her separate reality apart from *his* fears and desires. Paul momentarily considers this possibility, just as the narrative has made the reader aware of it as well. An intersubjective awareness, in other words, has temporarily interrupted Paul's more habitual narcissistic projections in relation to Miriam. Paul is not identical with the narrator, however, and the narrator, unlike Paul, continually plays with the tension between these two modes.

Paul's failure to comprehend Miriam's separate reality or otherness in fact fuels his sadistic bullying of her. He sees in her only a mirror of his own vulnerability, shame and fear, which arouses intense narcissistic rage. What he perceives as her terrible fragility again reflects his experience of his mother as too fragile to withstand the uninhibited expression of his passionate, bodily self. These narcissistic dynamics are especially apparent in the algebra lesson scenes, which Millett describes as "some of the most remarkable instances of sexual sadism disguised as masculine pedogogy which literature affords."[33]

Paul's sadistic fury is aroused precisely by Miriam's submissiveness and humility in the face of these lessons:

It made his blood rouse to see her there, as it were at his mercy, her mouth open, her eyes dilated with laughter that was afraid, apologetic, ashamed . . . [T]hings came slowly to her. And when she held herself in a grip, seemed so utterly humble before the lesson, it made his blood rouse. He stormed at her, got ashamed, continued the lesson, and grew furious again, abusing her . . . Once he threw the pencil in her face. (187–89)

Paul's expressions of rage and contempt when confronting Miriam's humiliating self-abasement are a defensive response to his own underlying shame. According to Andrew Morrison, rage and contempt are the affects most frequently associated with shame; they may, in fact, represent attempts to rid the self of shame: "underlying many expressions of rage is a feeling of shame—a feeling that reflects a sense of failure or inadequacy so intolerable that it leads to a flailing out, an attempt to rid the self of the despised subjective experience . . . Contempt represents . . . an attempt to 'relocate' the shame experience from within the self into another person, and thus, like rage, it may be an attempt to rid the self of shame."[34]

Interestingly, at the beginning of the novel, William exhibits similar bullying behavior toward his nightschool students. He would issue "snorts of impatience and disgust," and call names: "You great booby, you block-head, you thundering idiot and fool" (71). Léon Wurmser also discusses contempt as one of the most prominent "masks" of shame: it "lies in shaming others, in turning contempt from the self toward others. It is defense by reversal."[35] Mrs Morel's sons are caught up in the vicious cycle of shame, both their own and their mother's. The mother's deep feelings of narcissistic inadequacy, of emotional and bodily shame, are passed down relationally to the children who depend on and identify with her.

Miriam, too, suffers from a similar debilitating shame. Her fear of sexuality is essentially a fear of her own narcissistic inadequacy. When she considers having sex with Paul, she admits that she "was not afraid of people, what they might say. But she dreaded the issue with him . . . He would be disappointed, he would find no satisfaction, and then he would go away" (328). Her sense of profound self-deficiency, her fear, as quoted earlier, that "she had not in herself that which he wanted," proves once more to be the real source of her sexual inhibitions.

Miriam's perilous fragility again serves to infuriate Paul. In the scene leading up to their lovemaking, Paul's perception of Miriam's defenselessness is associated with images of death and destruction, and it characteristically provokes aggressive behavior. After climbing a cherry tree,

> He looked down. There was a faint gold glimmer on her face, that looked very soft, turned up to him.
>
> "How high you are!" she said.
>
> Beside her, on the rhubarb leaves, were four dead birds, thieves that had been shot. Paul saw some cherry-stones hanging quite bleached, like skeletons, picked clear of flesh. He looked down again to Miriam . . .

She seemed so small, so soft, so tender down there. He
threw a handful of cherries at her. She was startled and frightened. He laughed with a low, chuckling sound, and pelted her.
(329)

Aggressive feelings and destructive fantasies emerge, once
again, not from the experience of female/maternal power but
from the experience of acute female vulnerability. Miriam is in
the lowly, submissive position, seeming "so small, so soft, so
tender down there." Paul is in the position of power, and it is
the unconscious fear of overpowering and destroying the other
through one's own greedy, thieving love (like the birds, and as
in the doll and bread-burning episodes) that gives rise to the
deathly associations and, in this case, to the playfully aggressive
behavior.

When the narrator allows us inside Miriam's consciousness,
however, we discover that she is neither as defenseless nor as
vulnerable as Paul assumes. Her psychological defenses, in fact,
are quite similar to his. Just as Clara accuses Paul of never coming
out of himself or coming near to her, so too Miriam holds herself
back and never truly achieves intimacy with Paul. Her inner reserve protects against the fear of being dominated by him (just
as Paul holds back out of fear of being dominated by women in
general):

> She knew she felt in a sort of bondage to him, which she hated
> because she could not control it. She had hated her love for
> him from the moment it grew too strong for her. And, deep
> down, she had hated him because she loved him and he dom-
> inated her. She had resisted his domination. She had fought
> to keep herself free of him, in the last issue. And she *was* free
> of him, even more than he of her. (340)

Miriam finally confesses openly that their relationship "has
been one long battle," that he "had always fought away from
her," and that there had never been any real intimacy or "perfect
times" between them, as Paul would like to believe. This revelation, so unsurprising to the reader, is utterly shattering to Paul.

He is "aghast," stunned: "she whose love he had believed in when he had despised himself, denied that their love had ever been love . . . Then it had been monstrous. There had never been anything really between them—all the time he had been imagining something where there was nothing" (341). Once again Paul is confronted with his own false projections. He does not blame himself, however, but Miriam. He feels deceived and betrayed. "*You* never believed in me," he charges. "She had despised him when he thought she worshipped him" (342).

The accusation that Miriam "never believed in" him calls to mind a scene from a later novel, *Kangaroo*. Here the Lawrence alter ego character, Richard Lovatt Somers, has a disturbing dream in which a woman resembling both his wife, Harriett, and his mother appears "sullen and obstinate against him, repudiating him . . . [Her] face was swollen and puffy and almost mad or imbecile, because she had loved him so much, and now she must see him betray her love." He cries to her, "Don't you believe in me? Don't you *believe* in me?' " But the woman turns away "to the sullen and dreary, everlasting hell of repudiation." He wakes and immediately thinks of Harriett and his mother: "the two women in his life he had loved down to the quick of life and death," and yet he feels, "They neither of them believed in me."[36]

The mistrust of women so distinctive of Lawrence's work rises out of this deep-rooted conviction that his mother did not "believe in" him, that for all her narcissistic investment in him, she never trusted in his individual integrity or believed in him as a separate being in his own right. Nor does he have faith in her integrity as a separate, independent subject: the fantasy of Somers's dream is that the woman's mental disintegration results from his bad or untrustworthy love. The dream exposes, as does so much of Lawrence's fiction, the psychic consequences of failed intersubjectivity: the collapse into the oppressive, narcissistic polarity of idealization and repudiation—the all-good and all-bad splitting of the paranoid-schizoid state.

Miriam's worshipping love, like the dream woman's, proves to be false and empty. She had never really "believed in" him. Yet we have also seen how Paul has failed to believe in or fully comprehend Miriam's separate subjectivity, her independent reality or otherness. Paul and Miriam, finally, have never really believed in themselves or the other. In the last, pathetic scene between them toward the novel's end, each longs for the other's self-assertion to compensate for their own inability to claim themselves as subjects of desire. "He would leave himself to her," Paul thinks. "She was better and bigger than he. He would depend on her" (457). Each wants to be claimed, wholly and unequivocally, by the other—a dynamic that prefigures the theme of masochistic submission in much of Lawrence's later work.

Miriam sorely wants to put her arms around Paul's body, to "take it up, and say 'It is mine, this body. Leave it me!' . . . But she crouched, and dared not. She was afraid he would not let her. She was afraid it was too much" (462). The fear, once again, is that asserting one's real bodily passions and desires will be "too much": it will overwhelm, "destroy," or be rejected by the other. Rather, Miriam wants him to claim her: "Oh, why did not he take her! Her very soul belonged to him. Why would not he take what was his!" Paul, however, "could not bear it, that breast which was warm and which cradled him without taking the burden of him . . . She could not take him and relieve him of the responsibility of himself" (462).

Both Miriam and Paul suffer from such severe narcissistic loss and inner deficiency that neither can provide what the other needs. Both want the other to assume the "burden" of their tormented selves. Both are terrified of claiming themselves—of fully asserting their bodily, passionate being—and thus they look to the other to assert what they feel incapable of asserting. Miriam is as much a twin to Paul—a mirror of his tormented subjectivity—as she is the object of his rage and defensive projections. Jessie Chambers may not have felt rewarded by Lawrence's portrait of Miriam, but by granting Miriam an inner life so like his protagonist's, Lawrence is acknowledging an extreme closeness, indeed identification, with her character. Miriam's deep sense of shame, her self-mistrust, and her crippling inhibitions are the very problems with which Paul so exhaustingly struggles. His ultimate repudiation of her reflects a repudiation of his own projected weaknesses.

Yet Miriam's character is more than merely a bundle of Paul's projections. As with Mrs Morel's character, the narrative presents her particular history, her psychological and emotional conditioning, with compassionate insight. It also allows us to see Paul's misperceptions and misjudgments of her. In the end, Paul's repudiation of Miriam is balanced by the narrator's empathic recognition of the complexity and depths of her pain. By recognizing her suffering, her inner world, the narrator is recognizing Miriam's subjectivity as both like and separate from Paul's. The intersubjective consciousness of the narrative thus stands in tension with Paul's narcissistic projections, recreating for the reader a dynamic tension fundamental to human relational life.

Clara and Paul: Depersonalization and the Psyche/Soma Split

If Miriam's hot intensity uncomfortably mirrors Paul's inner shame and anxiety, making her a reflection or projection of his own undesirable self, then Clara, in her cool confidence and independence, represents for Paul a desirable otherness.[37] Clara's very remoteness and inaccessibility are indeed what make her so desirable to him. These qualities, first of all, duplicate those of his emotionally withdrawn mother. In the scene in which Paul and Clara attend the theatre, Paul's experience of Clara watching the play echoes, in several important respects, his experience of his mother viewing Lincoln cathedral:

> And he loved her, as she balanced her head and stared straight in front of her, pouting, wistful, immobile, as if she yielded herself to her fate because it was too strong for her. She could not help herself—she was in the grip of something bigger than herself. A kind of eternal look about her, as if she were a wistful sphinx, made him mad to kiss her. (375)

As in the cathedral scene, the woman's "immobile" stoicism, her fatalism, as well as her "eternal" and mysterious quality of inaccessibility are stressed. In this case, a merging fantasy immediately follows:

> He was Clara's white, heavy arms, her throat, her moving bosom. That seemed to be himself... There was no himself. The grey and black eyes of Clara, her bosom coming down on him, her arm that he held gripped between his hands were all that existed. Then he felt himself small and helpless, her towering in her force above him. (375–76)

The merging fantasy is provoked, once more, by the experience of the other's affective remoteness and impenetrability. We see here, as so often in Lawrence's fiction, the fantasy of the woman's "towering" force over the "small and helpless" self. Yet that fantasy significantly occurs in the context of Paul's perception of the woman's own helplessness, of Clara's yielding "to her fate because it was too strong for her." Again, the text makes us aware of an ironic reality: the boy/man's fantasy of the woman's dangerous omnipotence is precipitated by the reality of the woman's powerlessness and her stoic suffering in the face of it.

Clara's cool remoteness, however, also serves to make sex less threatening because Paul can more easily keep her depersonalized and invulnerable. Whereas Paul can never forget Miriam's neediness and personal frailty, Clara's detachment and seeming self-sufficiency allow him to unleash his sexuality without fear of destroying her. We are told that for Clara, "The naked hunger and inevitability of his loving her, something strong and blind and ruthless in its primitiveness, made the hour almost terrible to her" (397). Yet unlike Miriam, Clara can more easily contain and absorb this terrible, primitive force.

The peewits "screaming in the field" during Paul and Clara's lovemaking symbolically project the terror that is always bound up with sexuality for Lawrence. If a ruthless sexuality is to be unloosed, however, then that terror must be allowed expression as well, and the effect of such full-blown self-expression is liberating. A primitive, blind, and ruthless force has been released, and neither self nor other has been destroyed. As the following beautifully lyrical line suggests, a thrusting, assertive sexuality is safely contained—embraced within a balanced, wheeling universe: "They had met, and included in their meeting the thrust of the manifold grass stems, the cry of the peewit, the wheel of the stars" (398). The narrator indeed remarks a few lines later, "The night contained them."

The "baptism of fire in passion" that Paul experiences with Clara, however, is utterly without intimacy: "It was something that happened because of her, but it was not her" (399). For Paul, as for many Lawrence characters, an uninhibited self-assertion is possible only in the context of a depersonalized relationship in which neither self nor other is personally vulnerable. Depersonalization is also a characteristic defensive response to early narcissistic injury. If the infant's bodily being has not been recognized or affirmed, the child experiences his/her body and bodily functions as objectionable, shameful, and "bad." The continuity of the psyche/soma, in Winnicott's terms, is disrupted; the soma is split off from the psyche—one's body is not felt to be an integral part of one's personal subjectivity or experience of self.

Throughout Lawrence's fiction sexuality represents a *healing* of this split through *recognition* of the bodily self. Such a fantasy is evident in the scene in which Paul caresses Clara's naked body:

> She stood letting him adore her and tremble with joy of her. It healed her hurt pride. It healed her, it made her glad. It made her feel erect and proud again in her nakedness. Her pride had been wounded inside her, she had been cheapened. Now she radiated with joy and pride again. It was her restoration, and her recognition. (383)

The relationship between Paul and Clara, however, is far more complex than this fantasy about the restorative power of sex suggests. The intersubjective perspective of the narrative again endows the woman with her own afflicted inner consciousness that counters many of Paul's projections and fantasies about her. Clara, in fact, battles Paul's depersonalization of her, and in the next chapter she charges that he has never truly recognized her at all.

As quoted earlier, she cries, "About *me* you know nothing ... about *me*! ... You can't come out of yourself, you can't ... I feel ... as if it weren't *me* you were taking" (406–7).

This failure of recognition—the feeling that the other has failed to see or acknowledge the separate, real *me*—indeed distinguishes all of the characters' relationships in this novel. Paul, in the end, makes the very same complaint about Clara:

> She wanted him, but not to understand him. He felt she wanted the man on top, not the real him that was in trouble. That would be too much trouble to her, he dared not give it her. She could not cope with him. It made him ashamed. (451)

The fear, as usual, is that the other can "not cope" with the "real" me—the me that is troubled, anxious, and vulnerable, the me that is desperate for love. We see here the buried shame that rules the lives of so many of Lawrence's characters and is a key factor in their fundamental feelings of unreality and powerlessness. In the above passage, Paul continues: "So, secretly ashamed because he was in such a mess, because his own hold on life was so unsure, because nobody held him, feeling unsubstantial, shadowy, as if he did not count for much in this concrete world, he drew himself together smaller and smaller" (451).

Paul's experience of Clara, like his relationship with all the female characters in this novel, is thus profoundly contradictory. While she represents, in her ripe sexuality, a towering, fearsome force, she is equally felt to be too frail and shaky to withstand the force of his own terrible needs and desires—"Clara could not stand for him to hold on to" (151). The real issue, once more, is not the woman's power but the fear of her not being strong enough and the shame over the self's unmet, unmanageable needs.

Finally, one other incident in Paul's relationship with Clara deserves mentioning—the scene, restored in the unexpurgated Cambridge edition, in which Paul stealthily puts on Clara's stockings and is sexually aroused (381). Angela Carter sees Lawrence's fixation on women's clothes, particularly stockings, throughout his fiction as evidence of pure transvestism—"Lorenzo the Closet-Queen."[38] For Carter, Lawrence's art of "female impersonation" only reflects a deeper misogyny. Linda Ruth Williams interprets the stockings as a classic Freudian fetish—a symbolic phallus that defends against the horror of the castrated woman—while also emphasizing the multiple possibilities suggested by Paul's act: "the act manages to suggest narcissism, masturbation *and* straightforward heterosexual intercourse (Paul inserts himself into the stockings, which stand in for the absent Clara) . . . Paul is both his own masturbatory self as well as 'being' the sexiest part of Clara."[39]

Paul is certainly deriving pleasure from his female identification here, and perhaps it is pleasurable because he is alone and controlling it. Two other instances in the text also suggest Paul's identification as a girl in relation to both Clara and Baxter. At one point, the narrator states that Clara "saw his neck in the flannel sleeping jacket as white and round as a girl's" (384). Another time, when Paul runs into Baxter on the stairs—"he almost collided with the burly metal-worker"—Paul is whistling a tune entitled "Put me among the Girls" (391). The wish to be a girl is part of the larger fantasy of being ravished by a powerful, animalistic male. To be penetrated by the other is a way of absorbing his power and bodily vitality, and thus of reclaiming it as one's own. The intense ambivalence that such a fantasy inevitably entails, however—the terror of being overwhelmed and annihilated by the very animalistic masculinity one seeks—is also apparent throughout Lawrence's fiction.

Though the text reveals Paul's fantasies of appropriating and controlling Clara's sexuality, those fantasies, as usual, do not contain the whole story. Clara is not merely a sex object, as Millett maintains, "whom Paul nonchalantly disposes of when he has exhausted her sexual utility."[40] As discussed, Clara frequently points up Paul's misperceptions and shortcomings. Her character stubbornly resists his attempts to depersonalize her. She is indeed the object of Paul's narcissistic fantasies, yet she also maintains her integrity as a separate subject who withstands his attempts to objectify and assimilate her to the particular drama of his inner world. In such resistance—in the woman's maintaining her externality and otherness—lies the potential for real relationship and the hope implicit in Lawrence's best fiction.

Walter, Baxter and Paul: The Rejected Father and the Need for Recognition

The tension between repudiation and an empathic narrative identification also figures into the characterization of Walter Morel. Many readers feel that the dramatic presentation of Morel's character is far more sympathetic than the view of him we get through Paul's (and his mother's) eyes. Even after Walter's most brutal act in the novel, throwing the drawer at Gertrude, the narrator draws us into Morel's pained consciousness and informs us that Morel himself was far more damaged by the deed than was his wife:

> He lay and suffered like a sulking dog. He had hurt himself most. And he was the more damaged, because he would never say a word to her, or express his sorrow . . . Nothing, however, could prevent his inner consciousness inflicting on him the punishment which ate into his spirit like rust, and which he could only alleviate by drinking. (55)

The incident also evokes a familiar relational dynamic. The man comes to resent and dread the woman precisely because he has the power to harm or break her. The narrator comments: "He dreaded his wife. Having hurt her, he hated her" (57). As in the doll episode, hate for the female other emerges out of the experience of her destructibility, her vulnerability to one's own destructive impulses. In unconscious fantasy the woman is thus paradoxically at once powerful and powerless: the boy/man feels utterly dependent on her (she is all-powerful) but he has no faith in her dependability (she is powerless to withstand his self-assertive destructiveness). As Benjamin has argued, the mother's actual powerlessness and lack of agency in social and cultural life help create this trap by making it all the more difficult for her to survive her child's psychic destruction and become real to him.

Walter is caught in the polarizing stalemate that results from such intersubjective breakdown. Like his wife, he too "felt a sort of emptiness, almost like a vacuum in his soul" (63) which he attempts to dull through drink. His life with his mates at the pub becomes a refuge from the antagonism and emptiness of his home. The narrative nevertheless makes us aware of Morel's distinctly domestic, tender, and nurturing qualities—qualities that his children, particularly Paul, refuse to accept. When Paul is sick as a baby, we are told that "Morel wanted to hold the child, to soothe him. It would have done the man good to be able to nurse his sick baby. But the child would not be nursed by him. It would stiffen in his arms, and . . . would scream, draw back from the father's hands" (63). Later, when Paul is older and ill again, Morel stands hesitantly outside his door: "He felt his son did not want him" (91). Paul callously rejects all of his father's clumsy but touching attempts to comfort and reassure him.

The characterization of Morel is multidimensional, as is the psychology involved in Paul's rejection of him. Obviously Paul's enmeshment with his mother and her contempt for the father together play a vital role, as do Oedipal rivalry and Paul's inflamed need to possess his mother totally. In my view, however, what most prevents Paul from accepting and identifying with his father is Morel's explosive temper, his wild and unrestrained outbursts of anger toward the mother. These attacks are terrifying for the boy; he now must protect his mother not only from his own destructive impulses but from his father's as well. Morel's fiery temper thus exacerbates Paul's anxiety over his mother's psychic fragility. For the boy who fears his own rage and destructiveness, his father's fury becomes another inhibiting factor, another obstacle to the identification with masculine sexuality and the spontaneous expression of passion.

This dynamic is most apparent in the scene in which Paul, awakened from sleep, listens in terror to the "shrieking" of the ash tree outside the house as his parents quarrel violently in the room below. The tree is associated with Morel: he likes its shrieking noise—"It's music," he says, "It sends me to sleep" (84). To Paul, however, the tree's noise is "demoniacal" and mixed up with his father's drunken, violent behavior:

> Then he heard the booming shouts of his father, come home nearly drunk, then the sharp replies of his mother, then the bang, bang of his father's fist on the table, and the nasty snarling shout as the man's voice got higher. And then the whole was drowned in a piercing medley of shrieks and cries from the great, wind-swept ash-tree. The children lay silent in suspense, waiting for a lull in the wind to hear what their father was doing. He might hit their mother again. There was a feeling of horror, a kind of bristling in the darkness, and a sense of blood. (84–85)

The narrator tells us that not until Paul and the other children heard the soothing sound of the tap water drumming into the kettle "which their mother was filling for morning . . . could [they] go to sleep in peace" (85). Not until they were assured of their mother's safety, in other words, could they relax their defenses and allow themselves the self-abandonment of sleep.

Storch has also discussed the ash-tree's identification with the father. She associates it with a positive, specifically creative and liberating masculine force: Paul "must deny himself identification with this creative force and also with his father as a strong male. . . . Paul cannot identify with this liberating masculinity."[41] Paul is blocked from such identification, however, not simply by his mother's powerful hold over him and his father, as Storch maintains, but by the very nature of that masculinity itself, by its seemingly uncontrolled aggressiveness and frightening destructive potential.

Paul's dilemma is similar to that of a patient Winnicott discusses who was "in this position that he always protects the mother because he must preserve her in order to be able to have any rest or relaxation at all. He therefore has no knowledge that his mother might survive his impulsive act. A strong father enables the child to take the risk because the father stands in the way or is there to mend matters or to prevent by his fierceness."[42] Paul has no faith in his father's ability to mend, prevent, or stand in the way of his (Paul's) own destructive impulses; on the contrary, the father's temper only intensifies Paul's anxiety over his mother's safety. Winnicott describes his patient as adopting "self-control of impulse at a very early stage" and as being severely inhibited: "The inhibition had to be of all spontaneity and impulse in case some particle of the impulse might be destructive." The struggle *against* such inhibition is the very struggle that *Sons and Lovers,* indeed all of Lawrence's creative work, imaginatively enacts.

The son's rejection of his father, of course, only intensifies his need for paternal identificatory love. That need is made all the more desperate by the original failure of recognition in the mother-child relationship. Lawrence looks to an idealized father-figure not only to defend against the omnipotent mother of unconscious fantasy, as Storch and Ruderman insist, but also to bestow recognition of the bodily, passionate self that, having been unrealized, has become idealized.

Despite the overly Oedipal constellation of Paul's relationship with Baxter Dawes, the imagery and language of their fight scene (which prefigures the famous wrestling scene of Birkin and Gerald in *Women in Love*), suggest an even more primary, elemental desire at work. The fight is described in erotic, orgiastic terms that emphasize, above all, a perfect physical attunement and reciprocity between the two men:

> He [Paul] lay, pressed hard against his adversary, his body adjusting itself to its one pure purpose of choking the other man, resisting exactly at the right moment, with exactly the right amount of strength, the struggles of the other, silent, intent, unchanging, gradually pressing its knuckles deeper, feeling the struggles of the other body become wilder and more frenzied. Tighter and tighter grew his body, like a screw that is gradually increasing in pressure, till something breaks. (410)

To claim that this scene merely expresses Lawrence's latent homosexuality is analytically unsatisfactory—it doesn't explain enough. As James C. Cowan has discussed in relation to Birkin, the motives beneath the homosexual strivings are concerned not primarily with sexual gratification but with attempts to assuage early disturbances and divisions in the self—specifically, the split between the spiritual and the sensual, or the psyche and the soma.[43] The most blatant homoerotic scenes in Lawrence's novels—the bathing scene in *The White Peacock*, the wrestling scene in *Women in Love*, the sick-room scenes in *Aaron's Rod*, and the initiation rituals in *The Plumed Serpent*—all highlight the same fantasy: that of complete bodily attunement and mutual responsiveness between the self and an other like the self—an idealized masculine self. The homosexual fantasies, as Cowan argues, reflect, at the most fundamental level, attempts at magical, narcissistic repair. Because homosexuality is so tied up with narcissistic fantasies in Lawrence's fiction, it is prey to the same splitting and polarities— idealization and repudiation, domination and submission—that confound heterosexual relationships in his work. Paul's conflicted and erotically tinged relationship with Baxter raises issues that will be explored more fully in "The Prussian Officer" and *Women in Love*.

Paul: The Maternal Heritage

Both Mrs Morel's death and the novel's final scene display the paradoxical tensions so definitive of Lawrence's art. Paul directly hastens his mother's death by feeding her the morphine-laced milk. The act, as Storch suggests, reverses and vengefully attacks the original oral relationship between mother and child: by "denying life to his mother at the fundamental level," Paul is "making a statement of violence against the mother-child bond itself."[44] As so often in Lawrence's fiction, however, the unconscious fantasy does not contain the whole story. The act is also done in an attempt to relieve the mother of her real, excruciating suffering; it is equally an act of almost unbearable empathy. While watching his mother die, "It was almost as if he were agreeing to die also" (436). By killing her he believes he will be killing a vital part of himself as well. Thus for Paul, his mother's death on the one hand liberates or releases him and on the other relegates him to a deathlike state of horrifying nothingness and unreality. "The real agony was that he had nowhere to go, nothing to do, nothing to say, and *was* nothing" (456).

Many critics read the last scene in which Paul, fists clenched, walks "towards the faintly humming, glowing town, quickly" as a final repudiation of the mother, an embrace of the father's world, and a determined movement toward life. Others emphasize the "drift towards death" and read the ending more ambiguously.[45] In this final scene contradictory forces are again at play. At the same time as we see the workings of a profound despair, we see the seed of faith. Not only is the despair rooted in the maternal relationship but so too is the faith. At the end, Paul renounces a limitless narcissistic identification with his mother and in so doing discovers a limited self. This is, I believe, the psychological significance of one of the novel's most moving passages:

> On every side the immense dark silence seemed pressing him, so tiny a speck, into extinction, and yet, almost nothing, he could not be extinct. Night, in which everything was lost, went reaching out, beyond stars and sun. Stars and sun, a few bright grains, went spinning round for terror and holding each other in embrace, there in a darkness that outpassed them all and left them tiny and daunted. So much, and himself, infinitesimal, at the core a nothingness, and yet not nothing. (464)

The paradox of "at the core a nothingness, and yet not nothing" captures an emotional reality that acknowledges loss without annihilation, aloneness without disintegration. Paul turns his back at the end on a merged or narcissistic identification with the mother and on the despair and darkness to which such an identification inevitably leads: "He would not take that direction, to the darkness, to follow her" (464).

This type of renunciation is not the same thing as repudiation of the mother. Paul discovers that he can go on "being" in his mother's absence, and that discovery paradoxically implies her presence. Without some internalization of the loving, good mother, Paul would indeed have succumbed to the darkness.[46] Lawrence's faith in "being," his sense of belonging to a profoundly interconnected, living universe—in short, his religious sensibility—stems not from identification with an idealized father, as some have argued, but from hard-won faith in the primary maternal relationship.

In an object relational study of religious faith, John McDargh asserts, "Faith is integrally related to the development of the capacity to be alone,"[47] which includes the "capacity to tolerate dependency"[48] and "the capacity to tolerate ambivalence."[49] Lawrence's fiction dramatizes the exquisite struggle involved in developing the capacity to tolerate dependency, ambivalence, and aloneness. That *Sons and Lovers* gives such full play to the opposing, ambivalent forces in this struggle is testament to the capacity itself.

Notes

1. H. M. Daleski, *The Forked Flame: A Study of D. H. Lawrence* (Madison: University of Wisconsin Press, 1987), 43.

2. Mark Schorer, "Technique as Discovery," *Hudson Review*, Vol. 1 (spring 1948). Quoted from *D. H. Lawrence and 'Sons and Lovers': Sources and Criticism*, ed. E. W. Tedlock (New York: New York University Press, 1965), 167.

3. Geoffrey Harvey, *'Sons and Lovers'* (Atlantic Highlands, NJ: Humanities, 1987), 69.

4. Cynthia Lewiecki-Wilson, *Writing Against the Family: Gender in Lawrence and Joyce* (Carbondale: Southern Illinois University Press, 1994), 70.

5. Judith Arcana, "I Remember Mama: Mother-Blaming in *Sons and Lovers* Criticism," *D. H. Lawrence Review*, 20 (1989), 139.

6. Ibid. 143.

7. Lydia Blanchard, "Love and Power: A Reconsideration of Sexual Politics in D. H. Lawrence," *Modern Fiction Studies*, 21 (1975), 435. Cynthia Lewiecki-Wilson and Nigel Kelsey also focus on Mrs Morel as a victim

of patriarchy and its social and political constraints. According to Kelsey, in *D. H. Lawrence: Sexual Crisis* (New York: St Martin's, 1991), 87, "The Morel household is conditioned by a complex web of economic and politico-ideological relations." He points to scenes in which Mrs Morel laughs "when her oppression boldly exposes its nakedness to her" and argues that such laughter is a recognition of "the absurdity of one's emotional and material dependence on the various forms that oppression may take" (91). Lewiecki-Wilson, in *Writing Against the Family*, 75, similarly examines how Mrs Morel is robbed of her independent identity by patriarchy: "Morel controls her identity, despite her education or former social level . . . He has leased the home and has the paying job, even if she actually makes the home and judiciously distributes the money."

8. Jeffrey Berman, *Narcissism and the Novel* (New York: New York University Press, 1990), 205.

9. See Harry Guntrip, *Schizoid Phenomena, Object Relations, and the Self* (New York: International University Press, 1969).

10. Geoffrey Harvey, *'Sons and Lovers'*, 70.

11. In *D. H. Lawrence and the Phallic Imagination: Essays on Sexual Identity and Feminist Misreading* (New York: St Martin's, 1989), 95–96, Peter Balbert emphasizes the gender issue in this scene and believes it demonstrates Mrs Morel's "nagging and neurotic sexual envy of the state of manhood itself." The affective tone of the passage, however, does not convey envy but wrenching loss. Mrs Morel, due to her constrained and emotionally impoverished life, is indeed overly invested in the child. When Mr Morel claims the boy as belonging to the masculine world—the father's world outside the home—Mrs Morel's devastation is understandable. Critics seem to me more interested in blame than in the text itself. Both parents exhibit harmful and destructive behavior toward their children in this novel, yet the narrative also demonstrates an empathic awareness of the parents' individual plights. The novel portrays the complex web of conflicting relational needs and desires that, in infinitely various forms, characterize family life.

12. Dorothy Van Ghent, in "On *Sons and Lovers*," from *The English Novel: From and Function* (New York: Holt, Rinehart, and Winston, 1953), 249, sees the lilies and the white moonlight as representative of a "vast torrential force," a primal, nonhuman otherness associated with phallic power and eros, while Geoffrey Harvey, in *'Sons and Lovers'*, 73, says the whiteness of the moonlight and the lilies symbolizes Mrs Morel's "severe emotional

chastity." Elsewhere, John Stoll, in *The Novels of D. H. Lawrence: A Search for Integration* (Columbia: University of Missouri Press, 1971), 85, believes the phallic lilies serve as "an ironic commentary" on Mrs Morel, who has lost her passional nature; for Margaret Storch, in *Sons and Adversaries* (Knoxville: University of Tennessee Press, 1990), 189, the lilies, "reeling in the moonlight," confirm Mrs Morel's "terrible female power" and "evoke the mother's prohibition of the son's oedipal desires, transformed into a mystical taboo"; Lewiecki-Wilson, in *Writing Against the Family*, 90, believes the scene "deconstructs the myth of fixed gender division as it renders a sexually charged physical world by intermixing male and female imagery"; and in *D. H. Lawrence: 'Sons and Lovers'* (Cambridge: Cambridge University Press, 1992), 180, Michael Black emphasizes the multiple and competing symbolic possibilities of the scene, which, he argues, resists any easy algebraic equations: "One can't just say that the moon 'stands for' a will-driven feminine dominance which is cold; nor that the lilies 'stand for' a remembered passion now passing away; nor that the pollen on her face, easily brushed off, is her own participation in that passion."

13. See Gavriel Ben-Ephraim, *The Moon's Dominion: Narrative Dichotomy and Female Dominance in Lawrence's Earlier Novels* (East Brunswick and London: Associated University Press, 1981), for a discussion of the moon as a symbol of maternal power and dominance throughout Lawrence's early novels.

14. D. H. Lawrence, *The Woman Who Rode Away and Other Stories*, eds. Dieter Mehl and Christa Jansohn (Cambridge: Cambridge University Press, 1995), 230.

15. Jeffrey Berman, *Narcissism and the Novel*, 209.

16. Judith Arcana, "I Remember Mama: Mother-Blaming in *Sons and Lovers* Criticism," *D. H. Lawrence Review*, 20 (1989), 146–47.

17. Stephen A. Mitchell, *Relational Concepts in Psychoanalysis: An Integration* (Cambridge, MA: Harvard University Press, 1988), 103.

18. Ibid., 107.

19. D. H. Lawrence, *The Woman Who Rode Away and Other Stories*, 242.

20. According to Margaret Storch, in *Sons and Adversaries*, 99, "The body of the mother is, in fantasy, dismembered and destroyed, disintegrating in a flash of fiery consuming anger, and liquefied into the wax and sweat of elemental fluids . . . The scene is a vivid depiction of a child's sadistic fantasy against the mother." In *A 'Strange Sapience': The Creative Imagination of D. H. Lawrence* (Amherst: University of Massachusetts Press,

1984), 114, Daniel Dervin argues that the doll contains projections of both the bad mother and the badness within Paul himself: "Perhaps as Paul takes over the doll and decides its fate, it becomes a 'bad' self-representation that needs to be destroyed . . . It is from this point on that Paul ceases to be only a shadow-self." Dervin views the scene in a more positive light than Storch, arguing that for Paul "the immolated doll marks the dawn of imaginative power" (151).

21. Barbara Ann Schapiro, *Literature and the Relational Self* (New York: New York University Press, 1994), 67–68.

22. Michael Eigen, *The Psychotic Core* (Northvale, NJ: Jason Aronson, 1986), 179–180.

23. Ibid., 181.

24. Emmanuel Ghent, "Masochism, Submission, Surrender," *Contemporary Psychoanalysis,* 26 (1990), 124.

25. Margaret Storch, *Sons and Adversaries,* 103; see below, 146.

26. D. H. Lawrence, *The Fox, The Captain's Doll, The Ladybird,* ed. Dieter Mehl (Cambridge: Cambridge University Press, 1992), 49.

27. Ibid., 53.

28. See, for instance, Benjamin's book *The Bonds of Love: Psychoanalysis, Feminism, and the Problem of Domination* (New York: Pantheon, 1988).

29. Stephen A. Mitchell, *Hope and Dread in Psychoanalysis* (New York: Basic, 1993), 133.

30. In *Oedipus in Nottingham: D. H. Lawrence* (Seattle: University of Washington Press, 1962), Daniel Weiss sees both Miriam and Clara as mother-surrogates in the Oedipal conflict, with each representing one side of the Madonna-whore split. For Ben-Ephraim, in *The Moon's Dominion,* 110, Miriam is just another link in a chain of possessive women because "Paul is a man who needs to be possessed." For Mark Spilka, in *The Love Ethic of D. H. Lawrence* (Bloomington: Indiana University Press, 1955), 82, Miriam represents one of three "destructive forms of love" in the novel—"oedipal, spiritual, and 'unbalanced-possessive'." Feminist critics have tended to see her as one in a series of female stereotypes who exist exclusively to cater to Paul's needs. Miriam's role, according to Kate Millett in *Sexual Politics* (New York: Ballantine, 1969), 347, is "to worship his talent in the role of disciple."

31. Louis L. Martz, "Portrait of Miriam: A Study in the Design of *Sons and Lovers,*" in *Imagined Worlds: Essays on Some English Novels and Novelists in Honour of John Butt,* eds. Maynard Mack and Ian Gregor (London: Methuen, 1968).

32. Ross Murfin, 'Sons and Lovers': A Novel of Division and Desire (Boston: Twayne, 1987), 65.

33. Kate Millett, Sexual Politics, 355.

34. Andrew Morrison, Shame: The Underside of Narcissism (Hillsdale, NJ: Analytic Press, 1989), 13–14.

35. Léon Wurmser, The Mask of Shame (Baltimore: Johns Hopkins University Press, 1981), 24.

36. D. H. Lawrence, Kangaroo, ed. Bruce Steele (Cambridge: Cambridge University Press, 1994), 96–97.

37. Charles Rossman, in " 'You are the Call and I Am the Answer': D. H. Lawrence and Women," D. H. Lawrence Review, 8 (1975), 255–328, takes perhaps the most negative view of Clara. He emphasises her "coldness and aloofness" and her "rigid, egocentric isolation which has cut her off from all warm contact with others" (266). These traits are in fact responsible, he believes, for provoking her husband's brutality.

38. Angela Carter, Nothing Sacred (London: Virago, 1982), 161–68.

39. Linda Ruth Williams, Sex in the Head: Visions of Femininity and Film in D. H. Lawrence (Detroit, MI: Wayne State University Press, 1993), 133.

40. Kate Millett, Sexual Politics, 358.

41. Margaret Storch, Sons and Adversaries, 100.

42. D. W. Winnicott, Psychoanalytic Explorations, eds. Clare Winnicott, Ray Shepard, and Madeleine Davis (Cambridge, MA: Harvard University Press, 1989), 237.

43. James C. Cowan, "Blutbrüderschaft and Self Psychology in D. H. Lawrence's Women in Love," in The Annual of Psychoanalysis, Vol. 20, ed. Chicago Institute for Psychoanalysis (Hillsdale, NJ, and London: Analytic Press, 1992), 200–201.

44. Margaret Storch, Sons and Adversaries, 107; see below, 150.

45. Several critics share Daniel Weiss' view in Oedipus in Nottingham, 66–67, that the town is in "polar hostility to Gertrude, as the world of men" and that "In choosing the town Paul is accepting his father, an idealised image" and is thus embarked on a new, more positive direction. Other critics are more sceptical. Ben-Ephraim writes in The Moon's Dominion, 122, that "Paul Morel is too wounded and bereaved a young man to experience a beginning so hopeful and so new." Michael Black, in 'Sons and Lovers', 186–87, compares the last paragraph to "the dereliction, the despair, the sense of being impervious to death" that Ursula Brangwen experiences toward the end of The Rainbow. Lawrence, Black argues, "wills his central characters into the effort to move towards the world,

towards social human life" but much of the rest of his work shows them moving away from it. I share the perspective of critics like Geoffrey Harvey and Ross Murfin who stress the ambivalence and ambiguity of the novel's conclusion. In *'Sons and Lovers': A Novel of Division and Desire*, 131, Murfin claims that the last paragraph is "as self-divided and self-conflicted as Lawrence's characters."

46. James C. Cowan also makes this point in "Lawrence, Freud and Masturbation," *Mosaic*, 28 (1995), 94: "There is little question that despite the dangers of devourment and engulfment posed by the symbiotic merger with his mother, the imago of the nurturant and supportive mother was well established in Lawrence's internal representational world."

47. John McDargh, *Psychoanalytic Object Relations Theory and The Study of Religion: On Faith and the Imaging of God* (Lanham, MD: University Press of America, 1983), 81.

48. Ibid., 83.

49. Ibid., 92.

Images of Women in *Sons and Lovers*

MARGARET STORCH

❖　❖　❖

D. H. LAWRENCE'S response to women reflects his awareness of the fundamental power of women over men's emotional lives[1] and of strong female influence in his own society.[2]
This perception of female ascendancy was deepened by his close
relationship with his mother and by his early contact with the
women's emancipation movement. His resentment of female
domination was complicated and intensified by his relationship
with Frieda Weekley. Through Frieda, he became familiar with
the acceptance of matriarchal values, derived from Bachofen, of
the avant-garde group *die kosmische Runde*.[3] Through living at close
quarters with Frieda's forceful personality, his deep-seated resistance to female domination was aggravated into a particular form
of taunting invective.[4] He refers often to the powerful and overwhelming mother figure as the "Magna Mater." It is a term that
he applied to Frieda with variants such as the "Queen Bee," and
to Ursula in *Women in Love*. The response can also be found as the
mainspring of many important relationships within his works.
Lawrence's rebellion against the powerful mother has been noted

and regarded as a major element in his work. Marguerite Beede Howe defines this preoccupation in terms of the Laingian notion of the fear of engulfment.[5] If we study some recurring characteristics of the central male–female relationships, we will observe buried patterns that indicate the essential nature and source of his emotional reaction to women. Lawrence, in his earlier works, is likely not to be explicit about his antagonism towards women; indeed, an attitude of sympathy for women in their social condition is often uppermost.[6] The case of *Sons and Lovers* is especially interesting. In this autobiographical novel, Lawrence is apparently writing an account of a young man's Oedipal struggle, in which the father's authority is entirely despised and the mother wins emotional ascendancy over her female rival, a young woman of her son's generation, in order to establish absolute emotional control over her son. A close study of the novel reveals, however, that this surface pattern, in fact, conceals a fundamental antagonism towards the mother.[7]

D. H. Lawrence's *Sons and Lovers,* one of the first artistic works produced with an awareness of psychoanalysis, appears to be a classic Freudian text.[8] While writing the final draft of the novel, Lawrence was led by Frieda's insights into his earlier experience and also by her knowledge—through Otto Gross and others—of theory not yet widely known, to write of his emotional life with some objectivity. In so doing, he achieves a delicate balance between self-analysis and the evocation of sensuous immediacy. The triadic Oedipal pattern emerges sharply from the action of the novel: in the development of the relationship between the parents; in the conflict of the two sons, first William and then Paul, with the father; and in the emotional aridity of Paul's relationships with young women.

Yet does art reveal its fundamental impetus so readily? Is not the Oedipal pattern so deliberate and so close to the surface in *Sons and Lovers* that we are led to suspect that it must, in fact, conceal something else?

In 1913, when *Sons and Lovers* was published, Freud had not yet presented his own work on object relations,[9] which was later to provide a starting point for Melanie Klein. We find that it is Kleinian theory that leads us to the truest meaning of the novel.

Beneath the more apparent triadic Oedipal structure lie the dynamics of the early mother–infant dyad. The novel appears to be written out of loyalty to the mother, Gertrude Morel, on the part of the son, Paul Morel, whether against the aggressive father or the possessive sensual woman of the son's own generation; yet its true emotional core is a sense of hatred for the suffocating mother, leading to a series of fantasies in which the son destroys her, and culminating in her actual death at his hands. These key events are: the sacrifice of Annie's doll, Arabella, in Paul's childhood; the burning and symbolic entombment of the loaves of bread in the "Strife in Love" chapter; and the death of Gertrude Morel as an immediate result of an overdose of morphia administered by Paul. In each of them, we find a destructive anger that runs against the manifest devoted love for the mother in the text, corresponding to Melanie Klein's notion of the infantile defense mechanism of the splitting of the mother into a good aspect and a bad aspect.

The first episode is one of apparently motiveless violence in which the boy, Paul Morel, destroys his sister Annie's doll, with her frightened connivance:

> "Let's make a sacrifice of Arabella," he said. "Let's burn her." She was horrified, yet rather fascinated. She wanted to see what the boy would do. He made an altar of bricks, pulled some of the shavings out of Arabella's body, put the waxen fragments into the hollow face, poured on a little paraffin, and set the whole thing alight. He watched with wicked satisfaction the drops of wax melt off the broken forehead of Arabella, and drop like sweat into the flame. So long as the stupid big doll burned, he rejoiced in silence. At the end, he poked among the embers with a stick, fished out the arms and legs, all blackened, and smashed them under stones.
>
> "That's the sacrifice of Missis Arabella," he said. "An' I'm glad there's nothing left of her." (82–83)

The scene cuts beneath the familiarly "Oedipal" patterning of the novel to show a powerful anger against the mother. The "sacrifice" is an act of desecration against a figure who should be revered. This is apparent in the building of an altar, the title "Missis Arabella," and the aura of "wicked satisfaction" that emanates from defying a taboo. The body of the mother is, in fantasy, dismembered and destroyed, disintegrating in a flash of fiery consuming anger, and liquified into the wax and sweat of elemental fluids. When already blackened and "dead," the fragments are retrieved with aggressive phallic curiosity by means of a poking stick, and then further pulverized into nothingness, not "with" stones but "under" stones, suggesting both a final horror that cannot be looked at and the gravestones that cover the dead, which in turn have in their origins an impetus of aggression against the dead.[10]

The scene is a vivid depiction of a child's sadistic fantasy against the mother. The presence of Annie is an essential component of the scene. In this and the cognate episodes, her witnessing of the event and her connivance at Paul's action suggest that part of the emotional totality of anger against the mother is a fantasy of a sibling relationship that is transmuted into relationships with female peers in defiance of the mother's sensuous dominance.[11] The sister in earlier life can be a female figure who provides an alternative to the mother and who, like the son, strains against the mother's moral strictures.

In the structure of the narrative, the occurrence is closely related to Paul's conflict with his father. Immediately following this symbolic annihilation of the mother and a reference to his impetus against what he has destroyed—"He seemed to hate the doll so intensely, because he had broken it"—we find one of the central Oedipal scenes. Lawrence stresses Paul's opposition to his father and the Morel children's support of their mother against their father. He then shows us a triad of the mother with a black eye, the father shamefaced, and William glaring at the father (83). This significant juxtaposition is completed by a description of the ash tree, symbolic of the father's violence, which dominates the household and instills a fundamental fear in the children. We note, however, that it is also associated with freedom and the creative power of music:

> In front of the house was a huge old ash-tree. The west wind, sweeping from Derbyshire, caught the houses with full force, and the tree shrieked again. Morel liked it.
>   "It's music," he said. "It sends me to sleep."
>   But Paul and Arthur and Annie hated it. To Paul, it became almost a demoniacal noise. The winter of their first year in the new house, their father was very bad. The children played in the street, on the brim of the wide dark valley, until eight o'clock. Then they went to bed. Their mother sat sewing below. Having such a great space in front of the house gave the children a feeling of night, of vastness, and of terror. This terror came in from the shrieking of the tree and the anguish of the home discord. (84)

In the welter of emotions that are the condition of the boy's life, he must deny himself identification with this creative force and also with his father as a strong male. The emptiness, vastness, and sense of an unknown menace in the darkness, described above, make apparent his personal experience of psychic disintegration in the face of such conflicting pressures. The ambivalence of his response is, however, made plain in the treatment of Annie's doll, where Paul is behaving towards the mother in a way that reflects the father. Beneath the relatively superficial Oedipal structure, we see more fundamental feelings at work. Paul cannot identify with this liberating masculinity. His attempt to obliterate his mother's emotional hold over him is crushed, paralleling the father's futile act of aggression. The father's shame reflects the damaged masculine pride of father and son.[12]

The second episode displays a similar emotional configuration: Paul burns loaves of bread that his mother has given him the responsibility of tending as they bake in the oven. Paul is at his home with Miriam one evening during a phase of their relationship when he feels most strongly drawn to her and realizes how important it is for him to be able to discuss his work with her.

They are joined by Beatrice, a high-spirited and flirtatious young woman who teases them both and temporarily monopolizes Paul. At this stage, Miriam draws his attention to the fact that the loaves are burning. Beatrice in her flippant and mocking way aids Paul in covering up his neglect, grating the one badly burned loaf with a nutmeg-grater and then wrapping the loaf in a damp towel for Paul to hide in the scullery, or small back kitchen. The scene has a close parallel in the play *A Collier's Friday Night,* where the central figures are Ernest; his girlfriend Maggie who, like Miriam, is disliked by his mother; and another flirtatious and mocking Beatrice.

Correspondences between the two, and elements that emerge more nakedly in the play than in the novel, heighten our awareness of its significance.[13] In the play, the burned loaf is again grated, accompanied by even greater hilarity on the part of all three young people: Ernest Lambert (the Paul figure) and the two women. Again, it is wrapped in a damp towel and put in a small room, this time the pantry. Whereas in the novel a reference is made to the "swathed loaf,"[14] in the play, presumably the less carefully written text, it is the "shrouded loaf."[15] The use of the word "shroud" and the wrapping of the loaf to enclose it in a small dark space, the pantry, reflect a fantasy of killing and burying the mother. As with the episode of Annie's doll, in each of these versions of the loaf sequence, the son is accompanied by young women of his own generation, who offer him sensuous pleasure and escape from the mother's emotional dominance. The loaves of bread are a suggestive symbol of maternal power, since they are associated with the fundamental experience of nourishment, the center of the infant–mother relationship and its inherent conflicts. The essence of the fantasy lies in Paul–Ernest's assigned duty of tending the loaves as they bake. He has been given a constricting sense of responsibility to the mother, who governs the fundamental sphere of nourishment and sensuality. His temporary release from this responsibility is shown in the frivolity and promise of amoral, sensuous indulgence with which the burning of the loaves is surrounded, carried in each instance by a high-spirited, mocking, and indomitable young woman, Beatrice.

The complexity of the son's emotional situation is reflected in the three distinct young women who are associated with the scene. Beatrice offers a clear promise of liberation into sexual fulfillment. The sister, although her presence is admissible because she is the son's peer, here represents the mother's values and point of view. The deep emotional conflicts surround Miriam–Maggie, who is also linked with the mother's values, yet in a more complicated way.[16] It is she who is blamed for the burning of the loaves as the person who had distracted Paul–Ernest, blamed mockingly by Beatrice in the novel and with exasperation by Nellie in the play. Although Beatrice is apparently the object of Paul–Ernest's erotic fooling and flirtatiousness, it is clear that his deeper erotic feelings are more seriously directed towards Miriam–Maggie. Since, however, those instincts are frustrated, partly as a result of complex guilt in turn related to the mother, he gives rein to sensual impulses with Beatrice, who represents a condition of amoral emotional freedom.

The close connection between his feelings for Miriam and the loaf-burning episode, intertwined with awareness of maternal power, is very apparent. As Paul turns a fresh batch of baking loaves, he appears brutal and distant to Miriam: "There seemed to her something cruel in it, something cruel in the swift way he pitched the bread out of the tins, caught it up again" (247). The soft and vulnerable Miriam feels that he does not belong to her world but rather is a cohort of his mother, doing her harsh work, in which the baking pans become an implement of psychic control of dependents. Paul himself becomes a mother figure from whom the tender nursling Miriam desires loving sustenance but feels that he gives it grudgingly. As they study poetry together later, "She was really getting now the food for her life during the next week," while we are told that certain poems "nourished her heart" (248). Paul's final emotional loyalty to his mother makes Miriam experience the uncertain affections of a harsh mother. In other words, Paul takes on the dominance of his mother through his bond with her.

Earlier in the *Sons and Lovers* episode, Beatrice, the woman who is free from the sensual restraints associated with the mother, exerts her own control over Paul. As she and Paul tussle in a teasing, flirtatious way, she pulls his hair and then combs it straight with her own comb, tilting back his head to comb his moustache also (243). This signifies her female command of his maleness: we recall the anger and humiliation Lewis, in *St. Mawr,* feels when Mrs Witt wants to touch his head and cut his hair.[17] Here, Paul accepts Beatrice's treatment of him because it gives him access to her sensuality. The episode is redolent of passion and overtones of male sexuality: "It's a wicked moustache, 'Postle," she said. "It's a red for danger.—Have you got any of those cigarettes?" (243). The dangerous burning red of male virility is associated with the fire that burns the loaves in the oven; in the play we are told that the fire is "ramped" like hell.[18] The association links the force that rebels against the mother's hold and the force that desires sexual fulfillment, each of which also means a turning away from Miriam. The episodes in both novel and play are filled with references to Paul's many female admirers, which further links the suppression of the mother with fantasies of masculine prowess.

The relationship with the mother herself lies behind the responses to Maggie–Miriam and Beatrice. The mother is the moral and emotional center of Paul's life, and responses to her are split off in feelings towards other kinds of women. Thus, although the sexual unease surrounding Miriam is derived from the mother's sexual prohibitions, the relationship with the mother is experienced as a totality and a continuum, while that with Miriam is segmented and disjunctive, at the conscious level.

The burning of the loaves and the burial of the shrouded or swathed loaf is a reflection of the unthinkable and the unapproachable: the wish for the death of the repressive mother who curtails desire. In both the novel, *Sons and Lovers,* and the play, *A Collier's Friday Night,* the incident leads to a resolution of action that stresses its significance. In each case, the mother returns to the scene of the transgression, ill and suffering from a weak heart brought on by carrying bags of shopping for the family. In each case, it is an extra burden of meat that has been the final straw. The fantasy of the mother's death is, therefore, followed up by a premonition of her actual death, to be followed through in *Sons and Lovers.* Her maternal function and the moral power she wields through self-sacrifice are emphasized by the meat that she carries. The latent guilt at the destructive fantasy is transferred into a complete image of pity. As with the childhood episode of the annihilation of the doll in *Sons and Lovers,* the symbolic act of the destruction of the mother is followed up in both novel and play by a scene of emotional conflict with Oedipal overtones. The essential content of the sequence is similar in both works: the father, returning home drunk, wants to eat special food the mother is keeping for Ernest–Paul, clearly suggestive of the sexual generosity that she begrudges the father. This leads to a bitter altercation between husband and wife; the son intervenes and physical violence almost breaks out between father and son; the mother and son dispute heatedly over the time and attention that he gives to Maggie–Miriam. At the conclusion of the episode, he admits to his mother that he cares more deeply for her than for the girl, and they are tenderly reconciled.

Whereas in the earlier Oedipal configuration juxtaposed with the childhood doll fantasy, the father maintains a violent independence for the son to aspire to, here he is entirely crushed by the woman and her union with the son. The episode marks his final defeat. As he prepares for going to the pit in the morning, both the novel and play intimate that his son will never belong to this demeaning collier's world. In *A Collier's Friday Night,* the stage directions describe the movements of a broken man: *"Then he lurches round, and limping pitiably, goes off upstairs."*[19] Similarly, Morel in *Sons and Lovers* is a pathetic figure: "The elderly man began to unlace his boots. He stumbled off to bed. His last fight was fought in that home" (253).

In both works, this sequence of experience produces a moment of resolution: the working through of a fantasy of killing the mother and enjoying libidinal freedom with consorts who can stand against her; the guilty fear at the actual death of the mother with its consolidation of her supremacy over the father and other women in their emotional claims to the son. At the end of *A Collier's Friday Night,* the stage directions instruct the actors playing mother and son to speak in a particular way: *"There is in their tones a dangerous gentleness—so much gentleness that the safe reserve of their souls is broken.*"[20] In *Sons and Lovers,* Paul goes to bed in an intensely emotional state: "He pressed his face upon the pillow in a fury of misery. And yet, somewhere in his soul, he was at peace because still he loved his mother best. It was the bitter peace of resignation" (254). Each description of the emotional state refers to graduated psychic levels, the deepest level being "the soul," the elemental psychic state. In each, we are told that a point of acceptance has been reached after bitterly conflicting feelings have surfaced for a time. The acceptance brings with it a sense of gentleness or peace because the most fundamental state of the psyche—commitment to the mother, her dominance, and her taboos—is reaffirmed. However, it is a qualified gentleness because it denies the urgency of independence and desire. In the play, the "safe reserve" of the soul, the usual acceptance of external reality that makes it possible to live with deep psychic conflict, is broken, temporarily revealing what lies beyond. The final sequence of the episode in *Sons and Lovers* emphasizes the defeat of masculinity: the following day Paul's father tries to conciliate him, which is "a great humiliation to him." The sense of the cowed father, his male pride destroyed by the mother, is associated with the permanent effects of the experience for Paul, since submission to maternal dominance means a suppression of the possibility of male aspiration. The humiliation is shared by father and son.

The third episode in this sequence is the death of Gertrude Morel, hastened by Paul. The three acts, two fantasied and one actual, are linked by several similarities, indicating that they arise from the same psychic source. In each, Paul is accompanied by a young woman, either his sister or a woman with whom he has an erotic association. Paul and his co-conspirators plot together, knowing that they are breaking a strict taboo: this knowledge gives rise to the horrified fascination or hysteria of the females in each episode.

The chapter dealing with Mrs Morel's death is entitled "Release." The agony that Paul suffers upon her painful demise and his own great emotional loss is also a release from her powerful hold over him. There are certain parallels between the episode of actual death and the two fantasies of killing the mother found earlier in the novel that show how his mother's death releases Paul from the domination that could not be broken except in symbolic rebellion during her lifetime.

The central fact that reveals the association with the fantasies is that here Paul literally brings about her death and does so with the assistance of a female accomplice, his sister Annie. The three events are further linked by an association with fire. In the two fantasies, it is by fire, a displacement of urethral violence, that the mother image is destroyed. The moment when Paul first realizes that his mother is going to die is again related to fire. He is sitting in the kitchen smoking: "Then he tried to brush some grey ash off his coat. He looked again. It was one of his mother's grey hairs. It was so long! He held it up, and it drifted into the chimney. He let go. The long grey hair floated and was gone in the blackness of the chimney" (419–20). Fire is a presence here, yet it is curiously suppressed. Its light and heat are concealed, and it appears to turn living things like the hair to ash, without going through the intermediate stage of burning. Although we are not told that Paul is sitting by the fire, it is clear that he must be, because when he holds up the hair, it drifts up the chimney, necessarily drawn by the heat from a glowing fire. He is a strong agent, engaged in the masculine act of smoking, while his mother's life moves towards disintegration. Moreover, the ash from his cigarette turns into the hair of a dying woman and seems to cause its dissolution. The moment marks the knowledge that fantasy will become reality. The blackness into which the hair disappears reflects the infant's terror at the annihilation of his own being, which he has brought about through his destructive aggression. This sense of personal disintegration is experienced often from this point until the end of the novel, amid the turmoil of anguish that Paul endures.

Henceforth, fire is benign, symbolizing the sustenance of Mrs Morel's life. Its work of aggression is done. Paul lovingly tends the fire in his mother's sickroom to provide her with comfort. It is through an inversion of maternal power, the drinking of poisoned milk, rather than through masculine aggression, that she will be destroyed. The agent of annihilation has its source in the primary depths of the relationship.

Paul makes the decision to take his mother's life to spare her further suffering. The suffering, however, often seems to be his own, as he longs for her to die; but there is distinct ambivalence in the way he feels about the prolonged period of agony she suffers before she dies. He does not wish her to eat and puts water in the milk that he gives her: "And he would put some water with it, so that it should not nourish her. Yet he loved her more than his own life" (435). When he gives her the fatal draught of morphia, he puts it in the feeding cup of hot milk she takes before sleeping at night, making it a bitter potion that she drinks with difficulty. He seems almost to be forcing her despite her vulnerability: "He saw her frail fingers over the cup, her lips making a little 'moue.' " (438). When he tells Annie that she has drunk it and found it bitter, Annie laughs, "putting her under lip between her teeth." We notice here that in each of these episodes it is *milk* that is involved, the basic sustenance of life and the food that in the act of nourishment knits the bond between mother and child. In putting first water and then morphia in her milk, Paul is therefore denying life to his mother at the fundamental level and is, moreover, making a statement of violence against the mother–child bond itself. The fatal drink is given to her in a feeding cup, evocative of a child's cup. An elemental scene of nurturing in which the mother gives a soothing bedtime drink to the child becomes an act of imposing suffering and denying life as the mother, now a helpless child, is forced to drink. At the same time, an inverted mother–child relationship, in which Paul is the loving mother, is strongly suggested.

The final phase of Mrs Morel's life and the agonized process of her death are closedly interwoven in the narrative with references to Paul's unsatisfactory relationships with two women, Clara and Miriam. When he and Clara are together or are making love, Clara feels that he is a "make-belief" lover. With Miriam, too, Paul is unable to make true personal contact, precisely at moments of sensuous intimacy: "She could not kiss his agony.

That remained alone and apart. She kissed his face, and roused his blood, while his soul was apart writhing with the agony of death" (435). Paul's personal fragmentation and failure to maintain genuine feeling with these two women goes beyond the normal response, however painful, to a parent's impending death. As he is made more nakedly aware of his emotional dependence upon his mother, his inability to make deep emotional contact with women is more keenly present to him. The female accomplice who assists him in the three episodes of killing the mother is a symbol of the sexual liberation he hopes to achieve through destruction; that ultimate act of rebellion is finally, however, ineffectual.

Notes

1. Sandra Gilbert in "Potent Griselda: 'The Ladybird' and the Great Mother," in *D. H. Lawrence: A Centenary Consideration,* eds. Peter Balbert and Phillip L. Marcus (Ithaca, NY: Cornell University Press, 1985), 130–61, provides a comprehensive study of the theme of matriarchal power in Lawrence at play in "The Ladybird" and other works; Judith Ruderman in *D. H. Lawrence and the Devouring Mother: The Search for a Patriarchal Ideal of Leadership* (Durham, NC: Duke University Press, 1984) investigates the male's fear of being devoured by the mother figure in Lawrence's work.

2. Hilary Simpson in *D. H. Lawrence and Feminism* (De Kalb, IL: Northern Illinois University Press, 1982) gives an extensive account of Lawrence's contact with the women's emancipation movement. See especially 19–42.

3. Martin Green has shown the importance of this movement to Lawrence. He gives an account of Frieda's association with it and Lawrence's knowledge of it through her. See *The Von Richthofen Sisters: The Triumphant and the Tragic Modes of Love* (New York: Basic Books, 1974), 73–85.

4. Anne Smith provides a perceptive study of the quality of Lawrence's relationships with women, and especially Frieda, in "A New Adam and a New Eve—Lawrence and Women: A Biographical Overview," in *Lawrence and Women,* ed. Anne Smith (New York: Barnes and Noble, 1978), 9–48.

5. For example, see Marguerite Beede Howe, *The Art of the Self in D. H. Lawrence* (Athens: Ohio University Press, 1977), 18. Gavriel Ben-Ephraim in *The Moon's Dominion: Narrative Dichotomy and Female Dominance in Lawrence's Earlier Novels* (Teaneck, NJ, London, and Toronto: Associated University Presses, 1981) argues that males in Lawrence feel overwhelmed by female power, which they both resist and wish to be absorbed by. See, for example, 44, 223.

6. Carol Dix, in *D. H. Lawrence and Women* (Totowa, NJ: Rowman and Littlefield, 1980), stresses Lawrence's sensitivity toward women and feminist concerns. See, for instance, 22–23.

7. Mark Spilka, in *The Love Ethic of D. H. Lawrence* (Bloomington: Indiana University Press, 1955), 60–63, contends that the Freudian pattern is merely superimposed upon the narrative, and that the deeper emotional interest is the dualistic conflict between man and woman, which in turn is the true theme of the subsequent novels.

8. In "Lawrence's Quarrel with Freud," in *Freudianism and the Literary Mind* (New York: Grove Press, 1959), 151–76, Frederick J. Hoffman contends that the influence of Freud upon *Sons and Lovers* was rather superficial, despite the response of his contemporaries.

9. Freud's work on object relations would be presented in, for instance, "Mourning and Melancholia" (1917).

10. This sequence in the novel vividly recalls a Kleinian play situation in which a child's behavior toward representative small figures yields up deep analytic meaning. It has been discussed several times. Grover Smith, Jr, in "The Doll-Burner: D. H. Lawrence and Louisa Alcott," *Modern Language Quarterly,* 19 (1958), 28–32, points out the similarities between this episode and one in Alcott's *Little Women,* which Lawrence may have read, where a group of children burn a doll called Annabella in an act of sacrifice. Anne Smith relates Paul's destruction of Arabella to rebellion against his mother and to the sexual "sacrifice" of Miriam. I would argue that whether or not Lawrence knew Alcott's version, the power of his own scene of doll-burning comes from personal sources. Daniel Dervin examines the incident at length in a Winnicottian study in "Play, Creativity and Matricide: The Implications of Lawrence's 'Smashed Doll' Episode," *Mosaic,* 14 (1981), 81–94. He convincingly links the destruction of the doll with the child Paul's creation of a new and more assertive self.

11. In the 1927 paper "Criminal Tendencies in Normal Children," in *Love, Guilt and Reparation, and Other Works, 1921–45* (New York: Delacorte

Press/Seymour Lawrence, 1975), 175, Klein describes a fantasy of two brothers acting as accomplices to kill and eat the mother.

12. In "The *Sons and Lovers* Manuscript," in *D. H. Lawrence: A Centenary Consideration,* eds. Peter Balbert and Philip L. Marcus, 39–40, Mark Spilka contends that Paul suffers from a lack of male identity. In "Lawrence's Treatment of Women in *Sons and Lovers,*" from *Lawrence and Women,* ed. Anne Smith, 52, Faith Pullin argues that the "true love" in the novel is that between Paul and his father.

13. I am grateful to Nora Foster Stovel for first pointing out to me this correspondence.

14. A loaf in a child's fantasy can also stand for a baby (and here, therefore, a hated rival). It has been suggested that the word "swathed" reflects the meaning of the cognate "swaddled," therefore strengthening the sense of the baby as victim. I prefer to read "swathed" as "bandaged," conveying the notion of a mutilation that is covered up.

15. See *A Collier's Friday Night,* in D. H. Lawrence, *The Plays,* eds. Hans-Wilhelm Schwarze and John Worthen (Cambridge: Cambridge University Press, 1999), 39. The play was written between 1906 and 1909, and was never produced in Lawrence's lifetime.

16. Louis L. Martz in "Portrait of Miriam: A Study in the Design of *Sons and Lovers,*" in *Imagined Worlds: Essays on Some English Novels and Novelists in Honour of John Butt,* eds. Maynard Mack and Ian Gregor (London: Methuen, 1968), 351, describes the narrative technique that Lawrence adopts in the novel in order to manage "the deep autobiographical problems that underlie the book," whereby Paul's point of view is set against both the action and the portrait of Miriam.

17. See D. H. Lawrence, *St. Mawr and Other Stories,* ed. Brian Finney (Cambridge: Cambridge University Press, 1983), 56.

18. D. H. Lawrence, *The Plays,* 38.

19. Ibid., 53.

20. Ibid., 59.

Forms of Expression in *Sons and Lovers*

JACK STEWART

◆   ◆   ◆

*S*ONS AND LOVERS has been considered a breakthrough from the shallow aestheticism of *The White Peacock* and overripe Wagnerianism of *The Trespasser* to a "triumph of realism" in which Lawrence mastered his own painful experience. But to take *Sons and Lovers* as simply "realistic" is to neglect much of the novel's richness—or to expand the concept of realism beyond recognizable limits. Critics who put a high premium on realism tend to identify the completion of Lawrence's apprenticeship with the culmination of his career and to regard subsequent departures with suspicion. Graham Holderness theorizes a full range of stylistic development between the aesthetic experiment of *The White Peacock* and "the triumph of realism" in *Sons and Lovers,* while Nancy Kushigian condenses the entire pattern of Lawrence's early development into this one novel.[1] In proclaiming his *bildungsroman* his masterwork, Holderness tends to regard Lawrence's post-realist writing as a falling off, rather than a breakthrough. But Lawrence's mastery of realism released him, if not from youthful obsessions, then from any further compulsion to treat them directly in fiction.

In *Sons and Lovers,* the contingent and the essential—whatever lights up the writer's imagination as real—are conveyed through an objective style that interacts with subjective modes of vision. Rather than monolithic realism, a fluid interaction of styles animates and sustains an expressive image of life. Various styles frame and then penetrate the experience of a central self: realism supplies the bedrock, impressionism the atmosphere, symbolism the significance, and expressionism the vision. While literary realism and symbolism may have little to do with interarts comparison, I discuss them here as integral components of Lawrence's style that have much to do with his evolving vision and expression. I apply a series of lenses to the novel, not in order to label or categorize, but to give a fuller view of the complex integrity of Lawrence's art in its first full flowering. Realism clings to close observation of individuals in the social contexts from which their lives derive meaning. The first part of *Sons and Lovers,* which presents a history of the coal mines, a view of the town and people, and an account of the Morels' marriage, is authentic realism. Basing the narrative on his own experience, Lawrence describes "the actual conditions of living" (10), presenting individuals in family and community contexts. He renders feelings and actions with the authoritative insight of an insider and "[builds up] a real world . . . through an astonishingly detailed re-creation of a complex human environment."[2] Characters are embedded in a social matrix; conflicts can be traced to economic conditions and class differences; actions are generated within a fully realized setting.

Beyond depicting the environment, realism conveys the experience of living in a given place at a given time. "Rarely," writes Alfred Kazin, "has the realistic novelist's need to *present,* to present vividly, continually, and at the highest pitch of pictorial concentration . . . reached such intense clarity of representation as it does in *Sons and Lovers.*"[3] Jessie Chambers, disappointed with *Paul Morel,* urged Lawrence to get closer to reality, in the conviction that he "possessed the miraculous power of translating the raw material of life into significant form."[4] She felt that "the common round was full of mystery, awaiting interpretation" and that Lawrence, who "had the rare gift of seeing [the working class] from within," should become "an interpreter of the people to whom he belonged."[5] Lawrence's ability to express reality through sensory detail, dialogue, and physical action is a major element in the novel's success. It takes a flexible use of language to capture the movement of life at close range. But the realist writer has to detach himself from his milieu in order to see it clearly; imaginative distance, as well as intimate knowledge, is necessary.

In early 1914, Lawrence referred to *Sons and Lovers* as highly "visualised." Although he recalled his "joy in creating vivid scenes" and "accumulating objects in the powerful light of emotion," he told Edward Garnett that he would not write again in "that hard, violent style full of sensation and presentation."[6] As he gained perspective, he saw how the "autobiographical" novel was vital to his development as a writer; in facing the challenge of mastering his experience, he had developed his powers of realistic expression. The importance of visual representation to understanding is implicit in Garnett's remark that *Sons and Lovers* is "a piece of social history on a large canvas, painted with a patient thoroughness and bold veracity which both Balzac and Flaubert might have envied."[7] Lawrence had studied Balzac with enthusiasm. After reading *Eugénie Grandet* he declared: "Balzac can lay bare the living body of the great Life better than anybody in the world. He doesn't hesitate at the last covering . . . he goes straight to the flesh; and, unlike De Maupassant or Zola, he doesn't inevitably light on a wound, or a festering sore. Balzac is magnificent and supreme; he is not mysterious nor picturesque."[8] Seldom does Lawrence pour out such a paean of praise to a modern writer: he clearly derived much inspiration from Balzac's "level-headed, fair, unrelenting realism."

Garnett observes that *Sons and Lovers* "restores [working-class life] to its native atmosphere of hard veracity" but considers it "marred a little by a feeling of photographic accuracy in the narrative."[9] Documentation of surfaces is only one aspect of the novel's realism, however; the "expressive function" of the image in

Lawrence's style should also be recognized.[10] Tony Pinkney relates Lawrence's concrete visualization to imagism, and "the clipped, staccato hardness of the novel's language" to "the lives of the working people themselves."[11] Characterizing the modernist element in Lawrence's style as a combination of "linguistic hardness and Imagistic visualism," Pinkney suggest that *Sons and Lovers* might be called "the first Imagist novel."[12] But the "linguistic hardness" is limited to dialogue and documentation, while the "Imagistic visualism" appears chiefly when objects are enlarged in close-up or diminished by distance. Neither term accurately describes the numerous impressionist or symbolic scenes that add depth or atmosphere to the narrative. Pinkney applies the imagist thesis reductively when he describes scenes like those of Mrs Morel in the moonlit garden or Paul and Clara making love by the river as "crisply visualised episodes."[13] The "totalizing realist gaze" and the imagist/classicist "[focus] on minute details" do not form a simple dichotomy: isolating and totalizing functions complement each other, and the broad sweep is balanced by the close-up. According to Gestalt psychology, concrete particulars relate to each other within an overall vision that selects them for special attention and that they, in turn, sustain by their coherence. Several critics underline the atmospheric rather than merely documentary quality of Lawrence's style.[14] Pinkney's realist/imagist dialectic does suggest, however, that imagism may have contributed clarity and edge to Lawrence's verbal visualization.

Georg Lukács singles out the following aspects of realism: (1) closely observed, precise details and concrete phenomena of historically situated daily life; (2) understanding of social forces that underlie these phenomena and give rise to change; and (3) a human interest in life, progress, and fulfillment of the individual within the community. One difference between Lukács's theory and Lawrence's practice is that Lukács, following Marxist doctrine, sees realism as dealing with types rather than individuals, and as consequently anti-subjectivist and anti-impressionist. Keith Alldritt offers a more balanced view of visual and social representation when he defines "the true realism of the novel . . . [as] a matter of the alertness, the creative quickness of the narrative eye, which allows the phenomenal world of miner's home, colliery, farm, countryside and industrial landscape to figure in their actual full-ness and complexity of interaction, free from all authorial pre-disposition."[15] This perceptual immediacy, by means of which or-dinary details spring into life, may be technically related to imagism.

Lawrence's description of the miner's breakfast consists of prac-tical details yet conveys the energy, anticipation, and satisfaction of the man. It makes him real to the reader, arousing sympathy without asking for it, by combining, as Lukács would have it, the individual with the type, and the personality of Walter Morel with the physical circumstances of a miner's workday:

> He went downstairs in his shirt, and then struggled into his pit-trousers, which were left on the hearth to warm all night. There was always a fire, because Mrs Morel raked. And the first sound in the house was the bang, bang of the poker against the raker, as Morel smashed the remainder of the coal to make the kettle, which was filled and left on the hob, finally boil. His cup and knife and fork, all he wanted except just the food, was laid ready on the table on a newspaper. Then he got his breakfast, made the tea, packed the bottom of the doors with rugs to shut out the draught, piled a big fire, and sat down to an hour of joy. He toasted his bacon on a fork and caught the drops of fat on his bread. Then he put the rasher on his thick slice of bread, and cut off chunks with a clasp knife, poured his tea into his saucer, and was happy . . . He preferred to keep the blinds down and the candle lit, even when it was daylight. It was the habit of the mine. (37–38)

The casual efficiency of the style, based on close observation, con-veys to a middle-class audience the miner's love of comfort and cheerful acceptance of routine. The description of habitual prac-tices in the historic past might seem incidental, as it does not advance the narrative; but it functions as primary realism, estab-lishing the life-quality of the man in his independence and "all-roundness." Such descriptions emanate a genuine warmth.

Morel's character may be distorted to suit the balance of relationships, but here he stands firm in his wholeness and heartiness, free from any negative insinuation. In a single paragraph, Lawrence's realism reveals in close-up the pattern of a life, and of many lives.

Lukács maintains that "[the] characters created by the great realists, once conceived in the vision of their creator, live an independent life of their own; their comings and goings, their development, their destiny is dictated by the inner dialectic of their social and individual existence."[16] Lawrence treats the outer, physical/instinctual framework of Walter Morel's character objectively, while his inner, moral self is bent to fit the Oedipal pattern of the narrative and subjected to harsh judgment: "He had denied the God in him" (88). But by expressing the inner workings of Paul Morel's soul and psyche, as well as fleshing out his social and familial context, Lawrence allows the reader to understand the process that forms his protagonist's self. Rejecting his actual father and projecting a father image onto the distant pit-head, Paul dedicates himself to a quest for the unknown, or Promised Land.

Graham Holderness characterizes *Sons and Lovers* as a triumph of realism. The concept derives from Engels's critique of Balzac as expounded by Lukács and involves an imaginative response to reality that comes through *in spite of* the author's conscious intentions. Art that sets out to demonstrate preconceived ideas inevitably fails—"the novel gets up and walks away with the nail."[17] The hardest test of all is to achieve objective realism in an autobiographical novel. The author knows his environment from the inside and may render it accurately, but does he know himself or present himself fairly? Lawrence consciously strives to see Paul Morel as a character acted upon by social and psychological forces but remains subjectively involved in the outcome of Paul's relationships and in the choices that shape his destiny. For this reason, Pinkney, who identifies the text's "realist achievement" with Paul's personal claims to normalcy, sees a breakdown of realism in the novel's second half. Yet Lawrence's portrait of the artist does achieve a high degree of subjective realism. As Merleau-Ponty points out, "involvement in a point of view . . . makes possible both the finiteness of [one's] perception and its opening out upon the complete world."[18]

For the Russian critics, Belinsky, Chernyshevsky, and Dobro-lyubov, "art grew out of life and creatively reproduced it."[19] Applied to *Sons and Lovers,* this view has dual significance, depending on whether life is taken as primarily communal or personal. The miner in *Sons and Lovers* frequently commands attention *in himself* rather than in the role in which he is cast. While Lawrence later proclaimed a credo of "art for my sake" and saw the artwork as a supplement to, or overflow from, the artist's life, Lukács's emphasis is consistently objective: "artistic principles [are to be integrated] with the faithful reproduction of all the phenomena of life."[20] Lukács's aesthetic resembles Plato's theory of mimesis, with social forms replacing Platonic ideas: socialist or humanist realism, as he describes it, does not simply reflect the surfaces of life; it uncovers the causes of social conditions.

The struggle within Lawrence's narrative between subjective expression and cathartic control gives *Sons and Lovers* its scope, its ambiguity, and its power. In Merleau-Ponty's words, "[this] subject-object dialogue, this drawing together, by the subject, of the meaning diffused through the object, and, by the object, of the subject's intentions . . . arranges round the subject a world which speaks to him of himself, and gives his own thoughts their place in the world."[21] This explains how Lawrence can write oblique autobiography in describing the environment of his childhood in "Nottingham and the Mining Countryside" (1930). In *Sons and Lovers* he sought to master the volatile subjectivity of his material by giving it form. He wanted to achieve maturity of vision and produce "a restrained, *somewhat* impersonal novel."[22] But, paradoxically, "[he] is an author who writes better, not worse, for incompletely detaching himself from an autobiographical situation."[23] Lawrence achieves creative maturity in *Sons and Lovers* by setting aside cultural fantasies, like those of *The White Peacock,* which led him to impose a pastoral idyll on the mining countryside, and by coming to terms with the real environment in which he grew up. If an artist reveals the deepest emotional truth in himself, he will also reveal wider truths about his historical situation and that of his generation. The truth that he reveals, however singular, will be recognized by all whose consciousness has grown from similar roots. This is why Lawrence could claim that he had written "the tragedy of thousands of young men in England,"[24] and why Edvard Munch's expressionist drawings and woodcuts make such startlingly apt illustrations to *Sons and Lovers*.[25]

The strength of the novel's first part, which seamlessly integrates background and foreground, depends for its realization of the "underlying process of life"[26] on an accumulation of selected moments. As Lawrence's realism reveals the force of habit that molds character, Merleau-Ponty's phenomenology describes the perceptual process by which a fully rounded character is realized: "Seeing a figure can be only simultaneously experiencing all the atomic sensations which go to form it. Each one remains for ever what it is, a blind contact, an impression, while the whole collection of these becomes 'vision,' and forms a picture before us because we learn to pass quickly from one impression to another."[27] The miner's preparations for the day's work, his taking a cup of tea to his convalescent wife, his sullen or ferocious labors in the mine, and the pugnacious spirit in which he asks the minister to feel his sweat-soaked singlet (37–38, 41, 46) are good examples of the realism that makes a character convincing and presents an illusion of completeness through a selection of everyday details. Realism also dramatizes conflicts in relationships and reveals their social roots. Brutally realistic scenes, such as that in which Morel throws a drawer at his wife (53–55), modulate into symbolism as the action points beyond itself to deep-seated causes of dissension.

Morel's good nature, when unsullied by marital conflict, is expressed in cheerful work about the house, as when he hammers molten iron into shape or employs the children in making fuses. The task may be practical, but the sure-sighted, firmly handled description has ethical and aesthetic overtones: "He always had a beautifully sharp knife, that could cut a straw clean without hurting it" (88). Microscopic clarity of detail has microcosmic significance: "Then he set in the middle of the table a heap of gunpowder, a little pile of black grains upon the white-scrubbed board" (88). The meaning and danger of gunpowder and mining, even the relation between home and work, are compressed into this close-up that connects, as if by montage, the straw fuse and the "shot [fired to] blast the coal down." A realism that sticks to facts and matches words with lived experience can, through selective focus, suggest more than is said. Realistic observation has a metonymic function that matches the symbolic. Paul's fascinated observation and participation—"[he] loved to see the black grains trickle down a crack in his palm, into the mouth of the straw, peppering jollily downwards till the straw was full. Then he bunged up the mouth with a bit of soap" (89)—show his unconscious identification of work with craftsmanship, extending to his interest in painting and the decorative arts. Morel's "lavish" encouragement shows the pleasure in manual work he passes on to his artist son.

Pinkney, relating Lawrence's exact, attentive language to its object, sees this scene as imagist. But in imagism the image/object implies a poetic mood or idea, while in realism it is grasped more directly in its social context. Seen as it appears in itself, the object is placed in metonymic relation to a character's life, which tends to give it expressive qualities. While an imagist precision adds sharpness of focus, primary realism contextualizes lives through a series of juxtaposed objects.

Paul observes his mother's work at close range, and his direct awareness is recorded with painful, almost clairvoyant intensity:

> Once, roused, he opened his eyes to see his mother standing on the hearthrug with the hot iron near her cheek, listening as it were to the heat. Her still face, with the mouth closed tight from suffering and disillusion and self-denial, and her nose the smallest bit on one side, and her blue eyes so young, quick, and warm, made his heart contract with love. (90)

The still moment and synaesthetic image express Paul's heart-wrung response to his mother, arresting and framing her very being. While phenomenology "puts essences back into existence,"[28] Lawrence's realism tends to extract essences from existence. In the following paragraph, the focus switches to Mrs Morel's existence, as her brisk movements induce a glow of affection in the boy: "She spat on the iron, and a little ball of spit bounded, raced off the dark glossy surface. Then, kneeling, she rubbed the iron on the sack lining of the hearthrug, vigorously. She was warm in the ruddy firelight . . . The room was warm, and full of the scent of hot linen" (91). The realistic technique embodies being in action and signifies emotion in the motions that arise spontaneously in a concrete situation. This kind of realism, linking surfaces with essences, is strongly expressive of feeling without naming it. While Paul's respect, admiration, and love for his mother are compressed into a single moment, narrative "objectivity" highlights Mrs Morel's virtues of persistence, efficiency, and care. Another masterly scene, in which she shows her son a dish she has bought (98–100), combines the particular (her character) with the representative (the life of the townspeople, the Friday-night market, the family budget), in a way that Lukács considers the strength of social realism.

Lawrence describes the homecoming of William's coffin with dramatic realism, concentrating on material arrangements, physical movements, and social responses. The preparations are described with controlled objectivity: "Morel and Paul went, with a candle, into the parlour. There was no gas there. The father unscrewed the top of the big, mahogany, oval table, and cleared the middle of the room. Then he arranged six chairs opposite each other, so that the coffin could stand on their beds" (168). The rigorously controlled view of the event as it slowly unfolds is heightened at the climax by an expressionist use of language: "the limbs and bowed heads of six men struggled to climb into the room, bearing the coffin that rode like sorrow on their living flesh" (169). Synecdoche ("limbs and bowed heads") gives the scene an autonomy and monumentality as in expressionist sculptures by Ernst Barlach, Wilhelm Lehmbruck, or Käthe Kollwitz,[29] while the animistic simile of sorrow riding on the "living flesh" manifests intensity of emotion at a point of extreme confrontation between life and death. The finely maintained objectivity suggests that Lawrence may, after all, have learned something from Flaubert's realism; but how much more potent this scene is, with its sympathy for human suffering, that must not be weakened or diffused by sentiment. The effect of Lawrence's narrative technique, combining objective realism with the response of a participant, is to fuse personal sorrow with a profounder sense of human fate, elevating the individual to the universal. The severe reserve placed on emotional expression—limited to dramatic utterance, as the mother chants, "Oh my son—my son!" (169)—gives the moment its human and religious dignity.

Is realism an adequate term for such ritualization? Can it explain its power? Certainly not, if we think of Flaubert's realism, representing the commonplace and average with (in Joyce's terms) "a scrupulous meanness." The mystery of death-in-life is here obliquely expressed through an interplay of light and darkness. Candles or candlelight are mentioned five times, lamps twice; the darkness is "wide" but the night "faintly luminous"; the door "open[s] straight from the night into the room." The skill with which Lawrence combines symbolic and realistic techniques, integrating one within the other, gives the scene its reverberating power. The invisible—sorrow, fate—is made visible by expressionist means, while the cramped space, awkward movements, and overwhelming physical burden convey powerful emotion.

The homecoming scene in "Death in the Family" surpasses the social realism in which it is solidly grounded, using expressionist distortion, animism, and symbolism to project a participant's experience. Objective realism, lacking the intensity of built-in response, could not match this scene's effectiveness. While Lawrence's art heightens the sense of reality, it cannot be reduced to "realism." There is no meaning in a world untouched by consciousness, which infiltrates into objects, giving them significance: a subject–object dialectic shapes the image of reality. "Man can embody truth but he cannot know it," says Yeats,[30] or, as Paul tells Miriam, "God doesn't *know* things, he *is* things" (291). Realism in the novel is not so much an arrangement of facts as a realization of people, places, and actions within a structured vision of

living.[31] The difference between Lawrence's expressive ritualization
and conventional realism will be made clear by comparing the
coffin scene, on the one hand, with Paul's activities in the surgical
appliance factory, on the other.

The term "realism" is misleading if applied categorically to
writing in which a subjective viewpoint animates the description
of objects or a narrator imaginatively interprets them. In *Sons and
Lovers,* impressionist views, injecting an aura of life into surrounding drabness, are interspersed with realistic narrative: "The sky
overhead throbbed and pulsed with light. The glow sank quickly
off the field, the earth and the hedges smoked dusk" (14); "The
old brick wall by the Statutes ground burned scarlet, spring was
a very flame of green. And the steep swoop of highroad lay, in
its cool morning dust, splendid with patterns of sunshine and
shadow, perfectly still" (150). An alertness to light and landscape
is carried over from *The White Peacock*; but the style is swifter and
more dramatic, and the narrator has an eye for more than local
atmosphere. Here the focus on vital life ("a very flame of green";
"throbbed and pulsed") and its eclipse ("sank quickly"; "lay . . .
perfectly still") might be taken as foreshadowing William's fate, if
only in muted, metonymic fashion.[32]

While close-up scenes involving quarrels and violence are
harshly realistic, distant views of landscape and environment tend
to be impressionistic, providing relief from the claustrophobic domestic settings. After Morel kicks William, Mrs Morel takes Annie
and the baby to the cricket-field:

> The meadows seemed one space of ripe, evening light, whis-
> pering with the distant mill-race . . . Before her, level and solid,
> spread the big green cricket-field, like the bed of a sea of light.
> Children played in the bluish shadow of the pavilion. Many
> rooks, high up, came cawing home across the softly woven
> sky. They stooped in a long curve down into the golden glow,
> concentrating, cawing, wheeling like black flakes on a slow
> vortex . . . (49)

As often happens when impressionist passages are interspersed in
realist contexts, symbolic overtones are sounded, as in the figure

of the vortex. "The problem," as Merleau-Ponty puts it, "is to understand these strange relationships which are woven between the parts of the landscape, or between it and me as incarnate subject, and through which an object perceived can concentrate in itself a whole scene or become the *imago* of a whole segment of life."[33]

The sense of being there, experiencing the world through the character's eyes and ears, is built up with sensory touches, amplified by simile and metaphor: "Mrs Morel could hear the chock of the ball . . . could see the white forms of men shifting silently over the green, upon which already the under-shadows were smouldering. Away at the grange, one side of the hay-stacks was lit up, the other sides blue-grey. A wagon of sheaves rocked small across the melting yellow light" (49–50). The impression of animated peacefulness and privilege, in which white-clad men replace black, is a relief from the domestic battleground that Mrs Morel has momentarily escaped. The division of light on the haystacks, recalling Monet's motif,[34] and the light dissolving over the sheaves show an awareness of chromatic variations. Impressionist vision, endowing objects with complementary colored shadows and highlights, modulates into symbolism through a parallel intuitive process that endows Mrs Morel's second son with a prophetic aura:

> [She] watched the sun sink from the glistening sky, leaving a soft flower-blue overhead, while the western space went red, as if all the fire had swum down there, leaving the bell cast flawless blue. The mountain-ash berries across the field stood fierily out from the dark leaves, for a moment. A few shocks of corn in a corner of the fallow stood up as if alive: she imagined them bowing: perhaps her son would be a Joseph. (50)

Although the passage is predominantly visual, a metaphorical pattern runs through it, connecting refinement (the purity of a bell cast in fire) with upright and outstanding qualities (sheaves animated by light). Inner and outer vision converge, as Mrs Morel's consciousness, playing over the field with the sunset, projects her desires onto objects. While the text presents the visual field before her, her mind subsumes the natural in the biblical, forming a symbol. Paul is seen to have inherited this symbol-forming capacity when he links the steam and flame of the pit-head with the pillars of cloud and fire in Exodus. The illuminated corn-shocks suggest a symbolic analogy, while the psychological process, harmonizing imagination and environment, reveals the mother's ambition for her son. Symbols arise naturally from the real world, as the characters' responses trigger associated images from the unconscious. Lawrence, like Paul, goes beyond impressionism to symbolism, "[painting] rather definite figures that had a certain luminous quality . . . [and fitting these] into a landscape, in . . . true proportion" (345).

While Paul is recovering from an attack of bronchitis, his perceptions are slowed down and intensified. This convalescent phase, combined with the Oedipal situation that makes him so sensitive to his mother's feelings, stimulates his development as an artist. In reverie, he transforms objects around him, fusing sensory images with memories or fantasies. Despite his professed enthusiasm for the "life [and] warmth" of the working class (298), his view of the miners is mostly distanced and diminished. Lying in bed, he likes "[to] watch the miners troop home, small, black figures trailing slowly in gangs across the white field. Then the night came up in dark blue vapor from the snow" (92). Although Lawrence gives a wealth of factual data about the miners' working conditions, impressionist perspectives are frequently applied to the distant but ever-present mines. Subsuming details in atmospheric views—"Down in the great trough of twilight, tiny clusters of lights burned where the pits were" (85)—paradoxically conveys a more pervasive sense of living conditions.

As Paul convalesces and cultivates powers of observation, he becomes fascinated by the ephemeral in nature: "The snowflakes, suddenly arriving on the window pane, clung there a moment like swallows, then were gone, and a drop of water was crawling down the glass" (92). Images of snowflakes and water show Paul transforming his perceptions into impressions. As he contemplates the phenomena of metamorphosis, he himself is growing up and changing. The connection, to such a mind, of things small and

large, near and far, vertical and horizontal appears in a glimpse
"across the valley, [of] the little black train crawl[ing] doubtfully
over the great whiteness" (92), just as the water drop crawls down
the windowpane. The black-and-white schema recalls the "Japanese" patterning of van Gogh's sketches: Kazin finds the "mini-
ature" of horses feeding in the snow and miners trooping home
"exquisite as a Japanese watercolor."[35] The effect of symmetry in
disparate things reveals a mind in the act of comparing and or-
dering its impressions.

Interspersed with highly realistic accounts of work in the factory are impressionist views that provide distance and poetic relief
from the daily grind:

> From the train going home at night, he used to watch the
> lights of the town, sprinkled thick on the hills, fusing together
> in a blaze in the valleys . . . Drawing further off, there was a
> patch of lights at Bulwell, like myriad petals shaken to the
> ground from the shed stars; and beyond was the red glare of
> the furnaces, playing like hot breath on the clouds. (140)

For all its similes and metaphors, the scene is not merely decorative: Paul's viewpoint dramatizes a conflict between fantasy and
reality. His artist's eye selects and arranges groups of lights in
varying configurations and intensities, while his poetic imagination, playing off near against far, adds decorative or apocalyptic
images.

Paul develops his capacity for looking when he goes on ex-
cursions with his mother. In one emblematic scene,

> Mother and son stood on the road to watch. Along the ridge
> of the great pit-hill crawled a little group in silhouette against
> the sky, a horse, a small truck, and a man. They climbed the
> incline against the heavens: at the end the man tipped the
> wagon; there was an undue rattle as the waste fell down the
> sheer slope of the enormous bank. (152)

The group forms a Hardyesque silhouette that highlights a moment in successive generations of working lives. Paul "sketch[es]

rapidly" a scene that would certainly have attracted van Gogh, who sketched similar scenes in the coalfields of the Borinage. As an embryonic artist, Paul finds aesthetic form in industrial landscapes. His animistic image of the pit—"Look how it heaps together, like something alive, almost—a big creature that you don't know . . . And all the trucks standing waiting, like a string of beasts to be fed" (152)—is worthy of Émile Zola's voracious "Le Voreux."[36] The act of sketching sharpens Paul's appetite for the function and life of things. Looking with his mother stimulates his keenest awareness; he seems to see an image of his father's life, from which she has averted her eyes, shadowed forth in the trucks: "But I like the feel of *men* on things, while they're alive. There's a feel of men about trucks, because they've been handled with men's hands, all of them" (152). Paul's viewpoint expresses a vitalism in which material things are significant in proportion to the will and energy invested in them.

The scene from the grounds of Nottingham Castle, which Paul visits with Clara, is a painter's view of the industrial landscape[37], arranged in planes to emphasize variety and distance and fusing natural and man-made forms in a synthetic vision:

Away beyond the boulevard, the thin stripes of the metals showed upon the railway track, whose margin was crowded with little stacks of timber, beside which smoking toy engines fussed. Then the silver string of the canal lay at random among the black heaps. Beyond, the dwellings, very dense on the river flats, looked like black, poisonous herbage, in thick rows and crowded beds, stretching right away, broken now and then by taller plants, right to where the river glistened in a hieroglyph across the country . . . Great stretches of country, darkened with trees and faintly brightened with corn-land, spread towards the haze, where the hills rose blue beyond grey. (313)

This panorama dramatizes the act of looking, as the eye moves in leisurely fashion, contrasting line and mass, foreground and distance, clarity and haze. As Paul broods over it, the landscape loses its decorative detail and is submerged in symbolic vision. A powerful projection transmutes the texture of his vision from impressionist to expressionist: "All that remained was a vast, dark matrix of sorrow and tragedy . . . a dark mass of struggle and pain" (316). Paul sees before him what he feels inside himself and his community: the landscape, with its symmetrical design blurred and darkened, shifts into the somber register of his soul. His eyes merge natural, industrial, social, and sexual strata in a Munch-like vision of desolation.

Paul explains his painting to Miriam in terms of impressionism. He tells her that one of his sketches seems true to life "because there is scarcely any shadow in it—it's more shimmery—as if I'd painted the shimmering protoplasm in the leaves and everywhere, and not the stiffness of the shape . . . Only this shimmeriness is the real living. The shape is a dead crust. The shimmer is inside, really" (183). Intuitively, he has described the essential aim of impressionism: to paint the dance of life perceived by the eye and not the dead shapes conceived by the mind. As Edmond Duranty put it in *La Nouvelle Peinture* (1876), impressionists aimed "to render the trembling of leaves, the shimmer of water and the vibration of air drenched with light."[38] Paul struggles to express in words the vision that inspires his paintings—a "struggle for verbal consciousness [that] should not be left out in art."[39] At this stage of his apprenticeship, he clearly identifies the search for "real living" with impressionism, but for him the source of light is inside the leaves, a vital incandescence rather than a diffusely shed light. His insight into the life of matter emerges in the exchange with Miriam, and significantly his words "[give] her a feeling of life again, and vivif[y] things which had meant nothing to her" (183).

The vitalizing effect of impressionism eventually had its impact on a resistant public; now anyone can see a poppy field or a lily pond the way Monet painted them. As Georges Grappe said in *L'Art et le Beau*, for the impressionists "[it] is light that is all-powerful, that magnifies forms, brings out their beauty, renews their luster, metamorphoses their appearance, displaces their contours and quickens them": ultimately "all the forms [dissolve] in light."[40] In "Introduction to These Paintings" (1929), Lawrence looked back on his earlier enthusiasm for the impressionists:

Let us say what we will, but the real grand thrill of modern French art was the discovery of light . . . No matter how Cézanne may have reacted from the impressionists, it was they, with their deliriously joyful discovery of light and "free" colour, who really opened his eyes. Probably the most joyous moment in the whole history of painting was the moment when the incipient impressionists discovered light, and with it, colour . . . They escaped . . . from the dark procreative body which so haunts a man, they escaped into the open air, *plein air* and *plein soleil*: light and almost ecstasy.[41]

But after his apprenticeship phase, reflected in Paul's perceptions, Lawrence was no longer content with the impressionist dance of light without substance. Like Cézanne, he wanted to bring back objects and the body in all their solidity and integrity.

Another day Paul paints some trees in the sunset and exclaims to Miriam: "Now look at them and tell me, are they pine trunks or are they red coals, standing-up pieces of fire in that darkness. There's God's burning bush, for you, that burned not away" (183). With biblical myth and Blakean rhetoric, Paul projects his own sexual, religious, and aesthetic passion into the trees, so that the "dead crust" of shape is transfigured and the pine trunks vibrate with subjective intensity. As with the shimmering leaves, it is an epiphany, "a sudden spiritual manifestation." Impressionist vitalism takes on expressionist force, as in Van Gogh's *Pine Trees with Setting Sun* (1889), which Ronald Pickvance describes as "powerfully conceived with an almost brutal coloristic and symbolic imagery."[42] In Paul's symbolic vision, black trunks reddened by the setting sun signify a miracle of immanence, of matter *alive* and constantly transformed by the life-force as well as by perception. Blake meant something similar when he affirmed that the sun was not a golden guinea in the sky but a host of heavenly angels singing "Hosanna!"

Paul's vitalism makes Miriam see the pine trunks, that might have "meant nothing to her," as "wonderful" and "distinct." Once her perceptions are awakened, she in turn stimulates Paul in his struggle to express creative impulses. Her spirit flares up like the

tree trunks in the sunset in response to his painter's vision; but
to him she lacks the "ordinary," "fidgety" life-quality of leaves in
a breeze, as in the "shivering foliage" of Monet's *Poplars*, painted
with "a long, fidgety stroke."[43] The novel, combining Paul's point
of view with an omniscient narrator's, contrasts the life-quality
in the two characters, going considerably deeper than realism
could do.

Paul's mother and Miriam stimulate his development in complementary ways. His mother sits passively reading while he
sketches:

> And he, with all his soul's intensity directing his pencil, could
> feel her warmth inside him like strength . . . He was conscious
> only when stimulated. A sketch finished, he always wanted to
> take it to Miriam. Then he was stimulated into knowledge of
> the work he had produced unconsciously. In contact with Mir-
> iam, he gained insight, his vision went deeper. From his mother
> he drew the life warmth, the strength to produce; Miriam
> urged this warmth into intensity like a white light. (190)

He speaks, out of "the white intensity of his search," about Mi-
chelangelo, and "[it] felt to her as if she were fingering the very
quivering tissue, the very protoplasm of life, as she heard him"
(232): Miriam has clearly absorbed Paul's lesson about protoplasm
in the leaves and is now penetrating to a similar essence in him.
Later, as Paul talks of his hopes and fears, "his whole soul seemed
to lie bare before her. She felt as if she watched the very quivering
stuff of life in him" (289–90).

Paul has awakened a vital awareness of life in Miriam, just as
Cyril and Lettie awakened it in George and the young Lawrence
did in his friends. Paul's "white intensity" becomes Miriam's; it
represents an exclusively spiritual quality they stimulate in each
other. Responding to her yearning for "mystic participation," Paul
quickens this vital sense in the girl, then steals it back for his art.

> He saw her crouched voluptuously before his work, and his
> heart beat quickly . . . There was for him the most intense

pleasure in talking about his work to Miriam. All his passion, all his wild blood went into this intercourse with her, when he talked and conceived his work. She brought forth to him his imaginations. She did not understand, any more than a woman understands when she conceives a child in her womb. But this was life for her, and for him. (241)

Sexual energy is sublimated into artistic conception and gestation. But having served as a threshing-floor for Paul's ideas, Miriam cannot also serve in the Demeter role that Clara fills.

Lawrence increasingly supplements the novel's realism and impressionism with symbolism. Just as Renoir in *The Bathers* (1884–87) and Cézanne in *Women Bathers* (1898–1905) show classical tendencies supplanting impressionism, so Paul progresses to more organic yet vital forms of art:

He loved to paint large figures, full of light, but not merely made up of lights and cast shadows, like the impressionists; rather definite figures that had a certain luminous quality, like some of Michael Angelo's people. And these he fitted into a landscape, in what he thought true proportion. (345)

Paul's painting mirrors Lawrence's fiction. Lawrence also fits characters into landscapes with which they interact naturally and symbolically, and Paul's development prefigures his use of Renaissance models for concepts of organic character and form in *The Rainbow.*

In *Sons and Lovers,* Lawrence seeks to express psychological and spiritual meanings that lie beneath vividly realized material surfaces. Examples of such symbolism are the madonna lily scene, the sun baptism, the swing, Miriam's stroking the daffodils, Paul's feeling the blood-heat of eggs in a nest, his scattering cowslips on Clara's hair, the cherry-picking, the red carnations, the "baptism of fire," and the pit-head image. Paul tells Clara:

I like the rows of trucks, and the headstocks, and the steam in the daytime and the lights at night.—When I was a boy, I always thought a pillar of cloud by day and a pillar of fire by night was a pit, with its steam, and its lights and the burning bank—and I thought the Lord was always at the pit-top. (364)

He applies the Exodus symbol of God's guidance to his father's work and his own experience of being-in-the-world. The convergence of concrete reality and mythic symbol yields intimations of the unconscious, uniting fatherhood and godhead. Such symbol-formation shows a religious imagination at work, forging links between matter and spirit, finite and infinite. The same psycho-mythic process appears in a scene of children fighting around a lamppost at night, in which the boy's experience of hatred, terror, guilt, and revenge is illuminated by an apocalyptic symbol from the Book of Revelation: "Paul . . . [saw] a big red moon lift itself up, slowly, between the waste road over the hill-top; steadily, like a great bird. And he thought of the bible, that the moon should be turned to blood" (101).

Realistic and symbolic images depend alike upon concrete ver-isimilitude and sensory power. Van Gogh believed that "all reality is symbolic," objective forms evoking subjective responses, while Rudolf Arnheim maintains that "genuine culture [involves] the constant awareness of the symbolic meaning expressed in a concrete happening, the sensing of the universal in the particular."[44] As Lawrence seeks meaning among things and patterns in events, his imagination forges symbols from reality. Concentration on things produces images whose meaning, embedded in the object yet associated with a character, must be grasped in context rather than extrapolated. Images of lilies, roses, carnations, trucks, or pithead are saturated with a significance that flows through things from human lives. This homeophoric function accounts for the density of texture in symbolic scenes that are just as "full of sensation and presentation" as scenes of "hard, violent" realism.[45] "[The] categories of 'being' and 'meaning' coincide,"[46] as consciousness actively transforms objects of perception. Interactions between characters and places generate phenomenal images that function as symbols.

The episode in which Mrs Morel is thrust outdoors by her

drunken spouse is the first of a series of intense moonlight scenes in *Sons and Lovers, The Rainbow,* and *Women in Love.* Perfume, glistening leaves, vibrating moonlight, distant sounds, and swooning sensations merge in a mélange of impressions detached from mental control. The "mixing-pot" of Mrs Morel's experience modulates into a symbolic cluster that points beyond the moment; thrown back on nature in a moment of personal crisis, her being is rhythmically intermingled with night, moth, phlox, and roses. She is immersed in the bath of moonlight, the "tall white lilies . . . reeling" with her emotion. These flowers preside ominously over the prelude to Paul's birth, when "the child boiled within her" (34, 33).

The lilies are a complex symbol. As an extension of Mrs Morel, they symbolize spirituality intensified to the point of reification in opposition to the overbearing sensuality of her husband. The ambiguity of the symbol makes it all the more powerful and disturbing: the lilies' whiteness and fragrance are associated with the woman's aura, their pollen with the indifferent Life-Force that makes her its vessel. Odors are mixed; the lilies are slightly sickening, while "the raw strong scent" of the phlox is invigorating. The "fresh scent" of the white roses associated with "morningtime and sunshine" is an ironically displaced Apollonian symbol of Mrs Morel's conscious identity. Keith Sagar sees the scene as "a false epiphany," ushering Paul "not into a rich unknown, but into an all-encompassing mother-love" and suggests that "[the] blanched white light symbolizes the possession of his soul by women."[47] While I agree with Sagar's interpretation of "whiteness," I do not think that these images, suspended in a richly ambiguous matrix, can be read univocally from Paul's point of view. Such homeophoric symbols give the atmosphere and dynamics of experience, rather than specific foreknowledge of a character's destiny.

In the scene in which Miriam takes Paul to see her white rosebush, a mysterious effect is created by impressionist means: "In the old oak-wood a mist was rising and he hesitated, wondering whether one whiteness were a strand of fog or only campion flowers, pallid in a cloud" (195). The symbolic ritual that follows is centered on communion, holiness, and worship. Pausing at the threshold of the dark wood, "they saw the sky in front like mother-of-pearl," an image that hints at the source of Paul's inhibition. His uneasiness is partly fear of annoying his mother by being out late with Miriam; Mrs Morel's jealous judgment of the girl as "one of those who will want to suck a man's soul out till he has none of his own left" (196) projects her own possessiveness while expressing his fears. Paul's unconscious identification of Miriam with his mother casts a dark shadow over his feelings.

The white rose-bush is the counterpart of the fiery red pine-trunks, "God's burning bush," that Paul made Miriam see through his eyes. In these scenes of projection and empathy, each tries to initiate the other into his or her own vision, which is immanent in some form of nature. Now it is Miriam's turn to initiate Paul, and her iconic rose-bush—incandescent with spiritual power as his pine-trunks were with sensual—emanates a spell-binding *mana* of beauty and spirituality: "In bosses of ivory and in large splashed stars the roses gleamed on the darkness of foliage and stems and grass . . . Point after point, the steady roses shone out to them, seeming to kindle something in their souls. The dusk came like smoke around, and still did not put out the roses" (195). The ritual involves looking at and responding to an object that remains magically illuminated while its devotees are immersed in twilight. A strong sense of the numinous can be inhaled along with the "streaming scent" of honeysuckle. But it is excessive, unbalanced, overpowering—and before it Paul feels unmanned.

The scene symbolizes the threat of spiritual sublimation to Paul's precarious sexual being. But does he read Miriam's look correctly? "She was pale and expectant with wonder, her lips were parted, and her dark eyes lay open to him. His look seemed to travel down into her. Her soul quivered. It was the communion she wanted. He turned aside, as if pained" (195–96). The dialogic principle is sufficiently at work here to leave some doubt as to what Miriam expects and why Paul turns aside. At a conscious level, the sexual undertow of the phrasing foregrounds sublimation. Yet however heavy with virginal spirituality the scene may be, it remains profoundly erotic; Miriam's sensitivity lies vulnerably exposed, like an offering to her lover.

Paul recoils because he hates (fears) Miriam's capacity for spiritual loving as "too intimate." He laments that she "make[s] [him] so spiritual" (226), but the spirituality she arouses is his own. Miriam is identified with the talismanic roses, and her spiritual/sensual duality is suggested in a centripetal/centrifugal image: "She looked at her roses. They were white, some incurved and holy, others expanded in an ecstasy" (196). The narrator overdetermines the meaning of the scene, in order to justify Paul's reaction, by referring to Miriam's "worship" of the flowers (196). Anxious about the spiritual magnetism she has projected into "her" rose-bush, he interprets her desires arbitrarily. The formal and dramatic impetus of the narrative tilts such scenes toward a monologic reading that coincides with Paul's point of view—his fear of, and rebellion against, female spirituality, traceable to his mother's domination. Every detail fits, and the meaning is manifest; but the subtext subtly allows some of the ambiguity of undermined experience to seep through. The monologic voice leaves an impression of subjectivity, not only in Paul's experience but also in the narrator's interpretation of it.

The haunting power of the scene derives from Lawrence's symbolism, which maintains "the trembling instability of the balance."[48] The mingled sensory and psychological imagery creates an ambiguity that hovers over the source of the emotion. Miriam's "satisf[action] with the holiness of the night" is clearly attributed to her by external omniscience. As Paul reviews the encounter, he needs to believe that Miriam is satisfied with what dissatisfies him. Because his point of view is privileged, one knows what he feels; but who knows exactly what she feels? Her feelings are as yet unformed and depend largely on his responses. Paul's inhibition and sublimation, his penchant for the mystical, appear quite explicitly in a scene in the church at Alfreton, where he responds along with Miriam to the Pre-Raphaelite religious atmosphere and "[all] his latent mysticism quiver[s] into life" (203).

A scene in Paul's garden—referring back to Mrs Morel's experience in the moonlight—contrasts the scent of madonna lilies with that of carnations and irises (337–38). It is the prelude to Paul's breaking-off with Miriam and becoming reconciled with his mother. The garden presents a spiritual/sensual complex, in which images are "patterned" according to psychosomatic responses. As Merleau-Ponty observes, "my body is not only an object among all other objects, a nexus of sensible qualities among others, but an object which is *sensitive* to all the rest, which reverberates to all sounds, vibrates to all colours, and provides words with their primordial significance."[49] The tension of Paul's triangular relationship with his mother and Miriam has heightened his perceptions, as he intuitively seeks a way out. Lawrence's animism is powerful: the maternal aura that pervades and subdues Paul's consciousness seeks him out "stealthily," and "the air all round seem[s] to stir with scent, as if it were alive." The "dim white fence of lilies" is a barely visible barrier, its intoxicating aroma a living presence. All this correlates with the seductive attraction and deep-seated fear of all-absorbing mother-love.

The "keen perfume" of the carnations "[comes] sharply across the rocking, heavy scent of the lilies," evoking crosscurrents of loyalty in Paul. His sympathy for his embittered and exhausted mother is projected onto the lilies that "flagged all loose, as if they were panting"; yet their scent "[makes] him drunk," suggesting loss of control. He is still under the regressive spell of "the great flowers" when "like a shock he [catches] another perfume, something raw and coarse." There is no conflict between this sensual perfume and the spiritual perfume of the lilies, because Paul knows that his mother would rather condone a purely sensual relationship with Clara than a spiritual one with Miriam

The raw, coarse perfume that attacks Paul's senses stimulates him to hunt around in the dark until "he [finds] the purple iris, touch[es] their fleshy throats, and their dark, grasping hands" (338). The search moves from scent and dim vision to touch and possession, foreshadowing his "baptism of fire" with Clara. Anthropomorphic imagery embodies the female object of desire in "fleshy throats" and "dark grasping hands," male phallicism in the stiffness of the stalks. The fleshy irises are associated with

Clara, whose full throat and large hands, with their "almost coarse, opaque and white [skin], with fine golden hairs" attract Paul's artistic and sensual attention, while "her faint natural perfume . . . [drives] him wild with hunger" (270, 375). He is obsessed with Clara's physique and, at one point, actually identifies with her "white, heavy arms, her throat, her moving bosom" (375). Clara stimulates in him "that thickening and quickening of his blood, that peculiar concentration in the breast, as if something were alive there, a new self or a new centre of consciousness" (294).

The whole fragrance scene brilliantly yet unobtrusively epitomizes Paul's oscillation between three centers of consciousness. Having pondered the knot of his relationships in vain, he abruptly cuts it, gravitating spiritually toward his mother and physically toward Clara. He chews the petals of a carnation and spits them into the fire, sacrificing Miriam's love to his mother's will. Delicate pinks then give way to passionate reds, and Clara's scarlet petals, sprinkled on the earth "like splashed drops of blood," counterpoint Miriam's "pure white" roses with their "large splashed stars" (355, 195). Contrasting images reflect the *structure* of Paul's relationships rather than functioning as separate symbols.

A distinction of Lawrence's style is his power to link sensation and emotion with underlying forces. As language reaches out toward the unconscious, "individuality fade[s], and a primal stratum emerge[s], intoxicated, image-laden, Panic."[50] It is significant that Lawrence's writing of the final version of the novel (July–November 1912) coincided not only with his experience of passionate love with Frieda, with whom he had travelled to Germany in May, but also with the high point of European expressionism.

Expressionism in the arts (1905–20) was a revolutionary tendency that called for a complete break (*Aufbruch*) with the immediate past and a return to simpler, more primitive ways of living. Dissatisfied with civilization as they knew it, the expressionists wanted to prepare the way for a new humanity. They claimed the priority of personal experience over reason and convention, demanding the right to express visions that sprang from the unconscious, no matter how irrational or startling. Northern expressionism (originating in Dresden and Berlin) retained the human image, distorting it to bring out spiritual qualities or depersonalizing it as an element of nature or the city. Southern expressionism (centered in Munich) substituted animal forms or lyrical abstractions for human images, aiming at spiritual essences. Rejecting impressionism as superficial phenomenalism, expressionists "wanted . . . to look behind the outward appearance and to penetrate the forces which move the world."[51] Expressionist art springs from inner necessity projected into outward forms. It is presentational rather than representational, confronting the viewer with the artist's vision and aiming, by distortion, to shock him into awareness of hidden truths, sensations, and desires that have a universal basis.

Lawrence's lyrical description of Paul's and Clara's lovemaking employs expressionist elements of depersonalization, disorientation, animism, and universalism: "The naked hunger and inevitability of his loving her, something strong and blind and ruthless in its primitiveness, made the hour almost terrible to her . . . They had met, and included in their meeting the thrust of the manifold grass stems, the cry of the peewit, the wheel of the stars" (397–98). The human sounds and movements of lovers participate mystically in those of nature—there is an expressionist engagement with primal energies that breaks down isolated individuality. Paul's sense of oneness with the blindly thrusting grass stems is an erotic realization of transpersonal energies that obliterates personal love for Clara. Sexual and creative become one.

From such transports Paul gains a keener sense of physical reality and of the vital force that "rolls through all things" (Wordsworth, "Tintern Abbey"). The rhythmic rhetoric does not "symbolize" anything so much as manifest a universal dynamic. Submerging erotic sensation in sublimely simple images of nature and kinetic rhythms, Lawrence strives to express a preverbal experience through what Kirchner calls "the religious sensuality of art"[52]—"If so great a magnificent power could overwhelm them, identify them altogether with itself, so that they knew they were only grains in the tremendous heave that lifted every grass-blade its little height, and every tree, and living thing, then why fret

about themselves: they could let themselves be carried by life"
(398). The intensity, expansiveness, ritualism, mythicism, universality, extremism, pantheism, and vitalism all look toward
Lawrence's mastery of a fully charged expressionist language in
The Rainbow. The sexual rhythm that obliterates ego-consciousness
is "a pulsation in a little of the rhythm at life's Source."[53] But
because the experience is transcendent, the participants are only
vessels of the life-force, who do not meet as persons. The expressionist style marks a wide difference between ecstatic, impersonal states and normal, everyday experience, the province of
realism.

Expressionist overtones add resonance to impressions of the
Lincolnshire coast: "As they . . . looked round at the endless monotony of levels, the land a little darker than the sky, the sea
sounding small beyond the sand-hills, his heart filled strong with
the sweeping relentlessness of life" (400). The bare landscape and
exposure to empty space strike a lyrical, exultant note. But as
Paul watches Clara, she "grew smaller, lost proportion, seemed
only like a large white bird toiling forward" (402). The receding
and diminishing figure is the negative side of cosmic vision: Paul
sees Clara as dwarfed and dehumanized by surrounding immen-
sity—unlike Kirchner's bathers who are integrated with their seaside or forest environments. Distance invites a dangerous indif-
ference to identity: "She represents something," thinks Paul, "like
a bubble of foam represents the sea. But what is *she!* It's not her
I care for—" (402). He is not in love with an individual, but with
an archetype. Clara looms large only when the perspective
switches back to close-up and he watches her drying her breasts:
then, as Woman, she seems "even bigger than the morning and
the sea" (402). Expressionist language links Paul's sensations with
cosmic rhythms, as "[he becomes], not a man with a mind, but
a great instinct" (408). In the swelling rhythms and images of
Lawrence's vitalist manifesto, Paul achieves a subtle inter-
relatedness with the cosmos, recalling the Taoist belief "that the
artist . . . was brought into direct relation with the creative power
indwelling in the world."[54] The harmony of physical impulses,

freed from mental control, with the source of all life typifies a primitivizing strain in expressionism.

As Paul glances around before encountering Baxter Dawes, he sees "the houses [standing] on the brim of the dip, black against the sky, like wild beasts glaring curiously with yellow eyes down into the darkness" (409). The image is a grotesque projection of fear and aggression. In the fight that follows, the primitive autonomy of instinctual life is stressed: "He felt his whole body unsheath itself like a claw . . . Tighter and tighter grew his body, like a screw that is gradually increasing in pressure, till something breaks" (409–10). But he relents and takes a brutal beating. He returns to his mother and, shortly after he recovers, his life is overshadowed by her illness. Subsequent images of fatality and apocalypse suggest the dark world of suffering and death in Edvard Munch's paintings and woodcuts.

> The furnaces flared in a red blotch over Bulwell, the black clouds were like a low ceiling. As he went along the ten miles of high-road, he felt as if he were walking out of life, between the black levels of the sky and the earth. But at the end was only the sick room. If he walked and walked for ever—there was only that place to come to. (131)

Through expressionist projection of Paul's feelings, surrounding space is transformed into a rigid diagram. Monotonous, compulsive motion offers no escape from this dark, horizonless landscape, whose oppressive parallels signify claustrophobia and nightmare.

After his mother's death and the final parting with Miriam, Paul is left alone with nothing. His existential struggle against the "deathward drag" is projected onto blank space, as Lawrence makes his existence the core of being in an alien world: "Whatever spot he stood on, there he stood alone. From his breast, from his mouth sprang the endless space—and it was there behind him, everywhere . . . There was no Time, only Space" (464). The language is expressionist, with staccato sentence-forms, broken syntax, poetic parallelisms, exclamations, and monumental abstractions. Paul's despair is universalized, becoming an apocalyptic vision of the void, like Marlow's vision of "triumphant darkness" at the end of Conrad's *Heart of Darkness*. Emotionally tied to his dead mother, Paul is responding to a deep-seated death wish. He stands like cosmic man, alone at the center of a derelict world, suffering the anguish of alienation. He is divided between the pull of his dead mother's spirit, "gone abroad into the night," and his own body, stuck fast in the physical world.

> On every side the immense dark silence seemed pressing him, so tiny a speck, into extinction, and yet, almost nothing, he could not be extinct. Night, in which everything was lost, went reaching out, beyond stars and sun. Stars and sun, a few bright grains, went spinning round for terror and holding each other in embrace, there in a darkness that outpassed them all and left them tiny and daunted. So much, and himself, infinitesimal, at the core a nothingness, and yet not nothing. (464)

The extrasensory perception, distortion of spatial relationships, and profoundly religious reaching out to the cosmos match the ethos of Van Gogh's *Starry Night* (1889), in which stars and moon become spinning suns and constellations plunging waves. Expressionist form-language is marked by dynamism—"the backward-forward design, the poised or coiled tension path, the thrust and return and contrapuntal variations of the plastic elements."[55] In Lawrence's night vision, as in Van Gogh's field of gyrating forces, "the pressure of feeling . . . forces the bounds of the visible and determines the fantastic projections."[56] The artist's desire "to express his aspiration towards infinity in nature" produces visual apocalypse;[57] the centripetal pressure of space breaks down his enclosed identity, making way for an oceanic inflow and outflow of Being. In Lawrence's vision, the "few bright grains" of stars in the vast darkness and the rapturous "embrace" of opposites may be unconscious symbols of conception and gestation, as that infinitesimal "speck" of being, the self, struggles to be born from the womb of night. In a Manichean conflict Paul's desire to *be* narrowly overcomes his desire not to be, and the novel ends with his sudden conversion to the life-force, in an act of self-overcoming.

So exhaustively did Lawrence employ realistic methods, among others, in *Sons and Lovers,* that he surpassed the limits of realism and concluded: "I have to write differently."[58] The novel is a triumph of *art* ("art for life's sake," or "art for my sake," as Lawrence would say), in which an emerging modernist consciousness interrelates various forms of expression. The graphic realism on which Lawrence's vision is founded is supplemented by impressionist, symbolist, and expressionist language that deepens the image of experience and amplifies major themes. *Sons and Lovers* marks the watershed between Lawrence's apprenticeship to nineteenth-century traditions of realism and his achievement of a unique and innovative style, shaped by expressionism, primitivism, and futurism, in *The Rainbow* and *Women in Love.*

Notes

1. See Graham Holderness, *D. H. Lawrence: History, Ideology and Fiction* (Dublin: Gill and Macmillan, 1982) and Nancy Kushigian, *Pictures and Fictions: Visual Modernism and the Pre-War Novels of D. H. Lawrence* (New York: Peter Lang, 1990). Kushigian traces the growth of Paul's vision from a "nineteenth-century naturalistic consciousness through the stages of Pre-Raphaelitism, art nouveau and early Expressionism" (71).

2. Julian Moynahan, "*Sons and Lovers*: The Search for Form," in '*Sons and Lovers': Text, Background, and Criticism,* ed. Julian Moynahan (Harmondsworth: Penguin, 1977), 565.

3. Alfred Kazin, "Sons, Lovers and Mothers," in ibid., 597–610. The quotation comes from 605.

4. Jessie Chambers, *D. H. Lawrence: A Personal Record by 'E.T.'* (London: Jonathan Cape, 1935), 192.

5. Ibid., 198.

6. *The Letters of D. H. Lawrence,* Volume II, eds. George J. Zytaruk and James T. Boulton (Cambridge: Cambridge University Press, 1981), 132.

7. Edward Garnett, "From *Friday Nights,*" in *Twentieth-Century Interpretations of 'Sons and Lovers',* ed. Judith Farr (Englewood Cliffs, NJ: Prentice-Hall, 1970), 95.

8. *The Letters of D. H. Lawrence*, Volume I, ed. James T. Boulton (Cambridge: Cambridge University Press, 1979), 91–92.

9. Edward Garnett, "From *Friday Nights*," 95.

10. Dorothy Van Ghent, "On *Sons and Lovers*," quoted from its reprinted form in *'Sons and Lovers': Text, Background, and Criticism*, ed. Julian Moynahan, 529.

11. Tony Pinkney, *D. H. Lawrence and Modernism* (Iowa City: University of Iowa Press, 1990), published in Britain as *D. H. Lawrence*, 42, 44.

12. Ibid., 48, 42

13. Ibid., 47

14. See David Daiches, "Lawrence and the Form of the Novel," in *D. H. Lawrence, 'Sons and Lovers': A Selection of Critical Essays*, ed. Gāmini Salgādo (London: Macmillan, 1969), 164–70, especially 167–68, and Scott Sanders, *D. H. Lawrence: The World of the Five Major Novels* (New York: Viking, 1974), 23.

15. Keith Alldritt, *The Visual Imagination of D. H. Lawrence* (London: Edward Arnold, 1971), 41.

16. Georg Lukács, *Studies in European Realism* (New York: Grosset, 1964), 11.

17. The quotation is taken from the essay "Morality and the Novel," in D. H. Lawrence, *Study of Thomas Hardy and Other Essays*, ed. Bruce Steele (Cambridge: Cambridge University Press, 1985), 172.

18. Maurice Merleau-Ponty, *Phenomenology of Perception*, trans. Colin Smith (London: Routledge, 1962), 304.

19. Georg Lukács, *Studies in European Realism*, 107.

20. Ibid., 109.

21. Maurice Merleau-Ponty, *Phenomenology of Perception*, 132.

22. *Letters*, I, 184.

23. Laurence Lerner, "Blood and Mind: The Father in *Sons and Lovers*," in *D. H. Lawrence, 'Sons and Lovers': A Selection of Critical Essays*, ed. Gāmini Salgādo, 216–220, 219.

24. *Letters*, I, 477.

25. See Daniel A. Weiss, *Oedipus in Nottingham: D. H. Lawrence* (Seattle: University of Washington Press, 1962). In *Pictures and Fictions*, Nancy Kushigian claims that "the paintings of Vincent Van Gogh, Edvard Munch, Egon Schiele and other early expressionist painters provided pictorial images that the writer was able to use effectively to characterise a psychological state in Paul Morel" (37).

26. Keith Alldritt, *The Visual Imagination of D. H. Lawrence*, 42.

27. Maurice Merleau-Ponty, *Phenomenology of Perception*, 14.

28. Ibid., vii.

29. See Barlach's *Russian Beggarwoman II* (1907; plaster, under dark shellac) and *The Beggar* (1930; bronze), Lehmbruck's *The Fallen Man* (1915–16; bronze), Kollwitz's *Pietà* (1937–38; bronze) and *The Mothers: The War* (1922–23; woodcut), all in *German Expressionist Sculpture* (Los Angeles: Los Angeles County Museum of Art, 1984), catalogue nos. 7, 22, 91, 85, 82.

30. W. B. Yeats, quoted in Damian Grant, *Realism* (London: Methuen, 1970), 55.

31. Cf. Norman Bryson, *Word and Image: French Painting of the Ancien Regime* (Cambridge: Cambridge University Press, 1981), 8.

32. According to Roman Jakobson in "The Metaphoric and Metonymic Poles," in *Modern Criticism and Theory,* ed. David Lodge (London: Longman, 1988), 90, "the realist author metonymically digresses from the plot to the atmosphere and from the characters to the setting in space and time."

33. Maurice Merleau-Ponty, *Phenomenology of Perception,* 52.

34. See Robert Gordon and Andrew Forge, *Monet* (New York: Abrams, 1983), 160–62.

35. Alfred Kazin, "Sons, Lovers and Mothers," 608.

36. Compare Paul's description to the many animistic images used by Émile Zola to describe the mine in *Germinal* (1885).

37. Impressionist and post-impressionist painters were among the first to depict industrial landscapes. See Armand Guillaumin's *Sunset at Ivry* (1873); and Van Gogh's *The Factory at Asnières* (1887) in J.-B. de la Faille, *The Works of Vincent van Gogh: His Paintings and Drawings* (New York: Reynal, 1970), catalogue no. F318.

38. Edmond Duranty, quoted in Maria Blunden and Godfrey Blunden, *Impressionists and Impressionism* (New York: Rizzoli, 1980), 486.

39. D. H. Lawrence, *Women in Love,* eds. David Farmer, Lindeth Vasey and John Worthen (Cambridge: Cambridge University Press, 1987), 486.

40. Georges Grappe, quoted in Maria Blunden and Godfrey Blunden, *Impressionists and Impressionism,* 211. Cf. *Impressionists and Post-Impressionists,* ed, Alan Bowness (New York: Grolier, 1965), 9.

41. D. H. Lawrence, *Late Essays and Articles,* ed. James T. Boulton (Cambridge: Cambridge University Press, 2004), 197.

42. Ronald Pickvance, *Van Gogh in Saint-Rémy and Auvers* (New York: Metropolitan Museum of Art–Abrams, 1986), 149, plate 34.

43. Jacques Lassaigne, *Impressionism,* trans. Paul Eve (New York: Funk, 1969), 92.

44. Rudolf Arnheim, *Art and Visual Perception: A Psychology of the Creative Eye* (Berkeley: University of California Press, 1974), 454.

45. Ian Watt, in "Impressionism and Symbolism in *Heart of Darkness*," in *Joseph Conrad: A Commemoration*, ed. Norman Sherry (London: Macmillan, 1976), 37–53, distinguishes between *homeophoric* images, "[whose] symbolic meaning [is arrived at by] an imaginative extension of the *same* or *similar* properties as are normally possessed by the object," and *heterophoric* images, "[whose] symbolic meaning is carried by *something else* . . . [for instance,] another body of knowledge [such as the mythic]" (42).

46. Erich Neumann, "Creative Man and Transformation," in *Art and the Creative Unconscious: Four Essays*, trans. Ralph Manheim (Princeton: Princeton University Press, 1971), 149–205, 175.

47. Keith Sagar, *D. H. Lawrence: Life into Art* (Harmondsworth: Penguin, 1985), 99.

48. A phrase used by Lawrence in "Morality and the Novel," in D. H. Lawrence, *Study of Thomas Hardy and Other Essays*, 172.

49. Maurice Merleau-Ponty, *Phenomenology of Perception*, 236.

50. Gottfried Benn, *Selected Writings*, ed. E. B. Ashton (London: Bodley Head, 1961), 42.

51. Lothar-Günther Buchheim, *The Graphic Art of German Expressionism* (New York: Universe, 1960), 21.

52. Will Grohmann, *Ernst Ludwig Kirchner*, trans. Ilse Falk (New York: Arts, 1961), 84.

53. Sheldon Cheney, *Expressionism in Art* (New York: Liveright, 1958), 323.

54. Lawrence Binyon, *The Flight of the Dragon* (1911), quoted in ibid., 124.

55. Ibid., 58.

56. Meyer Schapiro, *Vincent Van Gogh* (New York: Abrams, n.d.), 100.

57. According to Schapiro, apocalyptic elements in *The Starry Night* include the "attempt to unite sun and moon into one figure [and] the tremendous flame-formed cypresses, the dark earthly vertical counterpart of the dragon nebula" (ibid., 100).

58. *Letters*, II, 142.

Sons and Lovers: Flight from the [S]mothering Text

LOUIS K. GREIFF

◆ ◆ ◆

THE 1960 SCREEN version of *Sons and Lovers* appeared over a decade after another Lawrence adaptation, *The Rocking Horse Winner,* yet it resembles its predecessor in a number of ways. Like Anthony Pelissier's effort, it is another relatively short, careful British production filmed in black and white. Yet the challenges of adaptation facing its director, Jack Cardiff, were absolutely the reverse of those Pelissier encountered. Pelissier needed to spin out and finesse a fifteen-page short story into a feature-length film. Cardiff, on the other hand, confronted a heavyweight novel, well over four hundred pages long, with the prospect of squeezing it into a movie about the same length as Pelissier's. This, in fact, is exactly what he did. The finished print of *Sons and Lovers,* including a scene excised by the censors, amounts to ninety-nine minutes of film—a paltry eight-minute increase in running time over *Rocking Horse.*[1]

The skills that Cardiff brought to this project—and to the challenge of effective adaptation—were primarily camera-related. *Sons and Lovers* was only his third directorial assignment, but he had a series of major successes behind him as director of photography, with credits including *The Red Shoes, The African Queen,* and *War and Peace.* Cardiff's official director of photography for *Sons* was Freddie Francis, an equally prominent and experienced cinematographer. Despite this, Cardiff was preoccupied with the photographic challenges of *Sons,* as a 1960 interview with *Films and Filming* reveals. Here, he discusses his decision to use black-and-white film with the Cinemascope camera, a combination suggestive of ambivalent transition between old and new technology. His remarks, however, reveal that he was experimenting with technique even in his choice to shoot in black and white. The film he used was new high-speed Tri-X. Its effect was to increase depth of focus and, as a result, to allow more "freedom of movement" while filming indoors or in subdued light.[2] Cardiff also talks about "pushing" the Cinemascope camera by exploring its potential for extreme close-up work when normally it is brought no nearer than six feet from its subject.[3] The more familiar Cinemascope panoramas are present in *Sons and Lovers* as well and may have provided a visual means of offsetting the condensation process and attempting to preserve some of the novel's original resonance and sweep.

Except for one comment on Dean Stockwell's "burning intensity" as an actor, Cardiff remains silent in his interview about his diverse cast.[4] They included distinguished veterans Trevor Howard and Wendy Hiller, appearing as Mr and Mrs Morel, and newcomer Heather Sears as Miriam Leivers. Just one year earlier, Sears had appeared as a girl somewhat similar to Miriam in Jack Clayton's *Room at the Top,* a film in which Freddie Francis worked as director of photography. Susan Brown—the character Sears portrayed in *Room*—paralleled Miriam in innocence, naïveté, and eventually lost virtue. She offered up her virginity to Laurence Harvey's Joe Lampton, and would do so a second time in *Sons,* making the identical sacrifice to Dean Stockwell's Paul Morel.

For Stockwell, this film represented the beginning of an adult acting career and a short-lived brush with stardom in his emergence as a young romantic lead. He had been a prominent child-actor in the 1940s. After leaving the profession for several years, he returned to enter what was to be, in Cardiff's words, the brief "burning intensity" phase of a very long and varied career—a career which remarkably would take him from the innocence of *The Boy with Green Hair* in 1948 to the perversity of *Blue Velvet* nearly forty years later. Stockwell burned intensely but all too briefly, starring in *Compulsion* (1959), *Sons and Lovers* (1960), and *Long Day's Journey into Night* (1962) as Edmund Tyrone, a figure similar to Paul Morel in sensitivity and youthful artistic inclinations. He then went into eclipse a second time, only to reappear two decades later as a character actor specializing in quirky and menacing roles.

Two more members of the cast who deserve mention here are Mary Ure, appearing as Clara Dawes, and Donald Pleasence as Pappleworth. Ure's career met an untimely end with her death in 1975 at the age of forty-two. Pleasence's career (like Stockwell's) took a turn toward the grotesque at about the same time with his appearance in such films as the Beatles' *Sgt. Pepper's Lonely Hearts Club Band* (1978), *Escape from New York* (1981), and the apparently endless *Halloween* series. Before their separate fates overtook them, Ure and Pleasence had enjoyed success on the British stage. Both were closely involved with the dramatic emergence of the Angry Young Men in the late 1950s and had acted together just one year before *Sons and Lovers* in the film version of John Osborne's *Look Back in Anger*. Ure, who was married to Osborne, brought her role from stage to screen. Four years later, Pleasence did the same with his part in Harold Pinter's *The Caretaker*. Recalling Heather Sears and Freddie Francis's recent involvement in *Room at the Top*, what all of this amounts to is the definite presence, in spirit, of the Angry Young Men among the cast and crew of *Sons and Lovers*, a spirit surely not identical to that of Lawrence's novel, yet parallel in its preoccupation with youth, sexual discovery, rebellion, and escape from the British working class.

As measured by the initial responses of critics, *Sons and Lovers* was a great success. Cinematography, direction, and acting all received favorable notices, with the greatest praise going to Trevor Howard. Stockwell got a somewhat less enthusiastic reception but largely among English reviewers who questioned the presence of an American (in fact, the cast's only American) as the star of a British film based on a British book.[5] This is not to suggest, however, that subjective opinions were limited to England. *Time* announced that the film included "everything important in Lawrence's 500-page novel."[6] Reviewing *Sons and Lovers* for the *New Yorker*, Whitney Balliett used his praise for the film and book as an excuse to attack *Lady Chatterley's Lover*, which he described as one of Lawrence's "lamentable later efforts" by comparison.[7] Largely unconscious of the irony, Stanley Kauffmann combined his comments on *Sons and Lovers* for the *New Republic* with a very nasty review of *Psycho*, leaving any specific comparison of Paul Morel and Norman Bates as devoted sons to the perverse imaginations of his readers.[8] Among the early reviewers, the most perceptive was Pauline Kael, who pointed out the strengths of the film but also understood its limitations, suggesting that at best it represented a cautious approach to the novel's potent and dynamic material.[9]

A second measure of the film's initial success came in the form of nominations and awards. *Sons and Lovers* went to the Cannes Film Festival as Great Britain's official entry in 1960. In America, the film received an Academy Award for cinematography and a half-dozen additional Oscar nominations—to Trevor Howard for best actor, to Mary Ure for best supporting actress, and to Jack Cardiff for best director. It was also nominated for best art direction, script, and picture. The best script nomination seems somewhat curious in that, almost immediately, the screenplay was singled out by critics as the weak point of the film. Writing for *Films in Review*, Henry Hart expressed praise for every element in *Sons and Lovers* except the screenplay, even suggesting that any apparent lapses in the performances of Stockwell and Sears were really the result of a defective script. Similarly, John Gillett in a *Film Quarterly* review suggested that a weak script resulted in compression "into a kind of *Reader's Digest* version" of the novel. Hart and Gillett also pointed out that Cardiff had to seek screen writing reinforcements well into the production process. T. E. B. Clarke and possibly others joined the project late to assist Gavin

Lambert, Cardiff's original scriptwriter and a man whose prior experience had been more critical and editorial than creative.[10]

What most troubled initial reviewers about the script was omission of detail and compression of the story as a whole. They called attention to this in order to criticize the film. Forty years later, it is possible to view the same condensation process somewhat more objectively and to regard it as a useful example of what tends to happen when a feature-length film grapples with a massive and powerful text. In *Sons and Lovers,* plot clearly suffers during this struggle. Despite losses, however, the screenwriters' strategies for adapting and compressing Lawrence's material are both interesting and enlightening to observe. In relation to the novel, for example, the beginning of *Sons and Lovers* on film is *in medias res* with a vengeance. Utterly absent are the Morels' courtship, young Gertrude Coppard's aspirations before meeting her future husband, and the reasonably happy early stages of their marriage. Also missing is Lawrence's vivid chronicle of Paul Morel's childhood and of the family's daily life as he and his siblings are growing up.

A second screen version of *Sons and Lovers* was released in 1981. Directed by Stuart Burge, with a screenplay by Trevor Griffiths, it appeared in seven episodes on BBC television. In contrast to Cardiff's ninety-nine minutes, Burge's adaptation takes up six and a half hours, allowing for a more expansive production as well as more opportunities to preserve detail from the text. As a result, much of the early novel cut in Cardiff's version now resurfaces. Gertrude's relationship with John Field, for example, along with her first encounter with Morel, their courtship, and their early married life all appear on television   not chronologically, as might be expected, but as flashbacks that occur as Gertrude has plenty of time to consider her past, having been locked out of the house by her husband. It is noteworthy that despite this wealth of time and opportunity, at least compared with Cardiff's film, the BBC screenwriter, Trevor Griffiths, still complains of having felt constrained. In his introduction to the published screenplay for the televised production, he writes that "there are the differences born of trying to incorporate a 500-page novel into a six-and-a-half-hour time slot. Much that is rich and textured has gone, where it has not been needed to support the narrative or serve the social relationships of the characters."[11]

Griffiths's introduction reveals several other points of contrast between the television production and the feature film. One is that Griffiths intended his screenplay as social and economic protest, far more emphatically than his predecessors Gavin Lambert and T. E. B. Clarke did, as well as a celebration of the working class. As a result, the mine scenes in the television production clearly suggest exploitation of labor for profit. Similarly, the scenes portraying Miriam, Mrs Leivers, and Gertrude Morel in domestic circumstances all imply the constraints placed upon women in general by late Victorian society. Partly because of the more overt class issue in the 1981 *Sons and Lovers,* Walter Morel (played by Tom Bell) and Baxter Dawes (played by Jack Shepherd) take on special prominence. Griffiths and his colleagues have deliberately conceived Morel to seem "as much victim as anyone else and, incidentally, much closer [than in the text] to the 'father' that Lawrence revalued towards the end of his own life."[12] The 1960 feature filmmakers also depict a "revalued" father through Trevor Howard's compelling performance as Morel but, as I hope to show, by way of a far less deliberate process. Baxter's friendship with Paul Morel, born of their struggle over Clara, is especially prominent in the television series, whereas it is virtually ignored on film. In fact, the 1981 Paul (played by Karl Johnson) seems to feel a grudging admiration for Baxter long before he decides to visit the older man in the hospital. This more developed and complex friendship becomes another way for the BBC filmmakers to explore their social and economic concerns while indirectly returning to the textual issue of fathers and sons.

With less than two hours of screen time at their disposal, Cardiff, Lambert, and Clarke were challenged by the demands of compression and acceleration in place of exploration. Thus, when *Sons and Lovers* opens on the large screen, Paul is already a young adult. During the first fifteen minutes, the 1960 film seems to be set in fast-forward, at least with regard to the text. Within three minutes, the audience hears of Miriam and learns that Mrs Morel is troubled by the girl's relationship with Paul. Within six minutes, we see Miriam and Paul together in an affectionate, idyllic meeting at the farm. Their postadolescent "lad and girl" lovemaking is interrupted, nine minutes into the film, by an explosion at the mine where Paul's father and brother Arthur are both working. Arthur's corpse is brought up from the mine shaft two minutes later, and, one minute after that, Paul's elder brother, William, comes home from London for the funeral. Paul finds work at Jordan's in Nottingham immediately afterwards and William begins courting Louisa Western. The fifteen-minute "overture" ends with William presenting Louisa's photograph to Paul and Mrs Morel as his train departs for London.

It would be absurd and, in fact, impossible to attempt such a pace much beyond the film's first few scenes. With Arthur's death and William's departure, viewing speed returns to normal, and for the next hour the audience is given a sustained account of one critical year in Paul Morel's life—the year of his and Miriam's sexual initiation, his affair with Clara Dawes, and his mother's death. Time and the need for compression still drive the filmmakers, but now their methods shift from fast-forwarding to the technique of condensation. Several major incidents within the film behave like Freudian dream structures in relation to the book. They are actually conflations of two or more textual events taken from different parts of the novel and melded together into a single screen episode.

Arthur's death at the mine, which completes the film's introduction, is the first such reconfiguration of the text. In Lawrence's novel it is not Arthur who suffers a mine accident but his father who is seriously but not fatally injured. Also, it is not the younger brother, Arthur, who dies in the novel but the elder brother, William. In effect, the screen version of *Sons and Lovers* merges the father's injury with the brother's death, so that the one film event resonates with the implications of both catastrophes. Arthur's death, like Walter's injury, suggests the ugliness and danger of work in the mine and confirms Mrs Morel's resolve to keep Paul away from it. At the same time, Arthur's death, like William's, is much more than merely an injury, even a critical injury. It is a "death in the family" (141) and, in text and film alike, the first tragic event that Mr and Mrs Morel have had to endure together.[13]

In the text, William's death is most of all a loss to Gertrude Morel, who has always favored her first-born son. She nearly follows him to the grave but is saved when Paul falls ill, reminding her of other maternal responsibilities and recalling her to life. An interesting shift in modulation on screen is that Arthur's death is most essentially a loss to his father and not to his mother. The emotional symmetry established in the film's initial scenes suggests that, of the two Morel boys remaining at home, Paul is his mother's child and Arthur is his father's. Arthur's death, then, has the early effect of isolating Walter Morel within his own household. This sets up a lonely and essentially defensive battle that Walter will be fighting against his family until the end and that will become one of the film's major achievements of both plot and character.

A second instance of film conflation involves a violent domestic quarrel and provides an example of failure rather than qualified success. Like Arthur's death, the quarrel is a composite of two textual episodes—the incident in which Morel strikes his wife with a drawer and the earlier incident in which he locks her out of their home. Where meaning is saved in the film reconstruction of "Death in the Family," it seems to be lost in this quarrel, leaving only the ugly and empty event before us. In the text, meaning within both confrontations of man and wife depends on Paul's intimate participation—as an infant and, even before that, as part of his mother's pregnant body. In the drawer scene, Paul is literally baptized in parental conflict and with his mother's blood. In the locking-out, he is likewise symbolically conceived amid the violent struggle of his progenitors.

On screen, Trevor Howard's Morel flies into a drunken tantrum at not getting his dinner. He throws a kitchen drawer to the floor, but does not strike his wife, then quickly puts her out of the house. Since Paul is already grown when this happens, none of the text's complexity of implication is possible. Instead, the scene climaxes with Paul's return home, rescue of his shivering mother, and confrontation with Morel, which nearly results in blows. Even this exchange of melodrama for meaning fails to work. In the Oedipal standoff between father and son, Dean Stockwell's Paul looks too delicate to fight. In turn, Trevor Howard's Morel looks too gentle, beneath his pit dirt and grimaces, to be capable of hitting anyone, least of all his son.

In the final fifteen minutes of the film an abrupt reversal of plot strategy takes place again. The technique of conflation is dropped, and the film returns to the fast-forward pace of its beginning. It is not difficult to understand why this happens, since the filmmakers' concluding challenge is to get Paul quickly out of everything he has gotten himself into, particularly his relationships with the three women in his life: Miriam, Clara, and Gertrude.

Clara and Miriam are disposed of with one brief scene of farewell apiece. Gone is the slow, agonizing process by which Paul frees himself from Miriam's stifling yet not wholly unwelcome embrace. Gone also is Paul's near-filial friendship with Baxter Dawes, which springs up after they lay violent hands upon one another. Since this is missing from the film, so too is Paul's ambiguous involvement in the reconciliation between Baxter and Clara, his actions as ex-lover and go-between in returning the strayed wife to her husband. Cardiff's Paul says a clean farewell to both women, and the former lovers simply move off screen.

While Paul and his mother cannot be parted quite this easily, Mrs Morel's death is also melded into the rush of the film's final quarter hour. As a result, it is far more peaceful and free of suffering than was Gertrude's death in Lawrence's text. Her slow, wasting cancer is transformed into a quick series of heart attacks, again as a concession to time but also as a way of sparing the imagined sensibilities of the audience. Similarly, Paul does not play a part in his mother's death as he does in the novel. Paul as mercy killer, like Paul as matchmaker to Clara, disappears in the filmmakers' reluctance to darken his image in any way or to complicate the straightforward goodness of the young hero.

Really, the only complication surrounding Mrs Morel's film

death has to do with Paul's painting and the interest she has always taken in his art. While ill, Mrs Morel has told Paul she would like to see the springtime daffodils, the implication being that she won't live long enough to do so. Paul resolves to paint the daffodils in order to grant her wish. He does, but she never sees them, dying just as he attempts to place the unfinished (and somewhat van Gogh-like) canvas in front of her. Although melodramatic, the scene manages to convey a suggestion interesting in part because of its opposition to the text. Lawrence's Paul speeds his mother's journey with morphine, giving her the final gift of death. The filmmakers' Paul gives her springtime flowers instead of the drug, as if trying to hold his mother back with images of renewal and life. Mrs Morel's film death is also interesting for biographical reasons. Like Paul presenting his canvas, Lawrence gave his own mother an advance copy of his first book, *The White Peacock,* when she was fatally ill.[14]

It seems logical to expect that a major reduction of plot is bound to overtake the film's characters as well. In fact, it does, yet with two exceptions significant enough to warrant special attention: Mary Ure's portrayal of Clara Dawes and Trevor Howard's portrayal of Walter Morel. The shrinkage of character on screen, however, is far more immediately evident to an observer than any expansion or gain. For example, one misses several important figures in the novel who have simply been dropped from the film: Paul's sister Annie, his childhood playmate and adult accomplice in their mother's death, and Miriam's older brothers, who for a time become Paul's closest friends.

Other memorable characters may be physically present yet absent in spirit, since they are reduced to flatness. The women who work with Paul at Jordan's suffer this fate, losing their distinctive personalities as they are merged into a comic chorus of observers to Paul's workplace courtship of Clara. Baxter Dawes is similarly flattened and cut. No trace remains of his softer side or of his paternal resemblance to Walter Morel. He survives in the film merely as a kind of prop—a threat to Paul and a clichéd image of the violently jealous husband. In fact, Baxter's reduction to one or two qualities provides an insight into the filmmakers' general strategy for adapting a novel that contains a remarkably full cast of round characters. With Baxter and several other major figures in *Sons and Lovers,* the film tends to maintain focus on a single human issue, omitting or else backgrounding all the rest.

This is very evident in the screen conception of Paul and Miriam. Their original complexity as a couple is largely absent, especially their ability to fuel their relationship by a unique synthesis of feelings and ideas. One cannot, for instance, conceive of Dean Stockwell and Heather Sears, in their portrayal of Paul and Miriam, discussing Paul's painting as these same characters do in the text and transforming words and impressions into erotic, ultimately mysterious energy:

> "Why do I like this so?" . . .
>
> "Why *do* you?" he asked.
>
> "I don't know—it seems so true."
>
> "It's because—it's because there is scarcely any shadow in it—it's more shimmery—as if I'd painted the shimmering protoplasm in the leaves and everywhere, and not the stiffness of the shape. That seems dead to me. Only this shimmeriness is the real living. The shape is a dead crust. The shimmer is inside, really." (182 83)

With such intricacies removed, what's left of the original Paul and Miriam is simply the sexual obstacle between them. Otherwise they are perfectly matched both youthful, optimistic, ar tistically inclined, and ordinary. Paul is a pleasant young man who paints (indifferently) and who yearns for his first sexual re lationship. Equally pleasant and colorless, Miriam neither paints nor wishes, under any circumstances, to have a sexual experience—not with Paul, not with anyone. He must have sex, and the very idea of it scares her to death. No question that this is a real issue between Paul and Miriam in the text, yet it is their one and only issue on screen. Like Baxter, this critical couple is pared down to a single conflict that serves as their raison d'être throughout the film.[15]

As with sons and their would-be lovers, so too with mothers.

Wendy Hiller's Mrs Morel is referred to as Gertrude just once in the film, the virtual disappearance of her given name accidentally suggesting her simplification as a human being. What remains of her is, again, a single trait—her obsessive, overprotective devotion to Paul. Actually, three mothers are present in the film, just as they are in the text: Paul's, Miriam's, and Clara's. The filmmakers, however, have called attention to them as a trio far more insistently than Lawrence ever did in the novel, so that the single human quality in each mother stands out boldly to create a sharp three-sided contrast of characters. Mrs Morel's excess of maternal love is opposed by Mrs Leivers's coldness to all of her children, especially Miriam. Rosalie Crutchley portrays her as a forbidding religious fanatic whose harshness is largely responsible for Miriam's inhibition and fear of sexuality. In contrast to these opposite extremes, the film presents the healthy normality of Clara Dawes's mother and implies that Clara's independence of body and spirit is at least in part the gift of maternal influence.

Clara's mother and Miriam's mother remain flat characters in their limited appearances. Far more visible, however, Mrs Morel does eventually undergo a slight rounding-out before the film ends. Despite her failed marriage and obsession with Paul, Mrs Morel occasionally and wistfully reminisces. In her happy monologues about the past, the film audience is allowed to glimpse what little spark remains of her youthful sexuality and once-passionate love for Walter. Plot also gains, or regains, dimensionality through Mrs Morel's on-screen memories. They afford the filmmakers an opportunity to put back a little of what was cut from the beginning chapters of *Sons and Lovers*.

A final pair of characters who suffer the simplification process are Paul's brother William and his fiancée, Louisa Western. The older brother never dies on screen, like his textual counterpart, but just fades away, returning to a London career and an eventual marriage to the attractive but shallow Louisa. Lost from the film, with the absence of William's death, is Lawrence's submotif of suffocation. In the novel, William dies of erysipelas, which begins with a chafing at the throat and spreads through his entire body. The suggestion is that William has been stifled, eventually strangled, by the dual constrictions of modern employment and modern romance. His workday collars have always seemed too tight, and in his final delirium he speaks to his mother about a ship's cargo of sugar which, like his engagement, has turned to rock (166). His love affair with Louisa has been something like an addiction, sexually euphoric yet debilitating in every other way. This is because although William compulsively desires Louisa's body, he detests the rest of her and holds no regard for her as a future wife or a human being. In Lawrence's hands, this minor but fascinating relationship becomes an ominous paradigm for the hazards of modern existence and also a specific prophecy for Paul, who could, by the very different agencies of his mother and Miriam, be hopelessly smothered himself.

What remains of William and Louisa is their visible sexuality, which becomes the film's simplified prophecy of Paul's future. William and Louisa serve as bridge characters, helping Paul cross from sexual frustration in his relationship with Miriam to sexual satisfaction in his impending affair with Clara. When William brings his fiancée home for the Christmas holidays, they kiss erotically, using the mistletoe as an excuse. Earlier in the film, when Paul attempted to kiss Miriam with similar fire, he succeeded only in angering and revolting her. He now watches his brother and Louisa carefully, and the difference between her response to the kiss and Miriam's is clear to audience and protagonist alike. Since the on-screen Louisa directs Paul, sexually at least, from Miriam toward Clara, the filmmakers have altered her appearance to suit her function. Whereas Lawrence's Louisa is dark-haired and dark-eyed, her on-screen counterpart resembles and anticipates the blonde and fair-skinned Clara Dawes

Any similarity between Louisa and Clara, however, begins and ends with this physical resemblance. William's superficial fiancée is the flattest character in a film largely peopled by flat characters. Mary Ure's Clara, on the other hand, is one of the few to escape being reduced to a single human dimension. She strikes the audience as a figure we don't know everything about and, in fact, can't know everything about—this quality tied in part to the skill of Ure's performance.

Beyond her ambiguity, yet related to it, Clara Dawes may be the only character in the film to strike the truly Lawrentian note—to survive cinematic transformation as a figure still his own in conception and spirit. The on-screen Clara effectively conveys a mixture of vulnerability and strength, a combination of qualities found not only in the original Clara but generally in the Lawrentian sisterhood. Ursula Brangwen, Ellen March, Yvette Saywell, and Connie Chatterley are all similarly conflicted figures. Also like her textual counterpart, Ure's Clara Dawes seeks to achieve a balance among three familiar Lawrentian forces—selfhood, sexuality, and the will to power. She is more than eager to be lost in the erotic moment so long as she can regain herself whole and intact afterwards—not merged with another or, worse, sacrificed to his needs. Beyond this, Clara Dawes in the film successfully projects the human urge to exert authority—to hold and apply power somehow and somewhere in the world. In text and film alike, this need informs Clara's political activity as a feminist and also explains her refusal to cut the tie with Baxter, a man to whom she does not belong but who clearly belongs to her.

It is not surprising, then, that the one film sequence which seems most Lawrentian in spirit and tone centers on Clara. This is the same scene that caught the censors' attention in 1960 by way of its postcoital intimacies between Clara and Paul. Their conversation takes place at a seaside hotel and has no exact counterpart in the novel. It is another cinematic conflation in which the filmmakers have combined several textual dialogues between the lovers into a single concentrated exchange. Speaking many of Lawrence's lines word-for-word, Clara accuses Paul not of sexual failure but of failure to acknowledge her as a separate being and failure to yield anything of himself: "About *me* you know nothing,—about *me!*" "But is it *me* you want, or is it *it?*" "You've never given me yourself." The words of this indictment fall like hammer blows. Clara speaks them while lying on the bed, her appearance suggestive of nudity under the covers. Paul stands over her, bare-chested. Despite these sensuous details, the lovers appear sundered from one another by way of their angry words and also by way of the filmmakers' visual composition of the scene. As Clara speaks, her face is framed by the brass bars of the bedstead, a pose suggesting imprisonment in the now-oppressive love affair and also inevitable alienation from Paul. The scene achieves an interesting intertextuality not only with *Sons and Lovers* but also with the later and darker *Women in Love* as well. As these lovers struggle with their dying relationship, they come to resemble Gudrun and Gerald in "Snowed Up," confined together in even more dangerous circumstances. At the outset of that chapter, Gudrun and Gerald also struggle in a shared hotel bedroom, physically close yet hopelessly separated and destined for a far more drastic parting than Clara and Paul.

Clara, then, gives us Lawrence whole, while most of the other characters in this film give us less. Curiously enough, Trevor Howard's rendering of Walter Morel somehow manages to go beyond Lawrence to give us more of a father than we have in the original text. The on-screen Morel is a many-sided figure, whereas Lawrence's coal miner seems simpler by comparison, flattened a bit, ironically a little like one of the characters in the film. Despite some winning qualities, the original Morel remains a negative presence and a negative force within the family. In the film, Morel's better nature and sensitivity show through, along with his coarseness and occasional brutality. As with the accurate rendering of Clara, this expansion of Morel can be understood partly in relation to the actor playing the role. While Trevor Howard effectively expresses both the dark and bright sides of Morel, he actually seems more convincing in his warm vitality than in his rages, as if there were an attractive human being slightly hidden under the pit dirt and nastiness. Seen from the past perspective of *The Rocking Horse Winner,* there is a clear relationship between this performance and John Mills's interpretation of Bassett. While Bassett is surely more wholesome than Morel, as well as more passive and deferential, both men represent a similar film tribute to unpolished and natural decency or, in other words, to a popular and idealized image of the British working man.

Beyond Trevor Howard's performance, the expansion of Morel

also represents the work of the film's director and screenwriters, who gave this figure qualities that Lawrence deliberately held back. The cinematic Morel is clearly the most vital member of his family, reflecting a gaiety and enjoyment of life on screen that mainly survive in Gertrude Morel's memories in the text. These warm qualities are especially evident in the film's Christmas Eve scene, where Morel sings a music-hall song and creates a memorable image that has no counterpart in the novel. In only one important respect does this expanded figure fall short of the original. The filmmakers, regrettably, have denied Morel any trace of his natural talent in the text as a teller of wonderful tales. With the omission of Paul and his siblings as young children, no opportunity remains in the film for their father to gather them about and fascinate them with stories of Taffy, the clever pit pony, stories which Lawrence wrote "would go on interminably" and which "everybody loved" (89).

What the on-screen Morel may lack in narrative gifts, he more than makes up for in sensitivity and intelligence. He is very aware, for example, of all the undercurrents and tensions within his family and often of the unexpressed feelings of his wife and son. This is revealed through several scenes in the film during which Morel confronts either Paul or Mrs Morel—not physically but with words and emotions. In one such scene between father and son, the morning after Mrs Morel has been locked outside, Morel correctly suggests that Paul's view of his parents' marriage is far bleaker than the reality itself, pointing out that it has endured many such crises and will continue to do so. In a later scene, after Mrs Morel's death, this same father perceives the suicidal potential in Paul's grieving and manages to turn him round in the direction of life—something which Paul, in the text, has to do entirely on his own. Morel tells his son that rather than "letting things slide," Paul owes himself and his dead mother a good struggle with life's possibilities. Morel even advises Paul to seize his independence by going to London in pursuit of his artistic career.

Given Lawrence's original conception of Morel, as an avoider and repressor of awareness, neither of these scenes would be possible in the text. Nor would the bedroom confrontation between Mr and Mrs Morel in which they argue over Paul's involvement with the married Clara Dawes. During this exchange Morel blames his wife for the affair, claiming that her intense possessiveness has prevented any relationship between Paul and a more eligible woman that might have led to marriage.

The Morel of Lawrence's text is not altogether unaware of the Oedipal triangle within his family, as is implied by his less-than-sober question, "At your mischief again?" when he discovers mother and son in a moment of intimacy (252). Yet the original Morel's awareness always remains largely inarticulate and subconscious:

> "Hm—hm! hm—hm!" he sneered.
>
> He went into the passage, hung up his hat and coat. Then they heard him go down three steps to the pantry. He returned with a piece of pork-pie in his fist. It was what Mrs Morel had bought for her son. (252)

In the film, it is Mrs Morel, instead, who seems the unconscious one, her husband having to explain to her that any son can escape the effects of a low father far more easily than he can avoid suffocation at the hands of a mother who loves too well. That Lawrence could have written a parallel scene into his novel, with a parallel explanation from Morel, seems difficult to imagine.

The film version of Morel is a mature and finished human being. Lawrence's Morel, by contrast, remains incomplete in many respects—still somewhat of a child despite his robustness and physical courage. This childishness becomes most evident just after Gertrude Morel's death when Paul suddenly realizes that his father is frightened by the presence of her corpse—afraid to look at his own dead wife, afraid even to remain in the same house with her: "His father looked so forlorn. Morel had been a man without fear—simply nothing frightened him. Paul realised with a start that he had been afraid to go to bed, alone in the house with his dead. He was sorry" (443).

The response of the on-screen Morel to death and to his own

dead is very different: he is resigned as a result of the past experience with Arthur and in no way frightened. This Morel, like his original counterpart, also fails to see his wife's body but not out of cowardice. In her last illness Mrs Morel has asked that they not see one another again—not obliterate what good memories remain of their marriage with more bitter ones. By refusing to view her in death, Morel is simply honoring his wife's final wishes.

Of the film's pair of fully realized characters, then, only Clara Dawes remains true to her textual counterpart. Morel the father does not because he proves to be deeper and more complete than the original. In a strangely prophetic way, however, Trevor Howard's Morel does remain true to Lawrence himself—not to the Lawrence of *Sons and Lovers* but to the more mature author and man who, ten years later, honestly reassessed his parents' marriage and his father's worth as a human being. Calling attention to this now well known reassessment, one of Lawrence's biographers, Jeffrey Meyers, writes as follows:

> In the late 1920s Lawrence . . . told his friends Rhys Davies and Achsah Brewster that he now understood and respected his father—"a piece of the gay old England that had gone"— much more than he had when he wrote *Sons and Lovers.* He thought his parents' quarrels were caused more by his mother's malicious taunts than by his father's drunkenness. He believed he had not done justice to his father, grieved over the hostile portrait and felt like rewriting the novel.[16]

Mark Kinkead-Weekes indicates that Lawrence's reassessment of his father may have begun much earlier than 1920, during the writing of *Sons* and even because of it. "As he grew more critical of his mother in writing *Sons and Lovers,* the sense may have grown of how much in his father's world had only been glimpsed in its pages."[17] It would seem from these biographical insights that an interesting relationship exists between the on-screen Morel and the unwritten Morel of Lawrence's evolving imagination. If the film character erases the original text of *Sons and Lovers,* he also inscribes a Lawrence text that never quite got written. Trevor Howard's Morel—vital, sensitive, and essentially good—emerges as a strange ghost, thirty years after the author's death, of the father Lawrence regretted not having created himself.

Beyond plot and character, a less literary film element needs to be discussed here. This can be described as the visual achievement of *Sons and Lovers* on screen—the extent to which it realizes itself as effective cinematic art. Here it would seem that Lawrence's original text has a great deal of direct help to offer the filmmakers. As raw material to be turned into film, the novel is already visually energized—not in a fixed way, like painting, but kinetically, something like accomplished motion picture art itself. Any reading of *Sons and Lovers* is surely an experience measured in dynamic scenes—each one startling when first encountered in the text, each one moving and memorable in the way that first-rate film should be and sometimes is.

The memory, at liberty within this novel and among such scenes, might take a reader back to William Morel's first haircut, or to Paul's sacrifice of the doll "Missis Arabella," an act which prefigures so much about his future relations with women of flesh and blood. The reader might also recall bread baking at the Morel household and how such a seemingly simple activity can be supercharged with human emotion and significance. Beyond these examples, there are several vivid scenes throughout *Sons and Lovers* exploiting nature as a means of revealing character and relationship. Paul Morel, for instance, repeatedly stabs at the earth with a stick, acting out the conflict within himself between sexual desire and sexual rage. Or Miriam Leivers, with equal frequency, embraces the flowers she finds so beautiful—roses, sweet peas, daffodils—all crushed and stifled, as Paul fears he will be, against her loving breast. Or Clara Dawes, more controlled in her admiration, caresses a stallion, expressing by the single gesture both her will to dominate the creature and her susceptibility to its power. Perhaps the most startling thing to be said about the film, at least in regard to its visuality, is that all of these scenes are absent—as if the filmmakers had refused outright Lawrence's generous gifts.

The swinging scene between Paul Morel and Miriam Leivers is one exception. Here Jack Cardiff and his associates have attempted to preserve a luminous moment from the text and to present it on screen. Despite the movement and intensity of Lawrence's original scene, the result of this effort proves to be a failure. In the novel, the swinging scene takes up only two compressed pages of text, yet reveals so much about Paul and Miriam as separate people and as a couple in conflict. When Paul swings, he loses his single, fixed being within the activity itself, within sensations powerful enough to dissolve him into the wider experience. This is something Miriam knows she can never do: "Away he went. There was something fascinating to her in him. For the moment he was nothing but a piece of swinging stuff, not a particle of him that did not swing. She could never lose herself so, nor could her brothers. It roused a warmth in her. It were almost as if he were a flame that had lit a warmth in her, whilst he swung in the middle air" (182).

When Paul swings Miriam, the implications of the scene turn directly erotic and predict their future incompatibility as lovers— their insoluble conflict between sexual searching, on his part, and sexual fear, on hers: "She felt the accuracy with which he caught her, exactly at the right moment, and the exactly proportionate strength of his thrust, and she was afraid. Down to her bowels went the hot wave of fear. She was in his hands. Again, firm and inevitable came the thrust at the right moment. She gripped the rope, almost swooning" (182).

None of these implications survives in the film. Only the external shell of Lawrence's scene remains. On screen, the sequence occurs just after Paul learns that a wealthy man has purchased one of his paintings and plans to become his patron. He rushes to the Leivers farm to tell Miriam the news and finds her sitting on the swing. After a few halfhearted efforts at pushing Miriam back and forth, Paul suddenly takes her place and begins boasting about his recent achievements as he stands up and swings. Any sense of eroticism is lost from the scene, as is Lawrence's suggestion about more intense realities and a meaningful freedom from self. What the film scene proves to be about, in fact, *is* self and nothing much else: Paul's egotistical celebration of his success and his ambition to become not a great artist so much as a famous and wealthy one. While he swings, he crows to Miriam, now standing beneath him, "I'm going to the top of the world. You coming with me?" He then disappears, leaving the swing empty as he jumps into a hayloft above it and deliberately hides from Miriam. As she looks for him, confused by the whole performance, he showers her with money—the four five-pound notes he has just received for his painting. Finally he reappears, sliding down from the hayloft, back to Miriam, and proclaims, "Women are all the same. They always want to drag a man down to their own level."[18]

Lawrence's memorable scene, then, is hopelessly damaged in the film and made to reflect materialism in place of human complexity, as well as a male smugness in Paul nastier than anything similar in the novel's original character. One conclusion that could be drawn from this failure is that the filmmakers were correct to omit virtually all of the major Lawrence scenes from *Sons and Lovers*. Despite their visual impact, these scenes are really inward visions and therefore impossible to film realistically without externalizing them and thus violating their essential spirit.

If many of Lawrence's visionary scenes in *Sons and Lovers* are either botched or avoided on screen, it also appears that none of the film's truly effective moments owes very much to the text at all. This is exemplified by several memorable sequences already mentioned here: the strong and honest confrontations between Morel and Paul or between Mr and Mrs Morel, the father's music-hall performance on Christmas Eve, and the censored bedroom exchange between Paul and Clara. Not one of these scenes has a textual counterpart in *Sons and Lovers,* suggesting that visually the filmmakers have gotten farther on their own than on anything derived from Lawrence. In addition, the film's visual or artistic unit of measure is not ultimately the kinetic scene at all, as it is in the novel, but something far more fixed. In an ironic reversal, the original text appears to be more cinematic than the movie, a work of literature in constant flux and motion as opposed to a film essentially static, "painterly," or even "textual" in its artistic accomplishments.

A simple instance of the still quality in Jack Cardiff's *Sons and Lovers* involves a trio of sketches and paintings employed in the film as literary symbols might be employed in a text. The works in question are three portraits done by Paul Morel during the film: one of his mother, the second of his father, and the third of Clara Dawes. In quite literary terms, what Paul portrays here are his own strong feelings—images of people in his life who rouse his love, or hate, or both. Where no such intense emotions exist, as with Miriam Leivers, the corresponding portrait is absent from the film. Paul's three portraits are purely the filmmakers' invention, their only textual basis being a sketch done by Lawrence's Paul not of Clara's face as in the film but of her hand and arm.[19]

The portraits of Paul's parents are also interesting as a related pair of images, behaving independently from the text yet in a purely literary way. Paul's drawing of his mother is idealized, depicting her as younger than her actual years and wearing a seductive bonnet in place of her usual dour one. The portrait of Paul's father is more naturalistically conceived and remarkably evocative of Lawrence's own *Contadini* painting in its general com-position and in the central figure's pose. Where the *contadino* looks down and away, however, Walter Morel looks defiantly out at the viewer, his face blackened by mine dust except for his eyes.[20]

In one of the film's earliest scenes, Morel and his son Arthur notice Paul's sketch of Mrs Morel as they come down to breakfast. Arthur makes good-natured fun of it, but his father ruins the portrait when he lays his greasy bacon fork upon it. The hostile gesture here strikes at wife and son together—at Paul's adoring tribute to his mother, and at Mrs Morel's own superior and lady-like image. Morel then tries to repair the damage by rubbing the drawing with his handkerchief. He succeeds only in blackening Mrs Morel's face, thus making it resemble his own. These hostile actions in the film, then, may have a touching side to them as well, by mutely expressing Morel's wish that he and his wife might be more alike.

An altogether separate visual metaphor, and one which proves to be more pervasive than the three portraits, involves the turning wheel. Wheels appear frequently in *Sons and Lovers* and provide the film with an image more capable of movement and change than a picture enclosed within a frame. The first wheel suggests mechanism and industry, but soon expands in meaning to involve death as well. The film's opening scene is of a rural landscape at dawn. The camera pans across this landscape until it reaches what the script describes as "an alien element; a coal mine," and in particular a large wheel that operates the mine shaft elevator.[21] As the camera pauses here, the wheel begins to rotate, frightening away a flock of pigeons roosting nearby. The audience sees this same wheel just a few scenes later when the mine elevator brings Morel up from the pit with his son's dead body.

A different cinematic wheel seems opposed to the industrial wheel—now rural, natural, and sexual in its connotations. This is the water wheel at the Leivers farm, an object prominent in Paul's first scene with Miriam and associated, throughout the film, with her and with the couple's evolving courtship. When they first become lovers, the camera focuses on this wheel turning in the water as the scene dissolves to black. Later, when Paul ends his relationship with Miriam on Christmas morning, the camera shows this same wheel now frozen in the winter stream.

A third wheel, introduced late in the film, complicates matters by bringing together the opposite suggestions of the first two and conflating sexual passion with dead mechanical process. This wheel appears at the close of the fire-side scene in which Paul and Clara first make love. As this warm and living image fades from the screen, it is replaced by a close-up of spinning bobbins at the factory where Paul and Clara work, an image suggesting furious yet utterly lifeless activity.[22]

No mine wheels, mill wheels, or bobbin wheels operate within the pages of *Sons and Lovers*. They are purely cinematic interpolations, yet they provide Cardiff's film with a way back to the novel and to Lawrence's own reaction against industry as ultimately an agent of death. A more problematic implication in the film's turning wheels, however, is that mechanical cycle and sexual cycle may somehow be related. A wheel appears somewhere on screen during every one of Paul's passionate adventures, perhaps implying that his initial sexual euphoria will eventually give way to mechanical repetition. Departing from Lawrence here into a kind of existential misogyny, the film counsels Paul to save himself by utterly rejecting the sexual merry-go-round. The film's closing message to its hero and audience alike is to climb straight to the top of the world alone—go as a man on your own, unencumbered by women who will drag you down into a vicious erotic spin. This is precisely what Dean Stockwell's Paul does to bring *Sons and Lovers* to a close. As the credits appear, he replaces the film's sexual turnings with a straight and narrow line of march. The film audience sees him approaching from a distance, walking toward the Bestwood railway station swiftly, directly, and with very little baggage. He boards the waiting train, which will accelerate his linear journey to London, conveying him to likely success as a man within a man's world.

The film seems to end here on a blatantly reductive note, especially so if we recall the poetic ambiguity of Paul Morel's "quickly" moving figure in the scene that closes the novel (464). Yet the screen imagery that prepares for this anticlimax is neither blatant nor reductive. It juxtaposes Paul's linear and exclusively masculine escape at the end with sexual convolution, ultimately feminine convolution, in that the film's turning mill wheels and spiraling bobbins always imply either Miriam or Clara. Such film imagery seems provocative in a way closer to current feminist discourse than to Lawrence's text. The film's closing combination of inventive metaphor and questionable suggestion provides a revealing statement about its own mixed results as a work of cinematic art. This final paradox therefore also raises the inevitable question of judgment. How is the reader/viewer ultimately to assess a filmed work of fiction as conflicted as *Sons and Lovers* is on screen between the compelling and the embarrassing? My own answer here is that Jack Cardiff's film achieves a marginal success or, perhaps more accurately, amounts to an interesting failure. Its embarrassments, counted up and tallied, far outnumber its handful of breakthroughs: the general shrinkage of Lawrence's characters and plot, for example, to suit the restrictions of ninety-nine minutes on screen—or the scenic opportunities offered by the text either muffed or simply ignored by the filmmakers.

On the credit side of cinematic reckoning, the film's achievements are few yet memorable when they do occur. Among the successes within *Sons and Lovers,* only Mary Ure's Clara Dawes pays direct tribute to the filmmakers and to D. H. Lawrence at the same time. In every other instance, the film soars, albeit briefly, only when it resists Lawrence, either altering his text or else leaving it out of the picture entirely. On the level of plot, Arthur Morel's mine death provides an example of such radical and artistically effective resistance. The same can be said, regarding character, of Trevor Howard's Walter Morel, a cinematic figure who actually complicates Lawrence's original. As to visual achievement, the film's most telling images are derived not from the text but from the filmmakers' own artistic resources—that curious grouping of still portraits, turning wheels, and linear progressions, for instance, absolutely uncinematic in conception yet effective on screen just the same.

By breaking free from Lawrence, then, the film manages a few moments of confident flight. Yet by eluding the writer, this film obliquely recovers him, too, as when Trevor Howard suddenly reminds us of a father Lawrence never acknowledged in his novel but eventually wished he had. There is a broader sense, as well, in which the film recovers Lawrence by the very act that rejects him. His text concerns the human need to throw off many kinds of dominations, especially the overwhelming maternal urge, which, if not resisted, smothers in the cause of nurturing and cripples in the name of love. Paul Morel is a young man who cannot move "quickly"—in the double-edged sense of vitally and fast—until he liberates himself from this force, as difficult and prolonged as the struggle might be. Like the novel's protagonist, the film *Sons and Lovers* moves "quickly" only in moments of successful escape from its parental and potentially smothering text.

Notes

1. Originally released by Fox in Great Britain, *Sons and Lovers* is not available on commercial videotape. A first-draft copy of the shooting script for *Sons and Lovers* is in the Lilly Library's collection at Indiana University in Bloomington. The final shooting script with on-set revisions, dated 8 December 1959, is available at New York University's Bobst Library. The film's brush with England's censors (paralleling Anthony Pelissier's experience in filming *The Rocking Horse Winner*) occurred over a bedroom scene, not present in the text, between Dean Stockwell's Paul Morel and Mary Ure's Clara Dawes. While the couple do nothing more than kiss, their state of mind and undress imply the aftermath of lovemaking. Quite suggestive and daring by 1960 standards, the segment had to be deleted in order for the film to receive Great Britain's A rating (Adult; no unaccompanied child admitted).

2. "Lawrence: The Script . . . and the Camera," *Films and Filming* (May 1960), 9.

3. Despite Jack Cardiff's emphasis on close-up work in *Sons and Lovers*, one serious critic of the film, Dennis DeNitto, seems to have missed the effect entirely. In "All Passion Spent"—his chapter on *Sons and Lovers* in Michael Klein and Gillian Parker's *The English Novel and the Movies* (New York: Frederick Unger, 1981)—DeNitto complains that "for some reason Cardiff has insistently kept his camera objective and distant from the characters": "Occasionally the director does indulge in close-ups or close shots . . . Generally, however, the camera is too discreet, as though embarrassed by emotional displays and tensions" (246). If an analytical film viewer like DeNitto remains unimpressed by Cardiff's close-ups or unaware of them, it is possible that moving in with the Cinemascope camera did not create the dramatic effect Cardiff had hoped for.

4. "Lawrence: The Script . . . and the Camera," *Films and Filming* (May 1960), 9. For further details on the making of *Sons and Lovers*, see Jerry Wald's "Scripting *Sons and Lovers*," *Sight and Sound*, 29 (summer 1960), 117. Wald, who produced the film, reveals that Montgomery Clift was the filmmakers' first choice to play Paul Morel. By the time production began, however, "the young actor whom we originally intended to play Paul, Montgomery Clift, grew too old, and we had to find a new Paul." It is interesting to consider what *Sons and Lovers* might have become on screen had Clift's troubled and complicated qualities as an actor replaced Dean Stockwell's youthful simplicity. Despite Clift's absence, the filmmakers must have been satisfied with their final product, because they

began work on another Lawrence film shortly after *Sons and Lovers.* T. E. B. Clarke, again working with Jerry Wald and Twentieth Century Fox, completed a final screenplay for *The Lost Girl,* dated 18 July 1961. A copy of the unpublished script remains in the hands of a private collector, and to date no film of *The Lost Girl* has been released.

5. Isabel Quigly, "Unlikely Lawrence," *Spectator* (July 1960), 21.

6. "The New Pictures," *Time* (1 August 1960), 58.

7. Whitney Balliett, "An Embarrassment of Talk," *New Yorker* (13 August 1960), 56.

8. Stanley Kauffmann, "Several Sons, Several Lovers," *New Republic* (29 August 1960), 21–22. In an essay entitled *"Sons and Lovers:* Novel to Film as a Record of Cultural Growth," Frank Baldanza includes a useful and informative summary of several reviews and early critical commentaries on Jack Cardiff's film. See *Literature/Film Quarterly,* 1 (1973), 64–70.

9. Pauline Kael, *I Lost It at the Movies* (Boston: Little, Brown, 1965), 72.

10. Henry Hart, review of *Sons and Lovers* in *Films in Review,* 11 (August–September 1960), 424; John Gillett, review of *Sons and Lovers* in *Film Quarterly,* 14 (1960), 41.

11. Trevor Griffiths, *Sons and Lovers: Trevor Griffiths' Screenplay of the Novel by D. H. Lawrence* (Nottingham: Spokesman, 1982), 11.

12. Ibid., 11–12.

13. See Frank Baldanza, "Novel to Film," for a related discussion of the film's constrictive effect on plot in *Sons and Lovers.* Baldanza refers to this general process as "foreshortening" and contends that it takes three different forms within the film—"telescoping," "substitution," and "simplification." While Baldanza's treatment of the first of these strategies parallels my comments on condensation, his examples and conclusions differ from mine. See, for instance, Baldanza's discussion of Arthur's death, which relates it to the father's injury but not to the elder brother's death (68).

14. John Worthen, *D. H. Lawrence. The Early Years, 1885–1912* (Cambridge: Cambridge University Press, 1991), 142.

15. Evidence from the 8 December 1959 final shooting script for *Sons and Lovers* suggests that the filmmakers intended Paul and Miriam to be more intellectual than they turn out to be in the finished film. This quality is not conveyed by anything resembling the intensely "felt thoughts" so characteristic of their relationship in the novel. Rather it is reflected in the script much more simply by having Paul and Miriam carry on conversations about literature. One such conversation involves the entire Morel family, oddly enough, in a discussion of Browning's

"Home Thoughts from the Sea." Another involves Miriam and her mother in an argument about Flaubert and whether or not his writings on love accord with Christianity. The only trace of such discussions surviving in the film itself is one dialogue between Paul and Miriam in which he refers to a sow in the Leivers barnyard as "The Dark Lady of the Sonnets" and "The Lady of the Lake." A moment later Paul mentions a book by Shelley, which he has forgotten to bring for Miriam. This leads to nothing more than a brief exchange about Mrs Leivers's disapproval of their reading material and of Paul's influence on Miriam in general.

16. Jeffrey Meyers, *D. H. Lawrence: A Biography* (New York: Alfred A. Knopf, 1990), 18.

17. Mark Kinkead-Weekes, *D. H. Lawrence: Triumph to Exile, 1912–1922* (Cambridge: Cambridge University Press, 1996), 55.

18. One shred of interest surviving in Cardiff's swinging scene is its odd and perhaps accidental parallel to a later Lawrence work. Just after Paul's comment about being dragged down by women, he sits next to Miriam in the Leivers barn and tells her, "I've got a heart that beats. Feel it." Paul's words repeat those of Henry Grenfel to Nellie March in "The Fox":

> "Do you think I haven't *got* a heart?"—And with his hot grasp
> he took her hand and pressed it under his left breast. "There's
> my heart," he said, "if you don't believe in it."

See D. H. Lawrence, *The Fox, The Captain's Doll, The Ladybird,* ed. Dieter Mehl (Cambridge: Cambridge University Press, 1992), 52. In the film, Miriam, like March, seems momentarily spellbound by news of the male heartbeat. Then both women are summoned back to reality by a cry from outside the barn—Banford's in "The Fox" and Mrs Leivers's in the *Sons and Lovers* film.

19. Paul's sketch of Clara is puzzling because it contradicts not only Lawrence's text but its own description in the script. In the film, the drawing is hastily done on the back of a leaflet Paul receives at one of Clara's suffragette rallies. It shows her exactly as she appears on the speaking platform—severe yet attractive, her hair upswept and covered by a stark black hat. The 8 December 1959 shooting script, however, describes a more openly seductive Clara in Paul's drawing, which "captures her essential femininity, as he sees it; there's a softness in her face; her hair falls to her shoulders, instead of being severely upswept" (67).

What motivated the filmmakers' change here, from final script to screen, remains uncertain.

20. As opposed to the sketch of Clara, Paul's painting of his father conforms to the way the filmmakers describe it in the script: "A portrait of Morel in which his [Paul's] father, with the grime of the pit like cracks on his face, has just come up from the mine. Looking up at sudden daylight, he blinks. There is something lost yet aggressive in his expression" (21).

21. Gavin Lambert and T. E. B. Clarke, "Sons and Lovers," Final Shooting Script with On-Set Revisions, 8 December 1959, 2, Bobst Library, New York University.

22. Described in the 8 December 1959 screenplay as the "whirling spindle of [a] spiral machine" (81), this third cinematic wheel is the only one to have attracted any critical notice. In "All Passion Spent," DeNitto suggests that "Visual symbols are . . . avoided [in *Sons and Lovers* on screen] while those that do appear are either patently obvious or undeveloped. The one exception is the shot of rotating bobbins after the one of Paul and Clara embracing" (246). DeNitto does not discuss this image further, nor does he relate it to the other turning wheels in the film.

Ideas, Histories, Generations and Beliefs: The Early Novels to *Sons and Lovers*

RICK RYLANCE

◆ ◆ ◆

The Puzzle of the Early Work: *The White Peacock*

What gave Lawrence's work its distinctive character in the second decade of the twentieth century? Reviewers of the first three novels appeared perplexed. There was confusion about the author's social milieu and gender, and irritation that provincial fiction should be so learned in literary and intellectual allusion.[1] His characters moved unpredictably between 'public-houses and dinner parties' and had deplorable grooming rituals: 'among their habits is a trick of messing and caressing and stroking each other's hair or arms'.[2] This zoological sneer loped after Lawrence throughout his career. Behind it lurked worries about evolutionary descent from the apes and, more worrying still, the possibility of degenerate reversion. But amid fretfulness about his carelessness with social and literary form, and his shocking lack of sexual reticence (a charge that began with *The Trespasser* in 1912), the central issue was bewilderment about his meaning. Few denied his talent; fewer still had a collected sense of where it led:

what does our author really mean by these pictures of wasted lives and ill-matched marriages? Is he a new prophet of the old fallacy of 'returning to Nature'? It sometimes looks like it, and yet the apologue which explains the title of *The White Peacock* does not suggest this as a moral, for surely the game-keeper who reverted violently 'to Nature' after freeing himself from his unnatural wife, 'the white peacock', did not make much of his experiment.[3]

This attempt to restore a troubling text to a recognisable message is clearly mistaken, but the misanthropic gamekeeper, Annable, *is* puzzling. He appears suddenly in the middle of the novel and fascinates the narrator, Cyril Beardsall, who likes his physique and outlaw style. The sexual and social ambivalence of such figures is often remarked. There is a homoerotic shimmer around Annable and, like Mellors in *Lady Chatterley's Lover,* he is better born and educated than he appears. The Cambridge-educated son of a 'big cattle dealer', his father's bankruptcy cut short his degree and, he tells Cyril, he became a curate before marrying into the gentry. His marriage foundered on differences of rank and culture as his wife was enthralled by 'souly' poets and painters. Annable became a piece of 'rough': 'I was her animal—son animal—son bœuf. I put up with that for above a year. Then I got some servant's clothes and went'.[4] His story captures something of the challenge of Lawrence's early work: hard to 'place' or explain, unconventional, rebarbative and dissident, it sets an interpretative problem. For Annable's life reverses stories articulating ideals of social integration, romantic harmony and cultural pride. A narrative about a worthy unfortunate and his lady-rescuer is given a sarcastic twist, as is a tale about artistic guardianship by the wealthy. And Annable's lost religious faith produces not soul-agony, but aggressive nihilism.

Annable reveals his life to Cyril among the gothic ruins of a derelict church. Symbolic of lost faith, the church takes its place with other ruins in a decrepit social order whose image would be fixed as a waste land by T. S. Eliot's famous poem eleven years

later. In *The White Peacock* there is the run-down estate, the eco-
nomically disintegrating farm, the 'degraded hall' of Colwick
Park, the London slums and the dilapidated shell of the Crystal
Palace.[5] The novel struggles with change from the outset, 'musing
in old age'[6] on a world beginning to appear unrecognisable. Violet
Hunt, in the left-wing *Daily Chronicle,* noted that 'there appears to
be no "county" at all, no great families, no squires, hardly even
a parson'.[7] There is, however, plenty of infrastructural alteration:
the agricultural depression, slum life in Nottingham, 'outcast
London', emigration. The volatility is reflected in George's impulsive career in farming, business and politics. Meanwhile, mining capital is entrenched nationally, instead of locally, by the
Tempest family, and Leslie moves smoothly into his role as a Tory
MP. The social façade of this life—fake pastoral picnics, charity
tennis parties 'for the Missionaries, or the Unemployed, or something',[8] the company of 'advanced' artists—feebly compensates
for Lettie's decline into stoic gloom.

Amidst structural upheaval, Annable's opinions are as uncom-
fortable as his alien name alongside Cyril, George and Leslie.

> He was a man of one idea:—that all civilisation was the painted
> fungus of rottenness. He hated any sign of culture. I won his
> respect one afternoon when he found me trespassing in the
> woods because I was watching some maggots at work in a dead
> rabbit. That led us to a discussion of life. He was a thorough
> materialist—he scorned religion and all mysticism . . . When he
> thought, he reflected on the decay of mankind—the decline
> of the human race into folly and weakness and rottenness. "Be
> a good animal, true to your animal instinct" was his motto.[9]

The ex-parson is now an extreme materialist, but the passage
disconcerts for other reasons. It is difficult, for instance, to evaluate the irony loaded into the third and fourth sentences. They
begin and end positively—'I won his respect . . . That led us to a
discussion of life'—but are punctuated by maggots munching on

a rabbit. The target of the irony is, however, uncertain. Is it Annable's nihilism? Is it Cyril himself, unalert to his own strange absorption in a carcass? Meanings are simply tangled in effects.

Techniques like this are common in Lawrence and were a source of early readers' confusions. But they are also a major source of that intricate valency of attitude, and open responsiveness to complex lives, which Lawrence treasured in the novel as a modern form. Asked about Annable by a shocked Jessie Chambers (his then girlfriend), his intentions were clear: ' "He *has* to be there. Don't you see why? He makes a sort of balance. Otherwise it's too much one thing, too much *me*." '[10] The reply indicates Lawrence's need to polarise his thinking, juxtaposing wavering Cyril against dogmatic game-keeper, refinement against brutality, gentility against poverty, youth against sour maturity.[11] But the unsynthesised dialectic, like the indefinite irony, is without resolution. The deliberate uncertainty embedded in style and structure matches uncertainties about historical and intellectual development in both the author and his characters. For Jessie Chambers, Annable 'seemed to be a focus for all Lawrence's despair over the materialistic view of life he felt compelled to accept for lack of an alternative'.[12] This is a key statement because it establishes the intellectual orbit of the early work. But the issue is not as straightforward as Chambers implies.

Lawrence and Nineteenth-Century Evolutionary Argument

For Lawrence's generation the word 'materialism' meant the denial of divine agency in the natural world. Natural processes, materialists believed, occurred as a result of the material properties of nature rather than by supernatural design or intervention.[13] Throughout the nineteenth century, therefore, materialism was a derogatory label fixed by Christians on developments in biology, the bio-medical sciences, psychology and other areas. One result was the familiar schism between science and religion emphasised in the debate on evolutionary theory. This emphasis is, in a sense, misleading because such developments affected sciences other than biology (such as physics and physiology), and because the theory of evolution itself had several very different strands within it which, in Lawrence's lifetime, were not yet ordered by the 'synthesis' of Darwinism and Mendelian genetics.[14] Nonetheless, evolution was perceived to drive a wedge between truth and orthodoxy, humanity and the cosmos. It also altered perceptions of humanity's physical embodiment. For Lawrence's generation, the relations of mind to body, and human to animal, were chronically disturbed, as reflected in the anxieties of his reviewers.

Jessie Chambers recalled Lawrence's encounter with materialistic ideas as traumatic:

> It came in full blast with T. H. Huxley's *Man's Place in Nature,* Darwin's *Origin of Species,* and Haeckel's *Riddle of the Universe.* This rationalistic teaching impressed Lawrence deeply. He came upon it at a time of spiritual fog, when the lights of orthodox religion and morality were proving wholly inadequate, perplexed as he was by his own personal dilemma. My feeling was that he tried to fill up a spiritual vacuum by swallowing materialism at a gulp. But it did not carry him very far. He would tell me with vehemence that nature is red in tooth and claw, with the implication that 'nature' included human nature. Yet . . . his dominant feeling seemed to be a sense of hopelessness.[15]

The recollection is generically familiar with its Tennysonian motifs ('nature . . . red in tooth and claw', 'spiritual fog') and crude choice between 'materialism' and 'orthodox religion' which produces 'hopelessness'. It illustrates the proximity of Lawrence's generation to the great Victorian thinkers (Huxley, for example, had died only in 1895).[16] In *Sons and Lovers,* Paul Morel's development beyond Christianity is gradually and carefully noted. He proceeds through sceptical questioning, mockery and agnosticism ('at the Renan *Vie de Jésus* stage') to an exposed, quasi-existentialist position at the close.[17] The novel is interested in the psychological eddies and scuffles of this development—Paul enjoys tormenting Miriam with his unbelief for instance—but there is no strong sense that the loss of religious belief is, in itself, desolating. Paul's eventual crisis has metaphysical components, but they are not a main cause.

The same was true for Lawrence. Like many, he was eager to find a way to negotiate between materialism and spirituality.[18] He was enthusiastic about William James's book *Pragmatism* in 1907 which, while favouring secular science, tried to respect spiritual needs. In 1909, he wrote to his old botany lecturer, the Unitarian Ernest Smith, that life 'seems to me barbarous, recklessly wasteful and destructive, often hideous and dreadful: but, on the whole, beautiful'.[19] This more balanced awareness needs to be read against Jessie Chambers's account because it reflects real, if complex, developments. Unitarian Christianity, with its conviction that matter and spirit were indivisible, helped scientists like Smith out of the impasse, and Lawrence noted Unitarianism's appeal for 'advanced' opinion in *Sons and Lovers* (301). The problem with some commentary on Lawrence's encounter with evolutionary and materialistic ideas is that it is captured by an 'either-for-it-or-against-it' paradigm. But Lawrence tried to think through available options and refused the revolving door of that classic Victorian stalemate. The characteristically angular, zigzag pattern of his intellectual development negotiated between opposed ideas, and the unsettled forms of his fictions respond to this. The early novels present disorderly stories or effects partly because he explores the limits of models of coherent explanation, beginning with Christianity and moving to evolutionary materialism.

Lawrence grappled with these issues during the composition of *The White Peacock*. His letter of 3 December 1907 to the Congregationalist minister in Eastwood, the Revd Robert Reid, is a formal announcement of doubt. Lawrence writes that he cannot reconcile faith with evidence of God's apparent tolerance of suffering in the slums of Nottingham and London.[20] But the case is not only moral or political. Lawrence uses evolutionary terminology to avoid the 'catastrophe' narrative presented later by Jessie Chambers. He describes his position as 'undergoing modification' and conducts an imaginary argument in which Reid suggests

that faith is 'belief in a hypothesis that cannot be proved'.
Lawrence replies:

> But sir, there must at least be harmony of facts before a hy-
> pothesis can be framed. Cosmic harmony there is—a Cosmic
> God I can therefore believe in. But where is the human har-
> mony, where the balance, the order, the 'indestructibility of
> matter' in humanity? And where is the *personal, human* God?
> Men—some—seem to be born and ruthlessly destroyed; the
> bacteria are created and nurtured on Man, to his horrible suf-
> fering. Oh, for a God-idea I must have harmony—unity of
> design. Such design there may be for the race—but for the
> individual, the often wretched individual?[21]

The letter develops Lawrence's already powerful wish for exploration through imagined scenes and polarised opinion. His the-
atrical (but not insincere) response—'But, sir, there must . . . '—
is spoken in character, taking the tone of the great Victorian
debates on materialism, and making use of language familiar from
scientific discourse, specifically relating to established precepts
like the 'indestructibility of matter', and the form of scientific
propositions (consistency in the data sustains the validity of
hypotheses, for example). Lawrence also makes what was, by that
time, a fairly common separation of the human from the cos-
mological.

By 1900 most advanced opinion agreed that disparate spheres
of knowledge (for example cosmology and ethics) need not bind
one another to common explanation. There was agreement about
this among liberal churchmen and scientific thinkers alike, not
least because it keeps opponents apart in their separate domains.
But the argument has other advantages. When the materialist
Huxley took this position in 'Evolution and Ethics', his influential
Romanes lecture in 1893, he illustrated how human values could
be extracted from materialistic determinism. Huxley saw ethics in
a dependent, but not determined, relation to nature. The strife
of the natural world, obeying the mechanisms of survival, was

undeniably brutal. But it did not follow that humanity should imitate such ethically inert behaviour. On the contrary, our ability to intervene ethically not only defines our humanity, it gives an evolutionary advantage because ethical behaviour emphasises co-operation rather than predation.[22] Such a position is not without difficulties (the origins and forms of these ethical standards remain unexplained, for instance), but it opens a different line of thinking, one which avoids the ethical void imagined by Jessie Chambers.

Typically, however, Lawrence did not follow this road straight-forwardly. The letter to Reid accepts this bifocal thinking, but reverses the evaluations. For Huxley, the natural order is trau-matic, the ethical order auspicious. For Lawrence, there may be 'Cosmic harmony', but humanity is caught in chronic confusion and suffering. This partly explains the apparently incoherent dis-integration of the human order expressed in the early fiction. His concern is with the chasm that opens between the human and the natural orders, between individual and group, and between experience and the perception of value. Writing to Reid, he calls these 'the great human discrepancies',[23] and it is this aching sense of discrepancy which gives the early novels their characteristic plangency.

'Art and the Individual: A Paper for Socialists', delivered at the Eastwood Debating Society three months later in March 1908, continues the discussion. Characteristically, in the polarising habit of Lawrence's thinking, it puts the opposite case. It argues that aesthetic culture is as important to socialism as the elimination of want. This is argued from an evolutionary perspective. Lawrence claims that evolutionary processes are not traumatic; in fact, they generate an aesthetically and spiritually inspiring sense of fittingness:

> Unconsciously, I think, we appreciate some of the harmony of this mutual adaptability, and that is how aesthetics come to be allied to religion, for they are a recognition . . . of the great underlying purpose which is made visible in this instance, and which it is, perhaps, the artist's duty to seek. This universal

Purpose is the germ of the God-Idea. It may be as the plant develops from the germ, it is twisted and clipped into some fantastic Jehovah shape, but—: [the paragraph deliberately breaks off][24]

Evolution reveals a harmony 'twisted and clipped' into distorted shape by religious orthodoxy, but religious feeling is not derided. In fact it harmonises with naturalistic understanding. Lawrence sees art and human culture playing a profound role in evolution because they foster the apprehension of the orderly growth which lies beneath a chaotic, apparently disorderly surface.

Lawrence's sources for this spiritually meaningful form of evolutionary development are a hybrid lot, not all fully absorbed.[25] But it is not a Darwinian vision. Darwinian evolution occurs through chance mutation and the random production of better-adapted forms. There is neither rule, order nor purpose in it. Instead, Lawrence draws upon an alternative theory which had considerable currency at the end of the nineteenth century (though it is now discounted), that associated with the French biologist Jean-Baptiste Lamarck. Lamarck believed that 'acquired characteristics' could be transmitted from generation to generation. This means that characteristics acquired by parents are passed to their offspring. These might be strong arms, or dextrous fingers, or advantageous mental attitudes. Successor generations may develop these 'acquired characteristics' or allow them to decline, but either way the important point is that humans, to some degree, can intervene in the evolutionary sequence which can, therefore, become purposive, orderly and unalienated.

It is not known whether Lawrence read Lamarck, but he found similar ideas in Schopenhauer's essay 'The Metaphysics of [Sexual] Love' (1818) which he read enthusiastically in 1906–7.[26] Schopenhauer took it for granted that '[i]n the child the qualities transmitted by both parents continue to live, fused and united into one being'.[27] Schopenhauer's essay often interests Lawrence scholars because of its unusually strong statement of the role of the sex-drive in human affairs, but it also offers a way of thinking about the relationship between generations:

What is decided by [the sex drive] is nothing less than the *composition of the next generation* . . . the being, the *existentia*, of these future persons is absolutely conditioned by our sexual impulse in general, so is their nature, their *essentia*, by the individual selection in the satisfaction of the impulse, i.e. by sexual love; and by this it is in every respect irrevocably fixed.[28]

Schopenhauer's sexual-reproductive determinism eventually alienated Lawrence, but his ideas do release an important theme, that '[t]he collected *love affairs* of the present generation, taken together, are accordingly the human race's serious *meditatio compositionis futurae, e qua iterum pendent innumerae generationes* [meditation on the composition of the future generation on which in turn innumerable generations depend]'.[29]

Love Choices: *The Trespasser*

The idea that a generation's love choices not only tell their own story but predict the historical sequence gave Lawrence important subject matter, though, like many, he was uncertain how to evaluate its implications. In *Sons and Lovers* it is said of Mrs Morel that 'She still had her high moral sense, inherited from generations of Puritans. It was now a religious instinct' (25). The implication is that sub-cultural habits can become a quasi-biological force (an 'instinct'). In *The Trespasser*, Siegmund's passion for Helena is similarly described: 'The changes in him were deeper, like alteration in his tissue. His new buds came slowly, and were of a fresh type'.[30] The emphasis on histological change (tissue alteration), and the use of botanical and biological vocabulary (buds of a fresh type), is very striking.

Equally important, however, is the fact that, in the dramatic action, these ideas are under enquiry. Mrs Morel's Puritan 'instinct' suggests cultural and trans-generational continuity, but it brings her into violent collision with her husband and, in the novel, she is the last of the line. In *The Trespasser*, Siegmund's deep-tissue change is, in fact, illusory. Half a page later Lawrence adds: 'Siegmund looked at her and continued smiling. His happiness was budded firm and secure'. The retrospective irony—the relationship is, in fact, radically insecure and Siegmund commits suicide—is a product of an unsignalled use of free indirect speech which now allocates the apparent objectivity of the botanical metaphor to Siegmund's consciousness, withdrawing its authority.

Lawrence tests models of coherent development, predictable growth and secure values. He tests them against a vision of splintering *incoherence* which emphasises lack of continuity, the lonely, often deluded abandonment of individuals, and the evacuation of received values. The action of *The White Peacock*, like that of *The Trespasser*, takes place largely within a single generation whose personnel become dispersed. *Sons and Lovers* examines two generations with similar themes of scattering and disconnection. *The Rainbow* (the next completed novel) covers three. It is as if each book looks further down the family tree to test what slow pattern might be found. In the first three novels, the chaotic record of the love choices, and the shortened historical perspective, obscure the signs that predict the future. *The White Peacock* is full of children, but there is an ominous sense of historical impasse.

Ancestral ghosts, however, haunt the present. The Saxton family in *The White Peacock* feel this strongly:

> "You do see yourself a bit ghostish—" said [George], "on a background of your ancestors. I always think when you stop in an old place like this you sort of keep company with your ancestors too much; I sometimes feel like a bit of the old building walking about; the old feelings of the old folks stick to you like the lichens on the walls."

His father agrees—' "That's why I'm going to Canada" '—and adds: ' "you stay in one place, generation after generation, and ... keep on thinking and feeling the same, year after year, till we've only got one side".'[31] The conspicuous reversal here—the living are as thin as ghosts and reified as one side of a wall—expresses an anxiety that transmitted values are deadly. The weight of absent generations bears heavily in *The White Peacock,* emerging in ghostly ruins and insubstantial identities. 'I myself seemed to have lost my substance,' remarks Cyril, 'to have become detached from concrete things . . . Onward, always onward, not knowing where, nor why'.[32] Feelings of personal emptiness and inhibition are widely distributed. They are accounted for by Lettie. ' "I have been brought up to expect it" ', she explains to George, ' "—everybody expected it—and you're bound to do what people expect you to do—you can't help it. We can't help ourselves, we're all chessmen".'[33] This is the other side of Annable's brutalist materialism. Annable declares 'be a good animal'; Lettie declares 'be a good social cipher'. Annable spurns humanistic values, but others are imprisoned by their social and behavioural inheritance. *The White Peacock* deploys its inconclusive argument around this uncongenial choice.

The second novel, *The Trespasser,* dramatises what became major Lawrentian themes, including the need to seek release from inhibiting social obligations, the discovery of personal authenticity through sexual passion and an energising vision of the sexual body which avoids Annable's gross reduction. The novel is a philosophical melodrama in which potential growth (described as a vitalistic urge) collides with ensnaring circumstance. This was a popular theme (in E. M. Forster, for instance), but the distinctiveness of *The Trespasser* lies in the complications in both perspective and analysis introduced into the narrative. The lovers appear united, but are quickly divided by their natures. Lawrence examines a collision between old and emergent forms of being, but refuses to sentimentalise their defeat into sad romantic tragedy.

On holiday on the Isle of Wight, the lovers try to live outside time: ' "There is *no* next week," she declared . . . "There is only the present" '; 'he wanted to . . . blaze up all his past and future in a passion worth years of living'.[34] But what calls Siegmund, particularly, back into time are his obligations to his children. Meanwhile, off Spithead, battleships cruise through heavily defended waters, fronting rival European nationalisms during a visit by the Czar. They act as reminders of social time. Helena and Siegmund temporarily choose to be isolated from family and community. But children and warships, personal and social time, press them towards defeat.

This, however, is by no means all the story. Siegmund's brain is in traumatic disorder throughout: 'Thoughts came up in his brain like bubbles, random, hissing out aimlessly. Once, in the startling inflammability of his blood, his veins ran hot, and he smiled'.[35] A grotesque simile is disconcertingly capped by a smile. It is one of many heavily materialised images used to describe Siegmund's and Helena's mental and emotional states. These are of various kinds: histological change (as we have seen), bodily wounds, the swarming of insects, the fertilisation of seeds, the running of machines and the smelting of metals.[36] The inconsistency of the group seems deliberate. It suggests the precarious uncertainty of their condition, but the images also subvert conventional descriptions of thought and the expected attributes of mind and body. Thus, blood possesses consciousness.[37] Or, when images are drawn from natural history, they do not suggest classifiable behaviour as they do when used by George Eliot, for instance. Instead, they have a rather ugly function, degrading individual significance or disempowering the human will.[38]

Such images make one uneasy. Is this description of Helena's transported state intended to be attractive or not? 'It seemed to her as if all the lightness of her fancy and her hope were being burned away in this tremendous furnace, leaving her, Helena, like a heavy piece of slag seamed with metal. She tried to imagine herself resuming the old activities, the old manner of living'.[39] The passage is obviously thematically pertinent, but the image 'slag seamed with metal' is disconcerting. It shows a modernist appetite for defamiliarising the rhetorics of interior life, but this only partially accounts for it. Comparing states of feeling to industrial smelting certainly avoids stereotype, but the metaphor also implies that mind-states are dramatically material rather than spiritual, and that they have multiple products, including waste. Processes of refinement produce ashes and slag, and this doubleness is essential to Lawrence.

Such rhetoric has complicated effects. As early reviewers discovered, it unsettles. But, in a distinctive and original way, it joins contemporary debates about materialism in life processes. These images press their heavy substance, but they are also flauntingly metaphorical and encourage imaginative exploration of their conceptual implications. This impressed one early reader who exclaimed over the 'wonderful interfusion' of 'physiology, psychology, and splendid poetry' in *Sons and Lovers*.[40] Like these images, the mind in Lawrence's work is neither exclusively physical process nor autonomous consciousness. Just as his revisionary and dramatising intelligence works between polarised issues, the images negotiate implications without simplifying reduction.

In 'Study of Thomas Hardy', written from September 1914, Lawrence argued that 'generations of ultra-Christian training', producing a de-eroticised and patriarchal culture, explain Angel Clare's failure to cope 'when he finds that [Tess] has, in his words, been defiled' in *Tess of the d'Urbervilles*. Angel's hysteria, for Lawrence, is symptomatic of an epochal crisis which also includes

> the great scientists and thinkers of the last generation, even Darwin and Spencer and Huxley. For these last conceived of evolution, of one spirit or principle starting at the far end of time, and lonelily [sic] traversing Time. But there is not one principle, there are two, travelling always to meet, each step of each one lessening the distance between the two of them. And Space, which so frightened Herbert Spencer, is as a Bride to us. And the cry of Man does not ring out into the Void. It rings out to Woman, whom we know not.[41]

It was shrewd of Lawrence to note the masculine bias of nineteenth-century science.[42] But his main criticism of evolutionary materialism is not only that it is womanless and sexless, but that it lacks dialectical exchange. His vision of biological development is curiously abstract (and is written in a distinctively religious register), but he is imagining a complex, polarised interaction which is, above all, unfinished. He rejects reductions of human origins and development to a limited causality, and his career as a novelist, despite his dogmatic outbursts, is committed to this kind of multi-aspected, exploratory understanding.

So Helena is both slag and metal and the divided qualities of both lovers prevent *The Trespasser* becoming sentimental. Their relationship grows increasingly awkward and divided as the novel develops. Lawrence renders this by swift alterations of point of view and use of free indirect speech. The narrative dissolves into their separate, limited consciousness, most clearly when episodic chapters switch rapidly from one to the other to reveal, without commentary, the detached imagined worlds of their relationship.[43] It is this that provides the literary energy of the novel.

Desire is solipsistic in *The Trespasser*. Helena, like Miriam in *Sons and Lovers*, wants a romantic lover: 'It was a gay, handsome boy she had to meet, not a man, strange and insistent'.[44] But, if she is troubled by grown-up desire, Siegmund's hopes of erotic translation are, in their way, equally dreamy: 'His dream was melted in his blood, and his blood ran bright for her. His dreams were the flowers of his blood'.[45] Their separate, eventually conflicting, mental planes collude in fantasy. Helena is the 'Dreaming Woman', but it is Siegmund who 'woke with wonder in the morning. "It is like the magic tales," he thought, as he realised where he was, "and I am transported to a new life, to realise my dream. Fairy tales are true after all".'[46] Torn between past and present, routine and potential selves, mind and body, duty and desire, social responsibility and fantasy, the lovers, like the characters in *The White Peacock*, have no clear vision of their aspirations.

Sons and Lovers: Point of View and the Unconscious

The manipulation of point of view and free indirect speech to expose the predicament of the isolated individual is also central to the narrative method of *Sons and Lovers*. It is used there with an assurance and precision only intermittently equalled in earlier work, as in this episode when Paul searches for his first job:

> And then, at ten o'clock, he set off. He was supposed to be a queer, quiet child. Going up the sunny street of the little

town, he felt as if all the folk he met said to themselves: "He's going to the Co-op Reading Room to look in the papers for a place. He can't get a job. I suppose he's living on his mother." Then he crept up the stone stairs behind the drapery shop at the Co-op, and peeped in the reading room. Usually one or two men were there, either old useless fellows, or colliers 'on the club.' So he entered, full of shrinking and suffering when they looked up, seated himself at the table, and pretended to scan the news. He knew they would think, "What does a lad of thirteen want in a reading room, with a newspaper," and he suffered.

Then he looked wistfully out of the window. Already he was a prisoner of industrialism. Large sunflowers stared over the old red wall of the garden opposite, looking in their jolly way down on the women who were hurrying with something for dinner. The valley was full of corn, brightening in the sun. Two collieries, among the fields, waved their small white plumes of steam. Far-off on the hills were the woods of Aldersley, dark and fascinating. Already his heart went down. He was being taken into bondage. His freedom in the beloved home valley, was going now.

The brewers' wagons came rolling up from Keston, with enormous barrels, four a side, like beans in a burst bean-pod. The wagoner, throned aloft, rolling massively in his seat, was not so much below Paul's eye. The man's hair, on his small, bullet head, was bleached almost white by the sun, and on his thick red arms, rocking idly on his sack apron, the white hairs glistened. His red face shone and was almost asleep with sunshine. The horses, handsome and brown, went on by themselves, looking by far the masters of the show.

Paul wished he were stupid. "I wish," he thought to himself, "I was fat like him, and like a dog in the sun. I wish I was a pig, and a brewer's wagoner." (114–15)

Dense, lulling detail carries a passage like this, so much so that one only slowly becomes aware of the distinct point of view. But the consciousness embedded there is clearly Paul's rather than

that of some impersonal observer. The dogged procession of dis-
piriting detail and the anxious awareness of others follows the
course of his mind. The self-pitying wistfulness and anger is his
too, as well as the painter's eye looking through the window to
observe the landscape as though it were a stylised picture of sunflowers, old walls, corn fields and distant labour in which even
colliery chimneys look pretty and wave their steam like feathers.
(The picturesque conventionality makes a point about Paul's cal-
lowness.) There is no formal marking of this transfer of voice
and perspective; the point of view is simply and delicately shifted
around the mind of the precocious thirteen-year-old as decisively
as the baby-language of the opening page of Joyce's *A Portrait of
the Artist as a Young Man* creates the consciousness of the infant
Stephen Dedalus.

Sons and Lovers has been discussed before in these terms (most
originally by Louis Martz in his path-breaking essay 'A Portrait of
Miriam'[47]), but the temptation has always been to limit the novel's
use of these techniques. In fact they are permanent features of
the style to which readers need to be consistently alert. But this
is more than a technical achievement. These techniques are central to the novel's concerns, not least because they convey complexity and avoid summative judgement. The passage describes
Paul's adolescent alienation from his community. But it also indicates the degree to which he has internalised versions of many
of its values. Thus his self-image is poor when he sees himself
through others' eyes (he thinks his masculinity is compromised
by 'living on his mother'). Though the passage opposes the world
of work to the world of art, the stylised nostalgia of Paul's vision
compromises its preferential claims and suggests, in part, that art's
value for Paul lies in escape and imaginative mastery, a mechanism through which he might feel not only released but superior.
Like the sunflowers, he can look down on those in whose presence he feels ashamed. Paul is squeezed between native and as-
pirant cultures and so the episode ends in aggressive self-loathing.
Like Annable, he wishes himself an animal, a dog or a pig—but
also a wagoner. The shocking thing is that he sees the last as
equivalent to the first two.

The internalisation of the attitudes of others through the skilful manipulation of point-of-view and free indirect speech produces a subtle account of how identity is formed interpersonally. This is a major concern. It is a development from the solipsistic self-absorption with which *The Trespasser* deals, and beyond the boundaries of ethical and metaphysical enquiry set by the debate over scientific materialism. *Sons and Lovers* continues to be concerned, very urgently, with the relations of mind and body and issues of subsocial and impersonal determination, but an additional, thickly described layer has been added. The novel is consistently attentive to psychological conditioning through the interrelation of personalities, not least, of course, in the relationship between Mrs Morel and her sons. Its dynamics include (as between Paul and Miriam) the interplay of desire and aggression, the adoption of postures of domination and deference, and the way in which potentially protean selves are reduced to smaller, more defensive entities.

One example concerns an aspect of the novel brought more vividly to light by the restoration of Lawrence's original text in the Cambridge edition. Among other material cancelled by Edward Garnett's editorial work on the original version of *Sons and Lovers* were substantial passages relating to Paul's elder brother William. This produced a more focused narrative and reduced the book's length, but unintentionally the patterns in the family dynamics are blurred. A two-page passage omitted from chapter 3, for instance, describes William attending a fancy-dress ball. He looks fine in his costume, but Mrs Morel disapproves for complex reasons. She has a compulsion to control a son growing up, jealousy of his girlfriends, fear that he might go 'the same way as his father' and a snobbery that the ball is held in 'a low town'. William attends the ball nevertheless, and enjoys himself, but '[h]e never knew how disappointed he was. The excitement of the moment, and of anticipation, was enough to carry him through the present. But all his hurt pride was built upon *her* seeing him. And afterwards, it always hurt him to think back on this ball' (76). There are several key issues here. There is William's need to project an image that his mother will approve of and authenticate; there is an account of the way pleasure turns to retrospective pain because that authentication is withheld; there is her manipulation of the situation. But above all there is the key point that all this develops *unconsciously*. William is not even aware of his own disappointment.

The subtlety of Lawrence's analysis is very telling, and over subsequent pages he builds a picture of the emotional structuration of William's personality through complex interpersonal interactions. Lawrence's images for this process are of grain-by-grain sedimentation, and the adding of small amounts to a mixture. It is a process described with great delicacy (as later for Paul) and it is important not to reduce or simplify what is happening as do cruder versions of psychoanalytic commentary. The formation of unconscious mental structures is exactly the issue, but Lawrence himself seems to me right to sense that psychoanalysis, like materialist determinism, is at best half a story. He resented Alfred Kuttner's early seizure of the book for psychoanalytic case-law and complained to a friend that ''complexes' are vicious half-statements . . . When you've said Mutter-complex, you've said nothing   no more than if you called hysteria a nervous disease. Hysteria isn't nerves, a complex is not simply a sex relation: far from it.—My poor book: it was, as art, a fairly complete truth: so they carve a half lie out of it, and say 'Voilà'. Swine!'[48]

As a recent article by Fiona Becket indicates,[49] Lawrence's psychological modernity does not consist of fellow-travelling with Freud, though their coincidence in intellectual history is of serious significance. The unconscious in *Sons and Lovers* is a complex and delicately formed structure derived from multiple sources including an embattled sexuality. But the novel is open and exploratory in its account of this formation. Indeed, the very word 'psychological' (widely used by early reviewers of *Sons and Lovers*[50]) usually suggested in this period not psychoanalysis, but materialist psychology in the nineteenth-century tradition. William James used it this way in *Pragmatism*, the book that influenced Lawrence strongly in 1907, and Lawrence's sister Emily shared the association, though she valued it negatively, deploring her brother's 'psychological set at the University, who ridiculed religion'.[51] In trying to understand Lawrence's distinctive achievement in the early work it is to this context that we should turn as readily as to other more familiar ground as he negotiated new, complex forms and ideas in a period of intellectual and personal transition.

Notes

1. See the reviews collected in *D. H. Lawrence: The Critical Heritage*, ed. R. P. Draper (London: Routledge and Kegan Paul, 1970)

2. Unsigned review, *Daily News*, 14 February 1911. Reprinted in *D. H. Lawrence: The Critical Heritage*, 40.

3. *D. H. Lawrence: The Critical Heritage*, 37.

4. D. H. Lawrence, *The White Peacock*, ed. Andrew Robertson (Cambridge: Cambridge University Press, 1983), 151.

5. See Ibid., 247 (Colwick Hall) and 260–61 (Crystal Palace).

6. Ibid., 1.

7. *Daily Chronicle*, 10 February 1911. Reprinted in *D. H. Lawrence: The Critical Heritage*, 38.

8. D. H. Lawrence, *The White Peacock*, 18.

9. Ibid., 146–47.

10. Jessie Chambers, *D. H. Lawrence: A Personal Record by 'E.T.'* (London: Jonathan Cape, 1935), 117.

11. For a discussion of the 'polarised' nature of Lawrence's thinking, see Robert E. Montgomery, *The Visionary D. H. Lawrence: Beyond Philosophy and Art* (Cambridge: Cambridge University Press, 1994), but other critics also recognise its centrality. An important discussion of the general area is to be found in Michael Bell, *D. H. Lawrence: Language and Being* (Cambridge: Cambridge University Press, 1992).

12. *D. H. Lawrence: A Personal Record by 'E.T.'*, 117.

13. William James's definition is helpful in a book that influenced Lawrence considerably in 1907: materialism is 'in the widest sense, explaining higher things by lower ones, and leaving the destinies of the world at the mercy of its blinder parts and forces. It is in this wider sense of the word that materialism is opposed to spiritualism or theism': *Pragmatism, A New Name for Some Old Ways of Thinking: Popular Lectures on Philosophy* (London: Longmans, Green, and Co., 1907), 93.

14. The literature on developments in evolutionary theory in the

period is, of course, extensive, but Peter J. Bowler, *Theories of Human Evolution: A Century of Debate, 1844–1944* (London: Johns Hopkins University Press, 1986), Robert J. Richards, *The Meaning of Evolution: The Morphological Construction and Ideological Reconstruction of Darwin's Theory* (Chicago: University of Chicago Press, 1992), and Robert M. Young, *Darwin's Metaphor: Nature's Place in Victorian Culture* (Cambridge: Cambridge University Press, 1985) are more than helpful.

15. *D. H. Lawrence: A Personal Record by 'E.T.'*, 112.

16. John Worthen describes this milieu in Eastwood: 'The process of questioning had begun almost a century earlier; but Lawrence was one of those people who came to consciousness in the earlier twentieth century with their Christian faith still untroubled. Religion in Eastwood's chapels was still an unassailable fact of life, its faith unquestioned and often unquestioning.' John Worthen, *D. H. Lawrence: The Early Years, 1885–1912* (Cambridge: Cambridge University Press, 1991), 173.

17. See *Sons and Lovers*, 230, 256, 263, 267, 298–99, 314.

18. Useful commentaries on Lawrence's interest in materialism include Roger Ebbatson, 'The Spark Beneath the Wheel: Lawrence and Evolutionary Thought', and Christopher Heywood, ' "Blood-Consciousness" and the Pioneers of the Reflex and Ganglionic Systems', both in *D. H. Lawrence: New Studies*, ed. Christopher Heywood (London: Macmillan, 1987), 90–103, 104–23; Robert E. Montgomery, *The Visionary D. H. Lawrence*; Daniel J. Schneider, *The Consciousness of D. H. Lawrence: An Intellectual Biography* (Lawrence: University Press of Kansas, 1986); and *D. H. Lawrence: A Personal Record by 'E.T.'*, especially Chapter 7.

19. *The Letters of D. H. Lawrence*, Volume I, ed. James T. Boulton (Cambridge: Cambridge University Press, 1979), 147.

20. Ibid., 40.

21. Ibid., 41.

22. T. H. Huxley, 'Prolegomena' and 'Evolution and Ethics', in *Collected Essays*, 9 volumes (London: Macmillan, 1893–94), Volume IX, 1–116.

23. *Letters*, I, 41.

24. D. H. Lawrence, 'Art and the Individual', in *Study of Thomas Hardy and Other Essays*, ed. Bruce Steele (Cambridge: Cambridge University Press, 1985), 133–42. The excerpt is from 138.

25. See D. H. Lawrence, *Study of Thomas Hardy and Other Essays*, xli–xlii, 271–75.

26. For commentaries on Lawrence's reading in Schopenhauer, see Michael Bell, *D. H. Lawrence: Language and Being*; Robert E. Montgomery,

The Visionary D. H. Lawrence; Daniel J. Schneider, *The Consciousness of D. H. Lawrence*; and Allan R. Zoll, 'Vitalism and the Metaphysics of Love: D. H. Lawrence and Schopenhauer', *D. H. Lawrence Review*, 11 (1978), 1–20. For Schopenhauer's general influence, see John A. Lester, *Journey Through Despair 1880–1914* (Princeton, NJ: Princeton University Press, 1968).

27. Arthur Schopenhauer, 'The Metaphysics of Sexual Love', in *The World as Will and Representation*, trans. E. F. J. Payne, 2 vols. (New York: Dover, 1966), Volume II, 536.

28. Ibid., 534.

29. Ibid., 534.

30. D. H. Lawrence, *The Trespasser*, ed. Elizabeth Mansfield (Cambridge: Cambridge University Press, 1981), 93.

31. D. H. Lawrence, *The White Peacock*, 200.

32. Ibid., 83.

33. Ibid., 120.

34. D. H. Lawrence, *The Trespasser*, 58–59.

35. Ibid., 66.

36. For examples, see ibid., 162, 159, 165–66, 93 and 198–99 respectively. An example of the last type is discussed below.

37. Ibid., 63.

38. For an example, see ibid., 165–66.

39. Ibid., 119.

40. Unsigned review in *Nation*, 12 July 1913. Reprinted in *D. H. Lawrence: The Critical Heritage*, 70.

41. D. H. Lawrence, *Study of Thomas Hardy and Other Essays*, 98.

42. For a discussion of the masculine bias in nineteenth-century science, see Evelleen Richards, 'Redrawing the Boundaries: Darwinian Science and Victorian Women Intellectuals', in *Victorian Science in Context*, ed. Bernard Lightman (Chicago: University of Chicago Press, 1997), 119–42; Adrian Desmond, *Huxley: Evolution's High Priest* (London: Michael Joseph, 1997).

43. See, for example, *The Trespasser*, 17–19.

44. Ibid., 74.

45. Ibid., 64.

46. Ibid., 72.

47. Louis L. Martz, 'A Portrait of Miriam: A Study in the Design of *Sons and Lovers*', in *Imagined Worlds: Essays on Some English Novels and Novelists in Honour of John Butt*, eds. Maynard Mack and Ian Gregor (London: Methuen, 1968), 342–68.

48. Lawrence to Barbara Low, 16 December 1916. See *The Letters of D. H. Lawrence*, Volume II, eds. George J. Zytaruk and James T. Boulton (Cambridge: Cambridge University Press, 1981), 655. Alfred Kuttner's article—'A Freudian Appreciation'—appeared in the *Psychoanalytic Review* in 1916. It is reprinted in the present volume.

49. See Fiona Becket, 'Lawrence and Psychoanalysis', in *The Cambridge Companion to D. H. Lawrence*, ed. Anne Fernihough (Cambridge: Cambridge University Press, 2001), 217–33.

50. See the reviews collected in *D. H. Lawrence: The Critical Heritage*, 58–80, and the Introduction by Helen and Carl Baron to the Cambridge edition of *Sons and Lovers*, lxiii–lxxi.

51. For William James see *Pragmatism*, especially Lecture II, 'What Pragmatism Means', where he distinguishes the study of psychology from rationalist philosophy. For Emily Lawrence, see John Worthen, *D. H. Lawrence: The Early Years, 1885–1912*, 178.

Interwoven Words, Interactive Feelings:
Paul Morel and *Sons and Lovers*

HELEN BARON

◆ ◆ ◆

THE PROCESS OF creativity is largely an enigma, but when
an author revises a written text, glimpses of that process may
be possible. Lawrence did not merely revise, but frequently started
a work from the beginning again and rewrote it completely. This
unique method of writing fiction, which often left for posterity two
or more differently composed versions of a story or novel, gives an
overwhelming amount of material for pondering Lawrence's particular creative process. It seems as if different ways of seeing and of
interpreting dominated his thought at successive writing periods,
and one can observe these by noticing the ways in which his use of
syntax, vocabulary, and imagery varies between versions.

When Lawrence abandoned the second attempt to write *Paul
Morel,* he revised the plot so radically that less than half the episodes from that draft survive into the fourth and final manuscript of the novel, which he renamed *Sons and Lovers.*[1]

The intervening third complete version is almost entirely lost,
so that the episodes in common between the second and fourth
manuscripts are separated by a now-invisible process of double

revision,[2] and by periods of composition which were twelve months apart in real time but, in some sense, a lifetime apart in Lawrence's experience. *Paul Morel* was written from March to July 1911 while Lawrence was teaching in Croydon, near London, and *Sons and Lovers* was written from August to November 1912 when he had just begun to live with Frieda Weekley beside Lake Garda in northern Italy.

Where the two novels have passages of narrative in common, fascinating comparisons can be made.[3] *Paul Morel* is not so much an embryo of *Sons and Lovers* as a separate work: not only is a great deal of the plot completely different, but the narratorial tones and strategies are worlds apart. This may seem an exaggerated claim, but the way in which the "same" episode becomes "other" as Lawrence rewrites it is a challenge to our approach to the activity of reading a novel.

For example, in a tiny vignette Lawrence describes the baby Paul's refusal to be held by his father. In *Sons and Lovers* the baby is eight months old:[4]

> It would stiffen in his arms, and, although usually a quiet baby, would scream, draw back from the father's hands. And Morel, seeing the small fists clenched, the baby face averted, the wet blue eyes turned frantically to the mother, would say in a kind of impatient despair:
>
> "Here, come an' ta'e him!"
>
> "It's your moustache frightens him," she replied, as she took the child and pressed it to her bosom. Nevertheless her heart hurt with pain. (63–64)

In *Paul Morel* there are remarkable differences, the very least of which is that the baby is *ten* months old:

> It would stiffen in his arms. On the whole a good, quiet, sad-looking infant, it would cry and press back from its father's hands, straining like a young hare. Morel felt the tiny hands pushing away at his chin, saw the baby's face averted, the wet

blue eyes turned back looking piteously for the mother, and he said, troubled:

"Come an' ta'e him, quick."

"It's your moustache frightens him," she said. But she would press the child on her bosom, and, as it pushed its face between her chin and her throat, snuggling up to hide in her, clasping her neck with small arms, she had much ado to prevent herself sobbing bitterly.[5]

As this brief drama was envisaged in 1911,[6] there was a free-flowing physical dynamic between each parent and the baby, which was reinforced by small lexical repetitions; but both these features were removed in the 1912 rewriting. In the earlier version, Paul's actions are linked from one parent to the other by repetition. Paul "would . . . press back" from Morel's hands, and later his mother "would press" him on her bosom. There is a contrast between the "father's hands" and the baby's "tiny hands." Paul's action of "pushing away at his [father's] chin" is repeated in reverse with his mother, when he "pushes" his face between her "chin and her throat." Having escaped from his father's "arms" he uses his own "arms" to cling to his mother. There is even a link between the idea that the baby cries and his mother struggles to resist sobbing, which is lost in the later version's more extreme contrasts of expression and suppression in the baby's "scream" and her hidden "pain."

When Lawrence rewrote this little scene, he reduced the amount of physical contact between the participants, as if he were a theater director instructing them to act in a more coldly impersonal manner toward each other. For example, where Morel had previously "felt" Paul's attempts to get away from him, the verb was changed to the nontactile "seeing," in the revision. The change from "press back" to "draw back" reduces the amount of physical contact between the baby and his father's hands, as does the change from the tiny hands pressing away at Morel's chin to the entirely noncontact image of small clenched fists. Even the change from "baby's face" to "baby face" is a move in a less personal, more abstract direction, away from the baby as a particular individual and toward "baby" as concept.

And yet, if one summarized the *plot* of this incident, the summaries of each version could well be identical. In the larger context of the narrative, the baby has an ear infection which makes him cry with pain, while the father, who is recuperating from an illness, sometimes fakes pain to win sympathy from his wife; and she is torn between the two. In the final manuscript, the narrator comments: "It would have done the man good to be able to nurse his sick baby" (63). A summary of this brief scene might read: the baby refuses to be nursed by his father, so the father asks the mother to take him and she experiences some distress.

But in the texture of the text there are yet more notations which indicate seismic shifts in perspective between these two versions of the tableau. For example, the change from "piteously" to "frantically" insinuates a darker note. It is a change from a viewpoint in which the baby is to be pitied by all—primarily by the father and mother, probably also by himself, and possibly by the narrator and certainly by the reader—to one in which "frantically" indicates a condition of panic experienced by the baby in isolation. There is a hint of potentially damaging extremes of harmful emotion. Similarly Walter Morel's response to the situation is given a more precise psychological interpretation in the change from "troubled" to "in a kind of impatient despair."

One of Lawrence's alterations in the fourth manuscript was the narrator's statement that Mrs Morel "took" the baby. But in the earlier version, despite the father's command, that action is omitted, with the result that the baby is responsible for the majority of the activity, with his three verbs, "pushed," "snuggling," "clasping"—and the mother is a sort of passive recipient of them. Her reaction, too, is revised to an isolating intensity: had she sobbed bitterly it would have been an action which involved her with her husband, dramatically; but the pain she senses in her heart is completely private.

The version of the episode in the fourth manuscript might be described as a distillation, and yet the revisions do not merely economize, they alter the quality from the mainly visual to the complexly and often ambiguously psychological. At the same time, more explanatory rhetorical signposts are introduced.

The omission of "she took" in the earlier manuscript is an interesting hiatus. It requires the reader to suppose the action, and therefore to contribute a word or image to the text while reading it. An option is left open, for example, for the imaginary insertion of "he placed the baby in her arms," which would give a very different emphasis. The reader is also required to interpret the one connection Lawrence does give: "But." What precise concession is indicated by "But"? The reader has to provide some sort of reason, such as: "She offered Morel the consoling excuse that the baby was only frightened of his moustache rather than of him as a person, but she nevertheless clasped the baby firmly to herself on taking it away from its father, as if she sympathized with and even shared the baby's rejection of Morel. Then it was the baby's continued efforts to get closer within her embrace that nearly reduced her to tears." The placing of the connections "but . . . and, as . . ." suggests that Mrs Morel's emotions are stirred by the baby's affectionate physical movements, his "snuggling up to hide in her," rather more than by the aversion for his father which they demonstrate. When Lawrence rewrote the passage, he moved his concessive notation further along, and used a more emphatic rhetorical word: "Nevertheless." But the apparatus of clarity does not make the meaning clearer. Why does her heart hurt? Is it her "heart" as a physical, emotional, or abstract entity? How could any "hurt" be experienced with anything *other* than "pain"? The tautology makes the grammatical simplicity illusory: hidden psychological complexity is implied.

Similarly, in the first line of the passage quoted, Lawrence provided a clarifying "although" when he rewrote. Readers of the earlier version have to provide that word themselves. And yet, at the same time, Lawrence took the connecting "and" away from the baby's two actions, to create the abrupt immediacy of "scream, draw back." The omission of "and" from a string of short clauses is a stylistic idiom which Lawrence used a great deal in the final manuscript of *Sons and Lovers* and it affects the illusion of simultaneity rather than sequence. But in *Paul Morel,* he tends to write lists more conventionally, as in the third sentence of the passage quoted above, where "and he said" makes the structure of the sentence into a list of clauses and thus justifies the absence of "and" earlier. At the same time this structure implies a comparatively free-flowing sequence of movements, an impression which is enhanced by the six "-ing" verb-endings in this version.

One cannot leave this discussion without offering some account of the animal simile in the *Paul Morel* text: "straining like a young hare." It is a striking feature, too, of the comparison between the two versions of Mrs Morel ironing, that Lawrence uses an animal simile in *Paul Morel*—"her movements were light, accurate as the dip and tilt of a gull"[7]—which is reduced in *Sons and Lovers* to "Her movements were light and quick" (91). Again, whereas in *Sons and Lovers* the young Paul "trotted after his mother like her shadow" (64), in *Paul Morel* there is another animal simile: "All day long he ran like a sickly fawn[8] at his mother's heel."[9] It is a feature, moreover, of the *Paul Morel* manuscript that many of the characters are presented to the reader with a rapid visual sketch which is often supported by an animal metaphor. For example, the parson is briefly drawn, after an illness: "He had gone thin, but still his jowl was heavy. He cocked his brows, smiling in his old manner as of a bird that listens and is uncertain."[10] By contrast, it is hard to find any indication of the parson's physical appearance in *Sons and Lovers*. The majority of these animal similes are entirely visual, and although the word "sickly" introduces a pejorative undertone, it is not nearly as *moralized* as Lawrence's animal metaphors tended to become later in this writing process. One example from *Sons and Lovers* of what I mean by "moralized" is Clara's disparaging characterization of Miriam as having a "blood-hound quality" (370).

Yet somehow the image of the young hare "straining" is not as innocent as the image of the gull's movements of "dip and tilt." The implication is that the young hare is being held against its will, and that, as a wild animal, its fear of capture by humans includes the fear of death. Immediately, for me, this brings to mind Lawrence's wonderful poem "Cruelty and Love" from *Love*

Poems and Others (1913), describing a woman who anticipates receiving the caresses of her beloved, while knowing that he has just killed a rabbit with those same hands. The poem focuses on the rabbit's terror at the man's approach, its entrapment in a wire snare against which it makes a "frantic effort," and the man's hard hands. There is an early version, entitled "A Beloved," which Lawrence wrote into one of his college notebooks in October or November 1909, where the rabbit is described as a "piteous brown ball" which "turns back his liquid . . . eyes."[11] The rabbit's liquid eyes are not tearful, of course, whereas the baby's "wet" eyes are. But the images overlap imaginatively, and there is a very slight hint that Morel is the quietly murderous gamekeeper.

Comparison, therefore, of these two different versions of a brief exchange between the Morels and baby Paul brings into sharp focus two contrasting narrational strategies, a contrast which centers around issues of physical gesture, lexical repetition, and the transmission of feelings.

A similarly revealing comparison is offered by the accounts of happy family evenings when Walter Morel tells the children stories about the pit ponies while they help him make fuses for use in the coal mine. The version in chapter 4 of *Sons and Lovers* (88–90), "The Young Life of Paul," is punctuated by explanatory comments from the narrator: "Morel had a warm way of telling a story. He made one feel Taffy's cunning . . . This story of Taffy would go on interminably, and everybody loved it" (89). Despite the narrator's ostensible enthusiasm, the word "interminably" seems to be fighting against the favorable intention of the rest of the sentence; and when the earlier version is set alongside this, the tone in *Sons and Lovers* suddenly seems remarkable by contrast for its languid, even sarcastic, drawl.

In *Paul Morel,* also, the narrator announces that the father is a good story-teller: "Morel put stores of interest and excitement in his voice. The children thrilled at the sinking and sudden rush of the sound." But what renders the claim credible in this text is that Morel performs his storytelling in such a way as to circulate emotions around the family:

"And 'e's comes into th' stall wi' a rattle, but when you're not looking, he slives an' shoves his nose in your jacket pocket where it hangs up, an' he snuffs, an' snuffs—" here Morel snuffed with his nose at Arthur, who rippled with laughter, till his mother smiled—"an' he snuffs till he finds a bit o' bacca, an' then he'll chew it, an' lift his head up an' chew— an' if it wor wrapped in paper, spit it out—" Morel did the action. Arthur again rippled with laughter: he had beautiful eyes. Paul would hold himself up and think:

"But is it nice—tobacco? How does it taste?"[12]

After a few more paragraphs of dialogue, the narrator comments: "Mrs Morel would listen, delighted. At such times she was fond of her husband—at such times Paul liked his father." Morel's comical actions set up a chain reaction (or perhaps ripples) within the family group: they make Arthur laugh and Mrs Morel smile; she feels fond of her husband and Paul likes him. The effect on Paul is more subtle, but marked with a tiny lexical repetition: Morel's linguistic reenactment of the way the pony would "lift his head up" to chew the tobacco makes Paul "hold himself up" in his curiosity about the taste; and in a few lines we are told that "Before he went to bed that night, Paul had nibbled a bit of tobacco from his father's pouch."[13] In the context of this circulation of feelings around the family group, small lexical repetitions have a reinforcing effect. The immediate reuse by Morel of the narrator's "till" in "till his mother smiled—an' he snuffs till he finds . . . ,' " by reinforcing the suggestion of *sequence,* gives the impression that Morel is aware of (or even trying to repeat) the effect that his playfulness with Arthur is having on his wife. The narrator also uses repetition and sequence ("At such times . . . —at such times") to underline the process whereby Paul relents toward his father in this situation: Paul's feelings effectively reach him via his mother and are suitably cooler, as if their strength is reduced by their reaching him at the end of the chain.

It first occurred to me that "chain reaction" would best describe what I had identified in the family drama Lawrence depicted here, before I realized that his word "rippled" actually suggests a version of chain reaction—that of a stone thrown into a pool. Whether Lawrence intended the scientific analogy when he wrote *Paul Morel* is hard to say, but it is fascinatingly endorsed by the following passage in *Fantasia of the Unconscious* (1922):

> A family, if you like, is a group of wireless stations, all adjusted to the same, or very much the same vibration. All the time they quiver with the interchange, there is one long endless flow of vitalistic communication between members of one family, a long, strange *rapport*, a sort of life-unison. It is a ripple of life through many bodies as through one body.[14]

By comparison, in the *Sons and Lovers* version of this scene, no one laughs or smiles, the mother is not manifestly present, and the energizing effect of Arthur's enjoyment is undercut by the narrator's "Meantime Arthur, still fond of his father . . ." (89). The implication is that his fondness will not last. There is a far more insidious, but buried, hint of this eventuality in *Paul Morel*, where Arthur's merriment at Morel's imitation of the horse spitting out the tobacco wrapping anticipates his teenage disgust when his father "hawked and spat in the fire" from the tea table.[15]

It is striking that Lawrence can use so slight a notation as the repetition of "up" ("an' lift his head up") to suggest Paul's curiously responsive body language ("would hold himself up"). This is a degree of subtlety which Lawrence had used earlier in *Paul Morel* to reinforce the description of Paul's fear at night (when his parents are quarreling) as a forcefully *physical* experience. In *Sons and Lovers* the children are described lying in bed after dark unable to distinguish the sounds of quarreling from the shrieking of the ash tree outside. "They lay with their hearts in the grip of an intense anguish" (85). In *Paul Morel* it is Paul alone whose awareness of his parents' raised voices is described, and there is no ash tree. Lawrence lists four different kinds of sound, including "the sudden bang of his father's fist upon the table"; and concludes "all these, sometimes, not infrequently, made hell in the child's soul as he lay, very straight and tight clenched, listening, while the blows on the table seemed verily to fall on him." A few lines later, Paul's method of controlling his fear of the dark is described: "With his heart beating fast, with his fists tight shut" he would recite poetry and hymns to himself.[16] The claim that he felt as if his father's fist was striking him is supported by the image of his whole body "straight and tight clenched"; whereas in the fourth manuscript, the word "grip" is used with different effect. The shift to the idea that the children's hearts are gripped in an anguish is a shift away from bodily sensations toward a more self-consciously psychological damage. This revision parallels that describing Mrs Morel's distress in the first passage discussed. Lawrence uses "heart" in both manuscripts to indicate feelings, but the change is typically from a simply physiological to a psychosomatic notation.

The repetition of "fist" a few pages apart may not strike the reader as significantly deliberate, but there are indications that Lawrence fully intended such lexical connections. For example, in one of the episodes in the second manuscript which Lawrence later discarded,[17] he had made Walter Morel complain to his friend Jerry that his head felt watery, and the narrator adds immediately: "Jerry's eyes watered in sympathy." Morel is in bed recovering from brain fever and Jerry has come to visit, secretly bringing him some beer. When Morel dare not drink much of it because of his head, the narrator again repeats the notation: "Tears came to Jerry's eyes. He dropped his head." The narration of this episode is overtly comic, as Lawrence somewhat emphatically satirizes the men's maudlin expressions of friendship. But because conversation is not the chief vehicle of their intimacy, Lawrence uses the same technique as earlier with the baby Paul, of focusing on a few salient physical features and oscillating between them. Jerry has had the forethought to bring some parsley for Morel to chew so that his wife will not detect the beer on his breath.

> "Now let me smell thee," said Jerry, putting his sharp nose near Morel's great moustache.
> "Thou'rt all right lad," he said. "If 'er's a nose like a needle 'er'll never know."
> Morel put out his hand from the bed, and laid it on Jerry's.

"Tha'rt a blessin' to me Jerry, thou art an' all!" he murmured. Jerry sniffed aloud.

Presently Mrs Morel came up. She glanced very keenly at her husband, then went up and put her hand on his forehead.[18]

The relations between the three characters are highlighted by interwoven words and gestures. The chief interweavings concern the noses (and sniffing), the synonyms of "sharp," and the ironical echo of Morel's hand gesture by his wife's. The physicality of the interactions is underlined by the three repetitions of the verb "put." The physical references are narrated in alternating sequence: Jerry's approach to Morel, his sharp nose, Mrs Morel's sharp nose, Morel's hand gesture, Jerry's sniff, Mrs Morel's keen glance, her approach and hand gesture. This oscillating between the characters and a limited range of physical references underlines the impression that the characters' dispositions are bound up together. Morel had earlier, in a merely practical manner, touched Jerry's hand which held the beer bottle: "Putting his trembling hand half over Jerry's, Morel adjusted the bottle to his mouth";[19] but in this passage his gesture is presented as purely sentimental, and in a sense it is rather surprising: a hint of exaggeration in Lawrence's satire.

From the standpoint of analyzing Lawrence's narrative ploys, the beer bottle plays a crucial part. It is the object which facilitates the release of emotions between the two participants. One might call it a transactional object or even a fulcrum—the leverage being applied by the narrator, not the characters. By introducing this object Lawrence is able to display a physical and emotional dynamic taking place between Walter and Jerry in a manner very different from that available to him if he had opted for dialogue— even though their talk would be about Morel's illness. The bottle enhances, sharpens, their preoccupation with Morel's condition. It provides scope for Lawrence's satire as Jerry leans over Morel's bed, helping him drink the forbidden substance. And, as a transactional object, the bottle functions to release physical gesture: it provides Walter Morel's first practical need to guide Jerry's hand so that he can drink while semirecumbent, which prepares the way for his later purely emotional gesture of putting his hand on Jerry's.

From a narratological point of view it would be possible to categorize the baby Paul, too, as having a similar function in the first passage discussed. The baby could be seen as the transactional object (indeed, Lawrence calls him "it") by means of which Lawrence narrates an emotional dynamic between the Morel parents more vividly than he might have been able to via dialogue alone. Something of this technique is being used in the other passages discussed, but it is harder to identify. In the descriptions of Paul's reaction to his parents' night-time quarrels it is clearly his father's fist which creates the focal point: it is the fulcrum which the author uses to indicate emotional pressure on the child. The use of the "fist" to focus the child's suffering makes the situation less open-ended, less psychologically invasive than the "anguish" felt by the children in the later version. By limiting the image to the physical blows, Lawrence limits the narrated experience to a dramatic, temporary moment, giving the illusion that the experience will be over as soon as the noises below cease.

The fuse-making sequence presents a more problematic case. At the moment in which it occurs in the narrative, the most evident fulcrum is Morel's storytelling, or perhaps Morel as storyteller. But in *Paul Morel,* it is significant that Morel's mimicry of the pony concentrates on his nose and mouth: "snuffed with his nose . . . ' . . . spit it out'—Morel did the action." This is consistent with Lawrence's depiction of Morel throughout the second manuscript, which focuses repeatedly on the area of Morel's face around his moustache. The moustache is mentioned in the moments of Morel's proximity with the baby Paul and with Jerry. When Paul is ill in bed and his father comes to say goodnight, "Paul turned his face hard away from his father, afraid of being kissed by that great moustache."[20] But in the fourth manuscript, Paul's dislike of his father's presence is presented as an emotion of general rejection: "The boy began to get feverish with irritation. His father's presence seemed to aggravate all his sick impatience" (92).

As I have indicated above, Morel's spitting gesture connects the earlier episode of mutual enjoyment between Arthur and his father during the family fuse making to a moment of intense mutual loathing later in *Paul Morel*, when Arthur is a teenager and quarrels with his father at the tea table. In this later scene Lawrence again uses a fulcrum to intensify the buildup of their antagonisms: he makes them physically tug the table to and fro between them. The situation is reminiscent of—and a fuller development of—a scene in act I of the 1909 play, *A Collier's Friday Night*:

> *The man gets hold of the table and pulls it nearer the fire, away from his daughter*
>
> NELLIE LAMBERT: Why can't you leave the table where it was! We don't *want* it stuck on top of the fire.
>
> FATHER: Ah dun, if you dunna.
>
> *(He drags up his arm-chair and sits down at the table full in front of the fire.)*[21]

Here, manifestly, the table as an object which father and child quarrel over helps focus the interplay of feelings between them: It dramatizes the unarticulated aspects of those feelings. *Paul Morel* is narrated in a manner which relates it closely to this early play. Lawrence did not continue to use the tea table tug-of-war in *Sons and Lovers*. He wrote to achieve dramatic intensity in a less visual-physical manner.

Elsewhere in *Paul Morel*, Lawrence makes charming play with this technique of setting an object between two characters to focus and enhance their exchange. He creates a delightful sequence in which the young Paul takes his pet rabbit, Adolphus, along with him in his pocket when paying a visit to Miriam Staynes and her mother. The rabbit is first used by the narrator as a transactional object between Paul and the invalid mother. Paul finds Mrs Staynes's resignation and lack of interest in the outside world a distressing contrast to his own mother's fighting spirit. But as their conversation proceeds, he feels "encouraged," and so he produces the rabbit and kneels before her with it in his hands. Their joint focus on the small animal produces a flow of emotion from her:

Adolphus sat between Paul's two hands, while the boy kneeled by the invalid chair, at the side of which stood the untouched orange; and Mrs Staynes, murmuring with trembling lips, touched Adolphus' shrinking brown head with her finger-tips. Paul remained quite still, holding his little offering. She, catching her breath with tears, leaned forward in her chair and softly touched the balled rabbit, which pressed back its young ears of oil-silk, and kept its young eyes wide-aglisten and alert. It was not trembling or afraid.[22]

The "untouched orange" was "perfectly set, with a silver spoon, and a bright little bowl of fine sugar"[23] as an elaborate compliment from Mrs Staynes's husband, of whom the narrator tells us "his prosperity had dribbled away, along with his virility." The ineffectuality of their marriage is delicately nuanced by Lawrence's "untouched/touched" in this passage. The orange is left alone in favor of the rabbit, which she touches (the word occurs twice), and while her lips are "trembling," the rabbit was "not trembling." Lawrence's verbal repetitions interlace the process of the subtle stimulation of feelings between the young boy and the neurasthenic woman. Here, the narrator is not telling the reader how to interpret his fiction but presenting a visual drama which offers a variety of emotions for contemplation, in a way that dialogue alone could not effect.

Lawrence's explicit use of a transactional object in this scene is attractively presented by "Adolphus sat between Paul's two hands, while the boy kneeled." Later on in the novel, he seems to have a similar narrative aim in view when describing the manner in which Paul presents his wages to his mother. The money is a kind of bargaining counter to gain from Mrs Morel an approval which she is reluctant to give. In *Paul Morel* Lawrence elaborates at some length a dialogue which he later distilled to a few crisp lines in *Sons and Lovers* (140). In *Paul Morel,* the issue requires lengthy and emotional treatment, with Paul "elated to a seventh heaven of pleasure to have so much silver" to give to his mother, so that he "gazed at her with beaming eyes," whereas she laughs repeatedly at his "self-gratification."[24]

These tangible offerings, which focus a relationship wherein Paul is endeavoring to have a mollifying effect on an older woman, are persuasive dramatically, but it may be harder to establish the idea that Lawrence also uses more intangible concepts to have the same fulcrum effect. However, there is a paragraph in *Paul Morel* introducing the onset of Paul's first attack of pneumonia which seems to spell out how the young Paul similarly presented his illness to his mother as a solution to her emotional blockage toward him. The clinching narratorial explanation is "Mrs Morel rebelled no longer":

> With a weary gesture, she took the lad and put back his hair from his forehead. Paul loved his mother very much. He left himself in her hands, not wincing when she pressed his bumped forehead. The touch of his mother's fingers was the only thing he cared about, all he wanted.
>
> "Where hurts you?" she asked.
>
> "Nowhere," he replied. Sensitive and therefore bilious by nature, he trembled uncontrollably.
>
> His mother sighed as she took off his cap and scarf.
>
> "I'd no business to let you go," she said grievously. "I might have known our William would not look after you."
>
> Whereupon William went out and wept into the scullery towel. Annie and Arthur looked on with solemn eyes.
>
> "Tell me where hurts you," Mrs Morel repeated.
>
> "I feel—sick," he replied tremulously.
>
> His mother's eyes contracted with irritable distress.
>
> "Eh child," she said, "I shall have nothing but trouble with you as long as you live."
>
> Which Paul Morel implicitly believed.
>
> Suddenly her manner changed.
>
> "Come and lie down," she said, very gently, soothingly. She beat up the bed of the sofa, and soon Paul was curled up on

the chintz-covered cushions he knew so well and liked so much during childhood. Mrs Morel rebelled no longer. She moved about quietly getting the children's dinners.[25]

Somehow, Paul has used his illness to negotiate a truce with his mother, a cessation of the coldness she tends to show because she resents her lot. He has brought about a situation in which "she rebelled no more" and became kind. The episode is treated very differently in *Sons and Lovers* (90) where Mrs Morel does not touch Paul or show any kindness. In *Paul Morel*, from the point of view of narrative technique, Paul's illness is as much a trans-actional object as he himself was between his parents when a baby, and as his rabbit was at the Staynes's house: it alters the emotional dynamic between the participants in the scene.

The pet rabbit, Adolphus, was discarded from the narrative after Lawrence abandoned *Paul Morel*, but in that manuscript he had made further use of the pet animal as a transactional object between the young Paul and his younger friend, Miriam. Follow-ing Paul's communion over Adolphus with Miriam's mother, he and Miriam depart to another room and develop imaginary games with the rabbit. It becomes, in effect, one of a series of transac-tional objects in their relationship. In this period they are ten and eleven years old, and each has very different fantasies of the rabbit as a play object, all of which the rabbit naturally evades. Because they are young, the transactional object functions (as in most of the situations discussed so far) as a vehicle for expressing emotion between two comparatively inarticulate individuals. When Paul and Miriam become adolescent, the transactional objects which figure in intense moments between them tend to provide a sep-arate and silent commentary in the midst of dialogues which are otherwise characterized by a precocious articulateness (on Paul's part).

In the "Lad-and-Girl Love" chapter of *Sons and Lovers*, Lawrence sets up a dynamic situation between Paul and Miriam which in-volves their joint reaction to the wild rose bush that she has discovered in the woodland (195–96). There is a kind of stifled communion between the two teenagers. In *Paul Morel* there is a similar incident in which Miriam wishes to show Paul a tree of yellow willow catkins. Clearly the two episodes serve a similar function in the narrative account of the developing relationship between Paul and Miriam. The striking difference between these similar episodes is not the species of plant chosen to be the transactional object (though, indeed, Lawrence moralizes the white rose bush as having a "virgin scent" in *Sons and Lovers* - 196), but that in the earlier version the two adolescents (they are eighteen and seventeen years old) gather bouquets from the tree of catkins, which they then place together and compare. Paul offers opinions on the differences between his bunch of twigs and hers; Miriam silently disagrees. The two handfuls of hazel branches function here as a narrative fulcrum between Miriam and Paul, but very differently from the way fulcrums are used by Lawrence earlier in the novel. Here the transactional object is a source of conflict which transmits complex emotions while simultaneously blocking their free expression. It focuses and yet holds in stasis certain conflictual attitudes between the participants. They pick the catkins together, but the effect is to hold them personally apart. The bouquets themselves dramatize an emotional, psychological dynamic which is active between the two teenagers, but of which they are themselves only partially conscious. Paul criticizes Miriam's bunch for containing some withered blooms and then removes his own, but Miriam brings it back to compare with hers:

> "What a difference!" she said.
> "Ay," he laughed. "Even when we are not conscious of it, I am selective and critical, and you're blind emotional."
> She laughed, dropped his hand, not liking his explanation.[26]

The conversation is largely one-sided in that Miriam does not expound her thoughts; but the narrator has already spoken on her behalf and undermined Paul's domineering expression of opinion. At the beginning of this episode, immediately before Miriam asks Paul to go along with her to see what she has to show him, Paul analyzes Miriam's character as "purely emotional." The narrator explains her silent reaction to his observations: "He was so blind with his heart, if perhaps wonderfully 'seeing' with his brain . . . He never *understood* how she loved him: his eye was too quick and critical."[27] Despite the fact, therefore, that their relationship is conducted in dialogue far more than that of other characters in the novel, there is also an undercurrent of inarticulateness in Miriam's silences and in Paul's tendency to be overly hasty and critical. The bunches of willow catkins provide more, therefore, than another opportunity for one-sided conversations; they also focus what is unspoken. In addition, they function like the beer bottle, as a narrative device which enables Miriam innocently to take hold of Paul's hand.

Thus, in passages of the second manuscript which were dropped from the final version of the novel, and in passages which survived but in revised form, it seems that Lawrence's conception involved a great deal more physical contact (of a nonsexual nature) between the participants. It will be evident, too, from the passages quoted, that there is a great deal of physiological focus on heads, hands, and hearts—where "heads" covers brows, eyes, face, forehead, hair, moustache, nose, etc. Descriptions of characters are largely visual and are limited almost entirely to heads and hands, while references to their hearts are used to indicate emotion of a straightforwardly physiological kind, such as fear or excitement, rather than anything of a more complex psychosomatic nature.

In *Paul Morel* Lawrence relies on techniques akin to those of the painter and the dramatist. He visualizes with intense focus but with comparatively little interpretative comment. He presents personal interactions through dramatic depiction, often using a transactional object to focus and stimulate exchanges of feelings between characters. The ways in which characters influence each other's feelings are made overt and visible. By contrast, in *Sons and Lovers* the emotional interactions between characters are hidden, complex, and controlled by the narrator's critical judgments.

Notes

1. *Paul Morel* is the "second" manuscript, because Lawrence claimed to have written a hundred pages of the first draft, but they have not survived. The opening seventy-two pages of the *Paul Morel* manuscript are now missing, but comparison with the same section of the third manuscript, which does survive, suggests that the opening chapters would also have had many similarities to *Sons and Lovers*.

2. Of the third manuscript, the first eighty-five pages survive (up to the account of Paul's motiveless crying, equivalent to page 65 of *Sons and Lovers*) and two short sequences of manuscript pages that were transferred forward bodily from *Paul Morel* into succeeding drafts and are now located within the final manuscript. These latter total fifteen small manuscript pages and belong to chapter 10, "Clara," of *Sons and Lovers*. The first describes Paul's dialogues with Clara about his paintings and her French reading; the second covers Paul's birthday present at the factory and his walk to the castle with Clara (*Sons and Lovers*, 306–7 and 311–17). Lawrence made a number of revisions to these pages, including the change of Clara's name from Frances Radford.

3. See Helen Baron, "Mrs Morel Ironing," *Journal of the D. H. Lawrence Society* (1984), 2–12.

4. Revised in MS: first "seven," then "six," then "eight." This passage was deleted in the final manuscript by Edward Garnett when he edited the novel for its first publication by Duckworth in 1913.

5. D. H. Lawrence, *Paul Morel*, ed. Helen Baron (Cambridge: Cambridge University Press, 2003), 9.

6. In the third manuscript the passage reads:

It would stiffen in his arms. Although a quiet baby on the whole, Paul would scream, would draw back wildly from his fathers arms. Morel saw the small fists clenched, the baby face averted, the wet blue eyes turned back wildly towards the mother, and he would say, in a kind of despair:
"Here, come an' ta'e him."
"It's your moustache frightens him," she said. But she would press the child on her bosom, as it clung to her neck, cleaved to her. (Ibid., 220–21)

7. Ibid., 9, 28.

8. In the third manuscript "like a fawn" occurs and is deleted. In

the final manuscript, the vestigial animal metaphor present in the verb "trotted" mixes uneasily with the simile "like her shadow."

9. D. H. Lawrence, *Paul Morel*, 13.

10. Ibid., 78.

11. The college notebook is Roberts E320.1 in Warren Roberts, *A Bibliography of D. H. Lawrence*, 3rd edition, revised by Paul Poplawski (Cambridge: Cambridge University Press, 2001). For the texts of "Love on the Farm" and "A Beloved," see *The Complete Poems of D. H. Lawrence*, eds. Vivian de Sola Pinto and Warren Roberts (London: Heinemann, 1972), I, 42; II, 910. Lawrence revised the poem for *Collected Poems* (1928) and retitled it "Love on the Farm." My concern here is to indicate his use of similar imagery and language in the period of writing *Paul Morel*.

12. D. H. Lawrence, *Paul Morel*, 15.

13. Ibid., 16.

14. D. H. Lawrence, *Psychoanalysis and the Unconscious and Fantasia of the Unconscious*, ed. Bruce Steele (Cambridge: Cambridge University Press, 2004), 77.

15. D. H. Lawrence, *Paul Morel*, 122.

16. Ibid., 16–17.

17. The MS pages 72–77 of *Paul Morel*.

18. D. H. Lawrence, *Paul Morel*, 7.

19. Ibid., 6.

20. Ibid., 32.

21. Nottinghamshire dialect for "I do, if you don't"; D. H. Lawrence, *The Plays*, eds. Hans-Wilhelm Schwarze and John Worthen (Cambridge: Cambridge University Press, 1999), 9.

22. D. H. Lawrence, *Paul Morel*, 44.

23. Ibid., 43.

24. Ibid., 73.

25. Ibid., 27.

26. Ibid., 86.

27. Ibid., 84.

Appendix

Sons and Lovers:
A Freudian Appreciation
[1916]

ALFRED BOOTH KUTTNER

❖ ❖ ❖

The following is a transcription of an article
which appeared in the *Psychoanalytic Review*,
Vol. 3, No. 3 (July 1916), 295–317. See the section
on the publication and reception of *Sons and Lovers* in the Introduction for details of Lawrence's
reaction to it.

*Note: Italics have been consistently supplied for
book titles; other errors in the original printing
have not been corrected; page numbers from the
Cambridge University Press edition of* Sons and
Lovers *have been added to quotations.*

Poets and novelists often strive for impressiveness in their crea-
tions by dealing in strange plots and adventures or in monstrous
and unnatural loves. The advantages gained may well be called
in question: to be grotesque is hardly ever to be great and the
bizarre may survive as a demerit after it is exhausted as a sensation. The great literature of life is after all built around the commonplace. *The Odyssey* treats of a bad case of homesickness, a thing
which we all understand perfectly. The drama of Œdipus depicts
an incestuous relationship, and we do not have to be told that

it is horrible. What distinguishes enduring literature is not novelty, but freshness of feeling, and that pointed insight into life which reveals a vivid personality keenly alive. *Sons and Lovers* has the great distinction of being very solidly based upon a veritable commonplace of our emotional life; it deals with a son who loved his mother too dearly, and with a mother who lavished all her affection upon her son.

Neither this distinction nor its undeniable freshness and often amazing style would of itself entitle Mr. D. H. Lawrence's novel to anything beyond an appreciative book review. But it sometimes happens that a piece of literature acquires an added significance by virtue of the support it gives to the scientific study of human motives. Literary records have the advantage of being the fixed and classic expression of human emotions which in the living individual are usually too fluid and elusive for deliberate study. The average man, subjected to what seems to him a kind of psychological vivisection, is apt to grow reticent, and mankind must often be convicted through its literature of impulses which under direct scrutiny it would acknowledge only with the greatest reluctance or else deny altogether. Literature thus becomes an invaluable accessory to the psychologist, who usually does well to regard with suspicion any new generalization from his researches for which the whole range of literary expression yields no corroboration. But if he can succeed in finding support there his position is immensely strengthened. For a new truth about ourselves, which may seem altogether grotesque and impossible when presented to us as an arid theory, often gains unexpected confirmation when presented to us in a powerful work of literature as an authentic piece of life. When at last we recognize ourselves we like the thrill of having made a discovery.

Sons and Lovers possesses this double quality to a high degree. It ranks high, very high as a piece of literature and at the same time it embodies a theory which it illustrates and exemplifies with a completeness that is nothing less than astonishing. Fortunately there can be no doubt as to the authenticity of the author's inspiration. For it would be fatal if the novel had been written with the express purpose of illustrating a theory: it would, by that very admission, be worthless as a proof of that theory. But it happens that Mr. Lawrence has already produced notable work, mainly some early and evidently autobiographical poems, which show his preoccupation with the identical theme. *Sons and Lovers* is thus truly creative, in that it is built up internally—as any masterpiece must be—out of the psychic conflicts of the author, and any testimony which it may bear to the truth of the theory involved will therefore be first hand.

The theory to which I have been referring is Professor Sigmund Freud's theory of the psychological evolution of the emotion of love as finally expressed by a man or a woman towards a member of the other sex, and the problem which Mr. Lawrence voices is the struggle of a man to emancipate himself from his maternal allegiance and to transfer his affections to a woman who stands outside of his family circle. What the poet has seen as a personal problem the scientist has formulated as a theory. I shall outline the problem first and then relate it to the theory. If the theory can succeed in generalizing the truth which Mr. Lawrence's novel presents the reader will realize with fresh force that fiction, to be great art, must be based upon human verities.

2

First we shall see how it happened that the mother in this story came to lavish all her affections upon her son. In the opening chapter Mrs. Morel, the wife of a Derbyshire coal miner, is expecting her third child, the boy Paul, who is to become the central figure of the story. Her life with her husband has already turned out to be a complete fiasco. He is a drunkard and a bully, a man with whom she shares neither intellectual, moral or religious sympathies. What strikes her most about Morel is that he presents a striking contrast to her father, who was to her *"the type of all men."* (18) For he had been a harsh, puritan type, given to theology and ignoring "all sensuous pleasure," (18) while Morel is the very opposite; warm, sensuous and indulgent, with a "rich ringing laugh" and a "red, moist mouth." (17) It is this sensuous quality in Morel which overwhelms and confounds her; she goes down before the sheer, impersonal male in him. After the sex illusion has worn off somewhat Mrs. Morel makes an attempt to draw nearer to her husband. But the clash of personalities is stronger than the transitory tie of their poetized passion and Morel's habitual drunkenness, his indulgent and shiftless ways, and his temperamental dishonesty are mercilessly flayed by his almost fanatically moral and religious wife. It is very easy for her to loathe him. At the time of the birth of her third child the breach is already irreparable. Mrs. Morel dreads the coming of another child, conceived unwillingly out of a loveless relation, and at the sight of it a sense of guilt steals over her. She will atone: *"With all her force, with all her soul she would make up to it for having brought it into the world unloved. She would love it all the more now it was hers;*[1] *carry it in her love."* (51) Towards Paul she feels, as to none of the other children, that she must make up to him for an injury or a sin committed by her and that he must recompense her for all that she has missed in her shattered love for her husband.

All the early formative influences in Paul's life radiate from his mother. Physically he is more delicate than the other children so that his illnesses tend to further her concentration upon him still more. Paul is a "pale, quite[2] child" who seems *"old for his years"* and *"very*[3] *conscious of what other people felt, particularly his mother. When she fretted*[4] *he understood, and could have no peace. His soul seemed always attentive to her."* (82) His mother and for a time his sister Annie are his only real companions. His brother William is too old to be his playmate and other children play no rôle in his early childhood. One vicious bond of sympathy unites all the Morel children; their common hate and contempt for their father. This feeling poisons the whole family life. Often, of a windy night in their creaking house, the children lie awake listening in terror for his drunken return, his banging fists and the muffled voice of their mother. The strain is greatest upon Paul. Towards evening he grows restless and stays near his mother, waiting for his father's coming and the usual scene of abuse and violence. Already at an early age these hostile feelings take definite shape. He often prays: *"Lord, let my father die."* And then, with a kind of guilty conscience: *"Let him not[5] be killed at pit."* (85) One incident in particular stands out in his memory. Morel has just blackened his wife's eyes and William, then already a tall and muscular youth, threatens to beat him. Paul aches to have him do it; it is his own wish which he cannot carry out. Later, when he is older, he almost does it himself, but for his mother's fainting, and his physical animosity, as if the memory of that earlier hate had lingered on in him. We must remember that Paul had been born into an atmosphere of parental violence; when still a baby his father hurled a drawer at his mother so that the blood had trickled down upon the child's head. Indelible among his earliest impressions must have been that gross and terrifying figure, threatening his life and that of his mother, whose convulsive movements to protect him must have aroused an answering quiver in the child.

The early relations between mother and child are full of a delicate and poetic charm. Paul's admiration for his mother knows no bounds; her presence is always absorbing. Often, at the sight of her, *"his heart contracts[6] with love."* (90) Everything he does is for her, the flowers he picks as well as the prizes he wins at school. His mother is his intimate and his confidant, he has no other chums. When Morel is confined to the hospital through an accident in the mine, Paul joyfully plays the husband, *"I'm the man in the house now."* (113) He is happiest when alone with her. By this time the interaction between mother and son is complete; she lives in him and he in her. In fact his whole attitude towards her is but the answer which she gradually evokes from him as her whole life finds expression in her son. *"In the end[7] she shared everything[8] with him[9] without knowing.* (112) . . . *She waited for his coming home in the evening, and then she unburdened herself of all she had pondered,[10] or of all that had occurred to her during the day. He sat and listened with his earnestness. The two shared lives."* (142) The emotional correspondence between them is striking, *"his heart contracted with pain of love of her"* (117) just as from the very beginning she has always *"felt a mixture of anguish in her love for him."* (90) Mother and son are one; the husband is completely effaced and the father exists merely as a rival.

But now Paul is to strike out for himself. He takes up an

occupation and finds himself attracted to women. His mother's whole emphasis has always been towards making Paul interested in some other occupation than his father's dirty digging, as a protest against the sordidness of the life that she herself has been compelled to lead with him. She therefore encourages the boy's liking for pretty things, for flowers and sunsets and fancy stuffs, and is delighted when his slender artistic endowment begins to express itself in pencil and paint. Her emotional revolt against her husband here takes an esthetic turn, as people are often driven to beauty by their loathing of the ugly, and it is interesting to note that Mrs. Morel's tendencies to estheticize Paul and to effeminate him go hand in hand, as if the two sprang from a common root. Paul never becomes a real artist. He uses his painting to please his mother and to court his women, but in the crises of his life his art means nothing to him either as a consolation or as a satisfying expression. As his painting is essentially dilettante and unremunerative, his mother apprentices him in a shop for surgical appliances where the process of effeminization goes on through his contact with the girls and women with whom he works. He himself has no ambition. All that he wants is *"quietly to earn his thirty or thirty-five shillings a week*[11] *somewhere near home, and then, when his father died, have a cottage with his mother, paint and go out as he liked, and live happy ever after."* (114) Not, like any normal boy, to strike out for himself, to adventure, to emulate and surpass his father, but to go on living with his mother forever! That is the real seed of Paul's undoing. We shall now trace the various attempts on his part to emancipate himself from his mother by centering his affections upon some other woman.

The first woman to attract Paul is Miriam Leiver, a shy, exalted and romantic girl who leads a rather lonely life with her parents and brothers on a neighboring farm. Paul's approach is characteristically indirect; he begins by avoiding the girl and cultivating her mother. Meanwhile Miriam, piqued by the neglect of this well-mannered boy, who seems so gentle and superior, has fallen in love with him. Paul is fascinated but uneasy and fights shy of personal intimacy with her. The intensity of her emotions frightens him and impresses him as unwholesome. He finds her growing absorption in him strangely discomfitting: *"Always something in his breast shrank from these close, intimate,*[12] *dazzled looks of hers."* (182) His feminine attitude towards her tends to reverse the usual method of courtship; it is Miriam who has to seek him out, to call for him and make sure of his coming again. Paul tries to approach her in two ways; through his art and as her teacher. Both methods are really self-defensive, they are barriers that he erects against Miriam to prevent anything too personal from arising between them, to keep his real self, as it were, inviolate. For as a painter he distracts her attention from himself to his work and as her instructor he wields an authority with which he can keep her emotions in check by overawing her. Something about her is always putting him on edge, he loses his temper at her very easily and feels a dawning impulse of cruelty. *"It made his blood rouse to see her there, as it were,*[13] *at his mercy."* (187) Sometimes he feels an actual hatred for her. And immediately he thinks of his mother: "He was *thankful in his heart and soul*[14] *that he had his mother, so sane and wholesome."* (184)

Paul resists every intimation that he is falling in love with Miriam. He indignantly repudiates his mother's insinuation that he is courting and hastens to assure Miriam: *"We aren't lovers, we are friends."* (209) And Miriam, who has already gone so far, tries to fortify herself with a prayer. *"Oh Lord, let me not love Paul Morel. Keep me from loving him, if I ought not to love him."* (208) But her love breaks through again and her healthier instincts triumph. Henceforth Paul can do with her as he will. But he can do nothing with her love because he cannot return it. Love seems to him like a *"very terrible thing."* (202) The honest and more impersonal passion that he feels for her frightens him. *"He was afraid of her. The fact that he might want her as a man wants a woman had in him been suppressed into a shame."* (216) He cannot even kiss her. And he hates her again because she makes him despise himself. They gradually move to the edge of a quarrel.

And now Mrs. Morel makes her appeal. Almost from the first she has mistrusted Miriam. She fears that Miriam will absorb him and take him away from her. *"She is one of those who will want to suck a man's soul out till he has none of his own left."* (196) Her jealousy revels in the exaggerated simile of the vampire. *"She exults—she exults as she carries him off from me. . . . She's not like an ordinary woman . . . she wants to absorb him . . . she will suck him up."* (230) So she throws down the gauntlet to her rival. She makes Paul feel wretched, as only a mother can make a son feel, whenever he has been with Miriam. Her comments grow spiteful and satiric; she no longer takes the trouble to hide her jealousy and plagues him like a cast[15] woman. *"Is there nobody else to talk to? . . . Yes, I know it well—I am old.[16] And therefore I may stand aside;[17] I have nothing more to do with you. You only want me to wait on you—the rest is for Miriam."* (251) It sounds like a wife's bitter reproach to her husband. Paul writhes under her words and hates Miriam for it. But Mrs. Morel does not stop there. She makes the final, ruthless, cowardly appeal.

"And I've never—you know, Paul—I've never had a husband—not—[18] really—"

He stroked his mother's hair, and his mouth was on her throat.

"Well,[19] I don't love her, mother," he murmured, bowing his head and hiding his eyes on her shoulder in misery. His mother kissed him,[20] a long, fervent kiss.[21]

"My boy!" she said, in a voice trembling with passionate love.

Without[22] knowing, he gently stroked her face. (252)   Thus she wins him back. He will continue to console her for her husband. There follows the scene where Paul almost thrashes his drunken father and implores his mother not to share the same bed with him. It is a crisis in his life: *". . . he was at peace because he still[23] loved his mother best. It was the bitter peace of resignation."* (254)

But there is some resistance in him still. For a time he stands divided between his two loves. *"And he felt dreary and hopeless[24] between the two."* (231) In church, sitting between them, he feels at peace: *"uniting his two loves under the spell of the place of worship."* (230) But most of the time he is torn between the two women. He does not understand his feelings. *"And why did he hate Miriam and feel so cruel towards her[25] at the thought of his mother?"* (231) His emotions towards Miriam are constantly changing. Sometimes his passion tries to break through. But it cannot free itself. *"I'm so damned spiritual with* YOU *always![26]"* (226) He blames her for the humiliating sense of impotence which he feels. It is all her fault. He transfers all his inhibitions to her and consciously echoes his mother's accusations. *"You absorb, absorb, as if you must fill yourself up with love, because you've got a shortage somewhere."* (258) When her love for him flames out to confound him he takes refuge by talking about his work. There at least some freedom is left for them both. *"All his passion, all his wild blood,[27] went into this intercourse with her, when he talked and conceived his work."* (241) But at last he tells her that he does not love her, that he cannot love her physically. *"I can only give friendship—it's all I'm capable of—it's a flaw in my make-up. . . . Let us have done."* (260) And finally he writes: *"In all our relations[28] no body enters. I do not talk to you through the senses—rather through the spirit. That is why we cannot love in common sense. Ours[29] is not an everyday affection."* (292) Thus he tries to spiritualize their relations out of existence. He would persuade himself of his own impotence.

Paul's whole experience with Miriam has thrown him back upon his mother; he gets away from Miriam by returning to her. *"He had come back to his mother. Hers was the strongest tie in[30] life. When he thought round, Miriam shrank away. There was a vague, unreal feeling[31] about her. . . . And in his soul there was[32] a feeling of the satisfaction of self-sacrifice because he was faithful to her"* (his mother) (261–2). *"She loved him first;[33] he loved her first."* (262) He is her child again and for a time he feels content. They go off on a charming excursion to Lincoln Cathedral. He behaves like a lover out with his girl, buying her flowers and treating her. Suddenly there surges up in him a childhood memory of the time when his mother was young and fair, before life wrung her dry and withered her. If only he had been her eldest son so that his memory of her could be still more youthful! *"What are you old for!"* he said, mad with his own[34] impotence. *"Why[35] can't you walk, why[36] can't you come with me to places?"* (282) He does not like to have such an old sweetheart.

At the same time his whole outlook upon life also grows childish again. When his sister Annie marries he tries to console his mother. *"But I shan't marry, mother.[37] I shall live with you, and we'll have a servant."* (285) She doubts him and he proceeds to figure it out. *"I'll give you till seventy-five. There you are, I'm fat and forty-four.[38] Then I'll marry a staid body. See!*[39] *. . . And we'll have a pretty house, you and me, and a servant, and it'll be just all right."* (286) His plans for the future have not changed. He thinks at twenty-two as he thought at fourteen, like a child that goes on living a fairy-tale. But it is a false contentment and he pays the penalty for it. In resigning the natural impulse to love he also resigns the impulse to live. Life cannot expand in him, it is turned back upon itself and becomes the impulse to die. Paul makes the great refusal. *"What is happiness!" he cried. "It's nothing to me! How* AM[40] *I to be happy? . . . He had that poignant carelessness about himself, his own suffering, his own life, which is a form of slow suicide."* (299–300) Mrs. Morel sees the danger and divines the remedy. *"At this rate*[41] *she knew he would not live* (300) *. . . She wished she*[42] *knew some nice woman—she*[43] *did not know what she wished, but left it vague."* (283) But now she knows that she can no longer hold her son to her exclusively.

At this point Paul begins to turn to another woman, Clara Dawes, a friend of Miriam. She is married, but lives separated from her husband. Paul has known her for some time before becoming intimate with her. She exerts a frankly sensual attraction upon him without having any of that mystical unattainableness about her which he felt so strongly with Miriam. Her presence has had the effect of gradually seducing him away from Miriam without his knowing it. There would be less difficulty with her. She is a married woman and is unhappy with her husband, like his mother. To love her would not be so momentous a thing, he would be less unfaithful to his mother if he had an affair with a woman who already belonged to someone else. Their relations threaten to become typical of the young man and the woman of thirty. *"She was to him extraordinarily provocative, because of the knowledge she seemed to possess, and gathered fruit of experience."* (307) The question of marriage would hardly enter; he could go on loving his mother. But still he is inhibited. *"Sex had become so complicated in him that he would have denied that he ever could want Clara or Miriam or any woman whom he knew.*[44] *Sex desire was a sort of detached thing, that did not belong to a woman."* (319) Clara's first service to him is to talk to him like a woman of the world and thus correct his self-delusion about Miriam: *". . . she doesn't want any of your soul communion. That's your own imagination. She wants you."* He objects. *" 'You've never tried,' she answered."* (321) Thus she gives him courage to do what he never could have done of his own accord.

The force which drives him back to Miriam is nothing but the sheer, pent-up sexual desire that has alternately been provoked and repressed in him. Now indeed it is a completely detached thing which does not belong to any woman. He has almost entirely succeeded in de-personalizing it. That is why he feels that he can let it run its course. But not in any personal way. *"He did not feel that he wanted marriage with Miriam. He wished he did. He would have given his head to have felt a joyous desire to marry her and have[45] her. Then why couldn't he bring it off? There was some obstacle; and[46] what was the obstacle? It lay in the physical bondage. He shrank from the physical contact. But why? With her he felt bound up inside himself. He could not go out to her. Something struggled in him, but he could not get to her. Why?"* (322) And Miriam does not insist upon marriage, she is willing to try out their feelings for each other. Theirs is a pitiful love-making. He cannot bear the blaze of love in her eyes; it is as if he must first draw a veil over her face and forget her. *"If he were really with her, he had to put aside himself and his desire. If he would have her, he had to put her aside."* (334) Love brings him only a sense of death: *"He was a youth no longer. But why had he the dull pain in his soul? Why did the thought of death, the after-life, seem so sweet and consoling?"* (334) Love has brought them no satisfaction, only bitterness and disillusion. He turns back to his men friends and to Clara's company and the old quarrel between him and Miriam breaks out afresh. He decides to break off his relations with her. But at last he is to hear the truth about himself from Miriam. *" 'Always—[47] it has been[48] so!' she cried. 'It has been one long battle between us—you fighting away from me.' "* (341) He tries to tell her that they have had some perfect hours. But he knows that these do not make up the healthy continuity of life. *"Always,[49] from the very beginning—always the same![50]"* (341) She has called him a child of four. It is the truth, and it goes to the heart of his vanity. She has treated him as a mother treats a perverse child. He cannot stand it. *"He hated her. All these years[51] she had treated him as if he were a hero, and thought of him secretly as an infant, a foolish child. Then why had she left the foolish child to his folly?[52] His heart was hard against her."* (342)

The full flood of his passion, freed of some of its incubus through his experience with Miriam, now turns to Clara. He tries to wear it out on her in the same impersonal way, and for a time lives in sheer physical ecstasy. With her at least he has had some solace, some relief. His mother has not stood so much between them. But it is only temporary, he cannot give himself to Clara any more than he could give himself to Miriam. Clara loves him or would love him if he could only rise above the mere passion that threw them together. " '*I feel,*' *she continued slowly, 'as if I hadn't got you,*[53] *as if all of you weren't there,*[54] *and as if it weren't* ME[55] *you were taking—*' '*Who then?*' '*Something just for yourself. It has been fine, so that I daren't think of it. But*[56] *is it me*[57] *you want, or is it* IT[58]*?*' . . . '*He*[59] *again felt guilty. Did he leave Clara out of count and take simply woman?*[60] *But he thought that was splitting a hair.*" (407) They begin to drift apart. He rehearses his old difficulties with his mother. "*I feel sometimes as if I wronged my women, mother.*" But he doesn't know why. "*I even love Clara, and I did Miriam; but*[61] *to give*[62] *myself to them in marriage*[63] *I couldn't. I couldn't belong to them. They seem to want* ME[64]*, and I can't even*[65] *give it them.*"

"*You haven't met the right woman.*"

"*And I shall never*[66] *meet the right woman while you live.*" (395)

His relations with Clara have brought about a marked change in Paul's attitude towards his mother. It is as if he realized at last that she is destroying his life's happiness. "*Then sometimes he hated her, and pulled at her bondage. His life wanted to free itself of her. It was like a circle where life wanted to turn back upon*[67] *itself, and got no further. She bore him, loved him, kept him, and his love turned back into her, so that he could not be free to go forward with his own life, really love another woman.*" (389) But his realization, as far as it goes, brings no new initiative. He is twenty-four years old now but he still sums up his ambition as before: "*Go somewhere in a pretty house near London*[68] *with my mother.*"

The book now rounds out with the death of Paul's mother. Mrs. Morel gradually wastes away with a slow and changeful illness; it is an incurable tumor, with great pain. Paul takes charge and never leaves his mother until the end. Their intimacy is occasionally disturbed by the clumsy intrusion of Morel, whose presence merely serves to irritate his wife. Paul and she commune with the old tenderness. *"Her blue eyes smiled straight into his, like a girl's—*[69] *warm, laughing with tender love. It made him pant*[70] *with terror, agony, and love."* (429) Their reserve drops before the imminence of death, it seems as if they would be frank at last. But there is also the old constraint. *"They were both afraid of the veils that were ripping between them."* (429) He suffers intensely. *"He felt as if his life were being destroyed, piece by piece, within him."* (429–30) But mingled with his love and his anguish at her suffering there now enters a new feeling: the wish that she should die. Something in him wants her to die; seeing that she cannot live he would free both her and himself by hastening her death. So he gradually cuts down her nourishment and increases the deadliness of her medicine. Here again he approaches close to the source of his trouble; he dimly realizes that he has never lived outside of his mother and therefore has never really lived. The feeling that he cannot live without her and the feeling that he cannot live a life of his own as long as she is alive, here run side by side. But when the death which he himself has hastened overtakes her, he cries with a lover's anguish: *" 'My love—my love—oh,*[71] *my love!' he whispered again and again. 'My love—oh,*[72] *my love!' "* (442)

But death has not freed Paul from his mother. It has completed his allegiance to her. For death has merely removed the last earthly obstacle to their ideal union; now he can love her as Dante loved his Beatrice. He avows his faithfulness to her by breaking off with the only two other women who have meant anything to him. He is completely resigned, life and death are no longer distinguished in his thinking. Life for him is only where his mother is and she is dead. So why live? He cannot answer, life has become contradictory. *"There seemed no reason why people should go along the street, and houses pile up in the daylight. There seemed no reason why these things should occupy space*[73], *instead of leaving it empty.* (454) ... *He wanted everything to stand still, so that*[74] *he could be with her again."* (455) But life in him is just a hair stronger than death. *"He would not say it. He would not admit that he wanted to die, to have done. He would not own that life had beaten him, or that death had beaten him."* (456)

The last chapter of the book is called "Derelict." The title emphasizes Mr. Lawrence's already unmistakable meaning. Paul is adrift now; with the death of his mother he has lost his only mooring in life. There is no need to follow him further; when he is through despairing he will hope again and when he has compared one woman to his mother and found her wanting, he will go on to another, in endless repetition. The author's final picture of Paul's state of mind is full of seductive eloquence: *"There was no Time, only Space. Who could say that*[75] *his mother had lived and did not live? She had been in one place*[76] *and was in another;*[77] *that was all. And his soul could not leave her, wherever she was. Now she was gone abroad in*[78] *the night, and he was with her still. They were together. And*[79] *yet there was his body, his chest,*[80] *that leaned against the stile, his hands on the wooden bar. They seemed something. Where was he?—one tiny upright speck of flesh, less than an ear of wheat lost in the field. He could not bear it. On every side the immense dark silence seemed pressing him, so tiny a spark*[81]*, into extinction, and yet, almost nothing, he could not be extinct. Night, in which everything was lost, went reaching out, beyond stars and sun. Stars and sun, a few bright grains, went spinning round for terror,*[82] *and holding each other in embrace, there in a darkness that outpassed them all,*[83] *and left them tiny and daunted. So much, and himself, infinitesimal, at the core of*[84] *nothingness, and yet not nothing."*

" 'Mother!' he whimpered—[85] *'mother!' "* (464)

3

Such is the condensed account of Paul's love-life. Textual testimony could hardly go further to show that Paul loved his mother too dearly. And shall we now say that it was *because* Mrs. Morel lavished all her affection upon her son? But then, most mothers lavish a good deal of affection upon their sons and it is only natural for sons to love their mothers dearly. Why should an excess of these sacred sentiments produce such devastating results? For it is undoubtedly the intention of the author to show us Paul as a wreck and a ruin, a man damned out of all happiness at the age of twenty-five, who has barely the strength left to will not to die. And why should we accept as a type this man who seems to bear so many ear-marks of degeneracy and abnormal impulse, who is alternately a ruthless egotist and a vicious weakling in his dealings with women, and who in the end stoops to shorten the life of his own mother? Surely the thing is deeper and due to profounder causes. But of these the author gives us no indication. Let us therefore assume for the moment that Paul is by no means a degenerate, but merely an exaggeration of the normal, unhealthily nursed into morbid manifestations by an abnormal environment. If that can be established it may very well be that the story of Paul's love-life simply throws into high relief an intimate and constant relation between parent and child the significance of which has hitherto escaped general observation. Perhaps all men have something of Paul in them. In that case their instinctive recognition of their kinship with the hero of the book would go a great way towards explaining the potency of *Sons and Lovers*. We are fond of saying something like that about Hamlet.

The theory which would enable us to assume such a point of view is at once concrete, humanly understandable, and capable of personal verification. For Freud holds that the love instinct, whose sudden efflorescence after the age of puberty is invested with so much poetic charm, is not a belated endowment, but comes as the result of a gradual development which we can trace step by step from our earliest childhood. In fact, according to Freud, the evolution of the mature love instinct begins as soon as the child has sufficiently developed a sense of the otherness of its surroundings to single out its mother as the object of its affections.[86] At first this is entirely instinctive and unconscious and comes as the natural result of the child's dependence upon its mother for food, warmth and comfort. We come preciously close to being born lovers. The mother is the one overwhelming presence of those earliest days, the source from which all good things flow, so that childhood is full of the sense of the mother's omnipotence. From her we first learn how to express affection, and the maternal caresses and the intimate feeling of oneness which we get from her form the easy analogies to love when we feel a conscious passion for another individual of the opposite sex. Our mother is, in a very real sense of the word, our first love.

As soon as the child is capable of making comparisons with other people it proceeds to celebrate the superiorities of its mother. She is the most beautiful, the most accomplished, the most powerful, and no other child's mother can equal her. But meanwhile the influence of the father, that other major constellation of our childhood, is also felt. Though not so gracious, he too is mighty, mightier than the mother, since he dominates her. His presence brings about a striking change in the attitude of the child, according to its sex. The boy, seeing that the mother loves the father, strives to be like him, in order to draw the mother's affection to himself. He takes his father as an ideal and sets about to imitate his masculine qualities. And the girl, becoming aware of the father's love for the mother, tries to attract some of his love to herself by imitating the mother. This is the process of self-identification which is already conditioned by the natural physical similarity where parent and child are of the same sex. Father and son, and mother and daughter, now have a common object of affection. But to the child this means at the same time an active rivalry, for the child is an unbridled egotist, intent upon nothing less than the exclusive possession of the affection of the beloved parent. It therefore manifests unmistakable signs of jealousy, even of frank hostility. So strong is this feeling that a careful examination of the unconscious childhood memories of thousands of individuals, such as is possible with the Freudian method of psychoanalysis, has yet to reveal an infancy in which a death phantasy about the rival parent has not played a part. The childish wish is ruthlessly realized in imagination; the boy suddenly dreams of living in a cottage with his mother after the father, let us say, has been devoured by the lion of last week's circus, while the girl revels in the thought of keeping house for her father after the mother has been conveniently removed. We may feel, then, that we were fellow conspirators with Paul when he prayed to God to have his father slain. For we have had the same wish in common: to eliminate the rival and celebrate a childish marriage with the parent of our choice.

From this naïve attitude the child is normally weaned by the maturing influences of education and by the absolute barriers

which its childish wish encounters. It is a slow and gradual process of transference, which continues through childhood and puberty. The child is tenaciously rooted in its parents and does not
easily relinquish its hold upon them. Even after it has acquired
a dawning sense of the meaning of sex it continues to interweave
its immature phantasies of procreation with its former ideal ad-
oration of the parent. Thus the girl, having had a glimmering
that the father has had something essential to do with her birth,
may assign to him a similar function in regard to her dolls, which
of course are her children. And the boy, similarly aware that his
father has played a mysterious part with regard to the mother
when she suddenly introduces another child into the nursery, is
likely to usurp the exercise of this function to himself. Both sub-
stitutions are merely more sophisticated ways of eliminating the
rival parent by making him unnecessary. It must be remembered,
of course, that the child can have none of our reservations as to
the direction which the erotic impulse may take, and therefore
quite innocently directs its crude and imperfect erotic feelings
towards its parent, from whom they must then be deflected. This
is most favorably accomplished when there are other children in
the family. The girl is quick to see the father in her brother and
the boy transfers his worship of the mother to his sister. The
father's manly qualities are used by the girl to embellish the
brother when she sets him up as a love ideal. From him again
she slowly extends her love phantasies to other boys of his and
her acquaintance. The boy on his part, dowers his sister with the
borrowed attributes of his mother and then passes from her to
other girls who in turn are selected on the basis of their similarity
to the sister and to the mother. In default of brothers or sisters
other playmates have to serve the same purpose. The enforced
quest of a love object other than the parent thus becomes the
great incentive of our social radiation towards other individuals
and to the world at large.

This process of deflection and transference, which is one of
the main psychic labors of childhood, is facilitated by a parallel
process that constantly represses a part of our thoughts to the
unconscious. The mechanism of repression, as the Freudian psy-

chology describes it, does not become operative until the age of
about four or five, for at first the child does not repress at all
and therefore has no unconscious. But the function of education
consists largely in imposing innumerable taboos upon the child
and in teaching it to respect the thou-shalt-nots. Thoughts and
feelings such as the cruder egotistical impulses and the associations with bodily functions, which seem quite natural to the
child's primitive and necessarily unmoral mind, gradually fall under the cultural ban proclaimed by parents and educators, so that
the unconscious becomes a receptacle for all the thoughts that
are rendered painful and disagreeable by the slowly developing
sense of shame and of moral and ethical behaviour. We "put away
childish things"[87] by putting them into the unconscious. Our ger-
minating sexual ideas and our naïve erotic attitude towards our
parents become particularly "impermissible" and we therefore
draw an especially heavy veil of forgetfulness over this part of
our childhood. But though we can forget, we cannot obliterate,
and the result of this early fixation upon our parents is to leave
in our mind an indelible imprint, or "imago,"[88] of both our
mother and our father. Our parents are always with us in our
unconscious. They become our ultimate criterion by which we
judge men and women, and exercise the most potent influence
upon our love choice. The imago of them that holds us to our
unconscious allegiance is a picture, not as we know them later,
old and declining, but as we saw them first, young and radiant,
and dowered, as it seemed to us then, with godlike gifts. We
cannot go on loving them so we do the next best thing; the boy
chooses a woman who resembles his mother as closely as possible,
and the girl mates with the man who reminds her most of her
father.

Such, according to Freud, is the psychological genesis of the
emotion of love. The normal evolution of love from the first
maternal caress is finally accomplished when the individual def-
initely transfers his allegiance to a self-chosen mate and thereby
steps out of the charmed family circle in which he has been held
from infancy. That this is difficult even under normal circumstance seems already to have been recognized in the Bible, where

Christ says with so much solemnity: "For this cause shall a man leave father and mother"[89]; as if only so weighty a reason could induce a child to leave its parents. Freud, in postulating the above development as the norm, proceeds to attach grave and far-reaching consequences to any deviations from this standard. The effect of any disturbance in the balanced and harmonious influence of both parents upon the child, or of any abnormal pressure of circumstances or wilful action that forces the child into a specialized attitude toward either parent, is subtly and unerringly reproduced in the later love-life. The reader himself will probably recall from his own observation, a large number of cases where the love-life has been thwarted, or stunted, or never expressed. He will think of those old bachelors whose warm attachment to their mother has so much superficial charm, as well as of those old maids who so self-effacingly devote themselves to their fathers. He will also recall that almost typical man whose love interest persistently goes where marriage is impossible, preferably to a woman already preempted by another man or to a much older woman, so that his love can never come to rest in its object; he will wonder whether this man too is not preserving his ideal allegiance to his mother by avoiding that final detachment from her which marriage would bring. He will notice a class of men and women who, even though their parents are dead, seem to have resigned marriage and live in a kind of small contentment with a constantly narrowing horizon. Or he may know of actual marriages that are unhappy because the memory of one of the parents has not been sufficiently laid to rest, and the joke about the mother-in-law or the pie that mother used to make, will acquire a new significance for him. And to all these cases thousands must still be added where neurotic and hysteric patients reveal with unmistakable clearness that the ghosts of the parents still walk about in the troubled psyches of these unfortunates, influencing life and happiness with paralyzing effect. These are all manifestations which the reader hitherto has observed only as results, without knowing the causes or trying to ascertain them. With the aid of the Freudian theory such examples may now help him to see, as perhaps he has already begun to see in Paul, the tremendous rôle that the abnormal fixation upon the parent plays in the psychic development of the individual. And in so doing he may perhaps also gain some insight into the part that his own parents have played in his normal psychic growth, just as disease gives us a clearer understanding of health or as Madame Montessori's study of subnormal children has enabled her to formulate general laws of education.[90]

4

We can now return to *Sons and Lovers* with a new understanding. Why has the attitude of the son to his mother here had such a devastating effect upon his whole life? Why could he not overcome this obstacle like other children and ultimately attain some measure of manhood? Why, in short, was the surrender so complete? In Paul's case the abnormal fixation upon the mother is most obviously conditioned by the father, whose unnatural position in the family is responsible for the distortion of the normal attitude of the child towards its parents. The father ideal simply does not exist for Paul; where there should have been an attractive standard of masculinity to imitate, he can only fear and despise. The child's normal dependence upon the mother is perpetuated because there is no counter-influence to detach it from her. But there is another distortion, equally obvious, which fatally influences the natural development. Paul's early fixation upon his mother is met and enhanced by Mrs. Morel's abnormally concentrated affection for her son. Her unappeased love, which can no longer go out towards her husband, turns to Paul for consolation; she *makes* him love her too well. Her love becomes a veritable Pandora's box of evil. For Paul is now hemmed in on all sides by too much love and too much hate.

If we now compare Paul's boyhood and adolescence with, let us say, the reader's own, we find that the difference is, to a great extent, one of consciousness and unconsciousness. All those psychic processes which are usually unconscious or at least heavily veiled in the normal psycho-sexual development lie close to consciousness in Paul and break through into his waking thoughts at every favorable opportunity. Everything is raw and exposed in him and remains so, kept quick to the touch by the pressure of an abnormal environment which instead of moulding, misshapes him. The normal hostility towards the father which is conditioned in every boy by a natural jealousy of the mother's affection, is nursed in him to a conscious hate through Morel's actual brutality and his mother's undisguised bitterness and contempt. And the normal love for the mother which ordinarily serves as a model for the man's love for other women is in him perverted into abnormal expression almost at his mother's breast, so that he is always conscious of his infatuation with his mother and can never free his love-making from that paralyzing influence. These powerful determinants of the love-life which we acquire from our parents would be too overwhelming in every case were it not for the process of submersion or repression already referred to. This repression usually sets in at an early stage of childhood and acts biologically as a protective mechanism by allowing us to develop a slowly expanding sense of selfhood through which we gradually differentiate ourselves from our parents. In this way the fateful dominance of the parents is broken, though their influence remains in the unconscious as a formative and directing impulse.

In Paul this salutary process never takes place because he cannot free himself from the incubus of his parents long enough to come to some sense of himself. He remains enslaved by his parent complex instead of being moulded and guided by it. One turns back to that astonishing scene at Lincoln Cathedral. Here Paul goes to the roots of his mother's hold upon him. For his passionate reproaches hurled at his mother because she has lost her youth, prove that the mother-imago, in all its pristine magic, has never diminished its sway over him; he has never been able to forget or to subordinate that first helpless infatuation. If only she could be young again so that he could remain her child-lover! With that thought and wish so conscious in him nothing else in life can become really desirable, and all initiative is dried up at the source. Paul cannot expand towards the universe in normal activity and form an independent sex interest because for him his mother has become the universe; she stands between him and life and the other woman. There is a kind of bottomless childishness about him; life in a pretty house with his mother—the iteration sounds like a childish prattle. Miriam feels it when she calls him a child of four which she can no longer nurse. Nor can Clara help him by becoming a wanton substitute for his mother. Only the one impossible ideal holds him, and that means the constant turning in upon himself which is death. Paul goes to pieces because he can never make the mature sexual decision away from his mother, he can never accomplish the physical and emotional transfer.

If now this striking book, taken as it stands, bears such unexpected witness to the truth of Freud's remarkable psycho-sexual theory, it is at least presumable that the author himself and the rest of his work also stand in some very definite relation to this theory. The feeling that *Sons and Lovers* must be autobiographical is considerably strengthened by the somewhat meager personal detail which Mr. Edwin Björkman supplies in an introduction to Mr. Lawrence's first play.[91] Mr. Lawrence was himself the son of a collier in the Derbyshire coal-mining district and his mother seems to have occupied an exceptional position in the family, showing herself to be a woman of great fortitude and initiative, who evidently dominated the household. Mr. Björkman is silent concerning the father, but gives us the interesting information that *Sons and Lovers* was written not long after the mother's death. This information is not sufficient, however, to warrant our inquiry going beyond the author's writings, a step for which, in any case, it would be necessary to have both his permission and his cooperation. We must therefore limit ourselves to the testimony of Mr. Lawrence's work. This consists of two additional novels, a volume of poems, and a play. What is truly astonishing is that all of these, in various disguises and transparent elaborations, hark back to the same problem: the direct and indirect effects of an excessive maternal allegiance and the attempt to become emancipated from it.

Reference has already been made to the poems. This is the way the author ends a love poem:

"What else—it is perfect enough,
It is perfectly complete,
You and I,
What more—?
Strange, how we suffer in spite of this!"[92]

Why, it may well be asked, should the perfection of love bring suffering? Certainly the love poems of adolescence are not as a rule colored with the feeling of suffering as unmotivated as this. But there is a second poem, entitled "End of Another Home-holiday" which in the short space of three pages states Paul's whole problem with unmistakable precision. The poet tells how dearly he loves his home and then continues as follows:

"The light has gone out from under my mother's door.
    That she should love me so,
    She, so lonely, greying now,
    And I leaving her,
    Bent on my pursuits!"[93]

How curiously that last line comes in, "Bent on my pursuits!" as if he felt that he ought to stay at home. Here we have again the son who cannot leave his mother; the mere thought of doing so fills him with self-reproach. In the next few lines the reproach deepens:

"Forever, ever by my shoulder pitiful Love will linger,
Crouching as little houses crouch under the mist when I
    turn.
Forever, out of the mist the church lifts up her reproachful
    finger,
Pointing my eyes in wretched defiance where love hides her
    face to mourn."[94]

Even inanimate things point the finger of reproach at him. A little later in the same poem the mother becomes a symbolic

figure, following the son through life like a Norn,[95] as she begs
for his love.

> "While ever at my side,
>   Frail and sad, with grey bowed head,
>   The beggar-woman, the yearning-eyed
>   Inexorable love goes lagging."
>   *
>
>   *
>
>   *

> "But when I draw the scanty cloak of silence over my eyes,
> Piteous Love comes peering under the hood.
> Touches the clasp with trembling fingers, and tries
> To put her ear to the painful sob of my blood,
> While her tears soak through to my breast,
>   Where they burn and cauterize."[96]

The poem ends with the call of the corncrake in the poet's ear,
crying monotonously:

> "With a piteous, unalterable plaint, that deadens
>   My confident activity:
> With a hoarse, insistent request that falls
>   Unweariedly, unweariedly,
>   Asking something more of me,
>   Yet more of me!"[97]

An interesting, tell-tale clew in these last lines shows how thoroughly this poem is Paul's and to how great an extent Paul and
the author are one and the same. For the careful reader will
remember that Paul too, coming home over the fields after vis-
iting Miriam is strongly depressed by the call of this same little
bird and immediately goes in to his mother to tell her that he
still loves her best and that he has broken off with Miriam. Has
not his mother too, "deadened his confident activity." Her influence could hardly be better described in a single phrase. The
whole poem is a protest against the terrible allegiance that the

mother exacts, just as Paul, towards the end of the book, reproaches his mother for the failure of his life. It can hardly be doubted that a vital part of the lyricist has gone into Paul.

In reading the two remaining novels and the play our attention is immediately struck by a curious sameness and limitation of motif that underlies them all. In each there is a deadly father or husband hate, a poignant sense of death, and a picture of marriage or love that does not satisfy. Siegmund, the husband in *The Trespasser,* is exposed to a hate so withering that he collapses before it. He is a kind and gentle musician, too effeminate for a man, and entirely devoid of initiative. The hatred of his wife and children is practically unmotivated, we are simply asked to assume it in order to follow him in his affair with Helena. This brings him no solace, he cannot come to rest in her, his love for her simply brings him the sense of death. It is the psychology of Paul transferred to a man of forty, and Helena's struggle to make his love for her real is much like Miriam's. In the play, *The Widowing of Mrs. Holroyd,* the wife seeks to escape from a brutal and drunken husband by eloping with another man. The death of her husband in a mining accident intervenes and brings her a sense of pity and remorse because she never tried to win and hold her husband's love. She had married him without love. Her son hates his father and wishes him dead. Blackmore, the man with whom she wanted to elope, has much of Paul in him; his belief that love can bring happiness is never more than half-hearted. The sense of guilt that the death of the husband brings to both of them, makes the elopement impossible. Death always supervenes upon the impermissible with Mr. Lawrence.

In *The White Peacock* the background is again a ruthless hate for the husband and father. One of the daughters says: *"There is always a sense of death in this house. I believe my mother hated my father before I was born. That was death in her veins for me before I was born. It makes a difference."*[98] We get a picture of women who marry meaningless husbands and men who marry unsatisfying wives. Lettie marries Leslie because George, whom she really loves, lacks the initiative to claim her, and George marries Meg after his abortive love for Lettie has made him despair of life. Neither he nor she come to any emotional satisfaction; Lettie consoles herself for her aimlessly empty husband by living in her children, and George ends his "Liebestod"[99] in drink. Lettie's brother, who tells the story, is almost sexless except towards his sister, whom he admires like a lover. One gradually gets a sense of monotony; happiness in love is always impossible in this fictional world of Mr. Lawrence, and hate for the parent or husband is the master passion. The motivation is often indistinct or inadequate in all three stories, and the artistry is inferior. They were evidently only preludes to *Sons and Lovers.*

In the story of Paul the author has reached the final expression of a problem which haunts his every effort. The creative labor of self-realization which makes *Sons and Lovers* such a priceless commentary on the love-life of to-day, accomplished itself but slowly in Mr. Lawrence, waiting, no doubt, for his artistic maturity and the final clarity which the death of his mother must have brought. And if, as I have tried to show, he has been able, though unknowingly, to attest the truth of what is perhaps the most far-reaching psychological theory ever propounded, he has also given us an illuminating insight into the mystery of artistic creation. For Mr. Lawrence has escaped the destructive fate that dogs the hapless Paul by the grace of expression: out of the dark struggles of his own soul he has emerged as a triumphant artist. In every epoch the soul of the artist is sick with the problems of his generation. He cures himself by expression in his art. And by producing a catharsis in the spectator through the enjoyment of his art he also heals his fellow beings. His artistic stature is measured by the universality of the problem which his art has transfigured.

567 WEST 113TH STREET
 NEW YORK.

Notes

Notes 1–14 and 16–85 record the variants between the text of Kuttner's quotations from the 1913 American *Sons and Lovers* published by Mitchell

Kennerley (recorded here as '1913') and the 1992 Cambridge University Press edition used in this volume (recorded as '1992'). Nearly all of Kuttner's quotations from *Sons and Lovers* were printed in italics in the *Psychoanalytic Review*; this has been ignored in the notes. The reading to the left of the square bracket records Kuttner's text; variant paragraph breaks (recorded as /) have been noted in indented quotations; variants in line breaks, opening capitalisation and closing punctuation are omitted. The 'Freudian slips' in the quotations recorded in notes 3, 42 and 67 are especially interesting. In the following, *OED2* refers to *The Oxford English Dictionary*, 2nd edition, 10 volumes (Oxford: Clarendon Press, 1989).

1. hers;] here; 1913 here, 1992
2. quite] quiet 1913, 1992
3. very] so 1913, 1992
4. fretted 1913] fretted, 1992
5. him not 1913] him 1992
6. contracts] contract 1913, 1992
7. end 1913] end, 1992
8. everything] almost everything 1913, 1992
9. him 1913] him, 1992
10. pondered, 1913] pondered 1992
11. week 1913] week, 1992
12. intimate, 1913] intimate 1992
13. were, 1913] were 1992
14. soul 1913] soul, 1992
15. I.e. cast off.
16. old. 1913] old! 1992
17. aside; 1913] aside, 1992
18. not—] not 1913, 1992
19. throat. / "Well,] throat. / "And she exults so in taking you from me—she's not like ordinary girls." / "Well, 1913, 1992
20. him,] him 1913, 1992
21. kiss. 1913] kiss: 1992
22. love. / Without 1913] love. Without 1992
23. he still 1913] still he 1992
24. hopeless 1913] hopeless, 1992
25. Miriam . . . her] Miriam, . . . her, 1913, 1992
26. YOU always!] *you* always! 1913 *you* always, 1992
27. blood, 1913] blood 1992
28. relations 1913] relations, 1992

29. common sense. Ours] the common sense. Ours 1913 the common sense . . . / Ours 1992

30. in] in his 1913, 1992

31. feeling] feel 1913, 1992

32. there was] was 1913, 1992

33. first; 1913] first, 1992

34. his own] his 1913, 1992

35. Why] *Why* 1913, 1992

36. walk, why] walk? *Why* 1913, 1992

37. marry, mother. 1913] marry mother—1992

38. seventy-five . . . forty-four 1913] seventy five . . . forty four 1992

39. See! 1913] See—! 1992

40. AM] *am* 1913, 1992

41. rate 1913] rate, 1992

42. she] he 1913, 1992

43. woman—she] woman—She 1913 woman—. She 1992

44. knew] *knew* 1913, 1992

45. have] to have 1913, 1992

46. obstacle; and 1913] obstacle. And 1992

47. Always—1913] Always, 1992

48. been] always been 1913, 1992

49. Always, 1913] Always—1992

50. same! 1913] same. 1992

51. years 1913] years, 1992

52. folly? 1913] folly. 1992

53. you, 1913] you—1992

54. there, 1913] there—1992

55. ME] *me* 1913, 1992

56. But 1913] But—1992

57. me] *me* 1913, 1992

58. IT] *It* 1913, 1992

59. 'He] He 1913, 1992

60. woman? 1913] woman. 1992

61. Miriam; but 1913] Miriam. But 1992

62. give] *give* 1913, 1992

63. marriage 1913] marriage—1992

64. ME] *me* 1913, 1992

65. even] ever 1913, 1992

66. shall never] never shall 1913, 1992

67. wanted to turn back upon] turned back on 1913, 1992

68. London 1913] London, 1992
69. girl's—1913] girl's, 1992
70. pant 1913] pant, 1992
71. oh, 1913] Oh 1992
72. oh, 1913] oh 1992
73. space] the space 1913, 1992
74. so that 1913] so 1992
75. say that] say 1913, 1992
76. place] place, 1913, 1992
77. another; 1913] another, 1992
78. in] into 1913, 1992
79. And] But 1913, 1992
80. chest, 1913] chest 1992
81. spark 1913] speck 1992
82. terror, 1913] terror 1992
83. all, 1913] all 1992
84. of] a 1913, 1992
85. whimpered—1913] whimpered, 1992

86. Kuttner's account of Freud is derived from a wide range of reading and cannot be sourced in any particular texts (information from John Turner): see e.g. N. G. Hale, *Freud and the Americans*, Vol. I, 1876–1917 (New York: Oxford University Press, 1971).

87. I Corinthians xiii. 11.

88. A word given a particular meaning by psychoanalysis at exactly this date: 'A subjective image of someone (esp. a parent) which a person has subconsciously formed and which continues to influence his attitudes and behaviour' (*OED2*): the first citation in *OED2* is from the 1918 American translation of Jung's *Psychology of the Unconscious* (1916).

89. Matthew xix. 5.

90. Maria Montessori (1870–1952), Italian educational reformer, evolved a theory of nursery education in which children are provided with facilities for practical play and allowed to develop at their own pace; books such as *The Montessori Method* (1912) and *Pedagogical Anthropology* (1913) had made her extremely well known before the First World War.

91. 'Introduction' to *The Widowing of Mrs. Holroyd* (New York, 1914), vii–x, reprinted in D. H. Lawrence, *The Plays*, eds. Hans-Wilhelm Schwarze and John Worthen (Cambridge: Cambridge University Press, 1999), 535–38; Edwin Björkman (1866–1951) was a Swedish-born novelist, translator and critic.

92. 'Bei Hennef', in *The Complete Poems of D. H. Lawrence*, eds. Vivian de Sola Pinto and Warren Roberts (London: Heinemann, 1972), I, 203.

93. Ibid., I, 63.

94. Ibid., I, 63.

95. One of the female Fates recognised in Scandinavian mythology (*OED2*).

96. *The Complete Poems of D. H. Lawrence*, I, 64.

97. Ibid., I, 64.

98. D. H. Lawrence, *The White Peacock*, ed. Andrew Robertson (Cambridge: Cambridge University Press, 1983), 28.

99. 'Love's-death': description by Richard Wagner (1813–83) of the mystic love duet at the end of Act II of his opera *Tristan und Isolde* (1865); today usually applied to the death of Isolde at the end of the opera.

Suggested Reading

Editions of Sons and Lovers

'Sons and Lovers': A Facsimile of the Manuscript, edited by Mark Schorer. Berkeley. University of California Press, 1977.

Sons and Lovers, edited by Helen Baron and Carl Baron. Cambridge: Cambridge University Press, 1992. Republished with different editorial matter by Penguin Books, 1994.

Paul Morel, edited by Helen Baron. Cambridge: Cambridge University Press, 2003.

Reference Books on D. H. Lawrence

Cowan, James C. D. H. Lawrence: An Annotated Bibliography of Writings About Him. 2 vols. De Kalb, IL: Northern Illinois University Press, 1982, 1985.

Draper, R. P., ed. D. H. Lawrence: The Critical Heritage. London: Routledge and Kegan Paul, 1970.

Poplawski, Paul. D. H. Lawrence: A Reference Companion. Westport, CT: Greenwood Press, 1996.

Preston, Peter. *A D. H. Lawrence Chronology.* Basingstoke: Macmillan, 1994.
Roberts, Warren. *A Bibliography of D. H. Lawrence.* 3rd edition, revised by Paul Poplawski. Cambridge: Cambridge University Press, 2001.

Biographical Sources

Chambers, Jessie. *D. H. Lawrence: A Personal Record by 'E.T.'* London: Jonathan Cape, 1935.
The Collected Letters of Jessie Chambers, edited by George J. Zytaruk. A special edition of the *D. H. Lawrence Review,* Vol. 12, Nos. 1–2 (spring–summer 1979).
The Letters of D. H. Lawrence, Volume I, edited by James T. Boulton. Cambridge: Cambridge University Press, 1979.
Nehls, Edward, ed. *D. H. Lawrence: A Composite Biography.* Volume I. Madison: University of Wisconsin Press, 1957.
Worthen, John. *D. H. Lawrence: The Early Years, 1885–1912.* Cambridge: Cambridge University Press, 1991.
──────. *D. H. Lawrence: The Life of an Outsider.* London: Allen Lane, 2005.

Collections of Essays on *Sons and Lovers*

Bloom, Harold, ed. *D. H. Lawrence's 'Sons and Lovers'.* New York: Chelsea House, 1988.
Farr, Judith, ed. *Twentieth-Century Interpretations of 'Sons and Lovers'.* Englewood Cliffs, NJ: Prentice-Hall, 1970.
Rylance, Rick, ed. *'Sons and Lovers'.* Basingstoke: Macmillan, 1996.
Salgādo, Gāmini, ed. *D. H. Lawrence, 'Sons and Lovers': A Selection of Critical Essays.* London: Macmillan, 1969. Published in America as *D. H. Lawrence, 'Sons and Lovers': A Casebook.* Nashville, TN: Aurora, 1970.
Tedlock, E. W., ed. *D. H. Lawrence and 'Sons and Lovers': Sources and Criticism.* New York: New York University Press, 1965.

Books Devoted to *Sons and Lovers*

Black, Michael. *D. H. Lawrence: 'Sons and Lovers'.* Cambridge: Cambridge University Press, 1992.

Draper, R. P. *'Sons and Lovers' by D. H. Lawrence.* Basingstoke: Macmillan, 1986.

Finney, Brian. *D. H. Lawrence: 'Sons and Lovers'.* Harmondsworth: Penguin, 1990.

Harvey, Geoffrey. *Sons and Lovers.* Atlantic Highlands, NJ: Humanities, 1987.

Moynahan, Julian. *'Sons and Lovers': Text, Background, and Criticism.* New York: Viking Press, 1968.

Murfin, Ross C. *'Sons and Lovers': A Novel of Division and Desire.* Boston: Twayne, 1987.

Salgādo, Gāmini. *D. H. Lawrence: 'Sons and Lovers'.* London: Edward Arnold, 1966.

Books Containing Treatments of *Sons and Lovers*

Alldritt, Keith. *The Visual Imagination of D. H. Lawrence.* London: Edward Arnold, 1971.

Balbert, Peter. *D. H. Lawrence and the Phallic Imagination: Essays on Sexual Identity and Feminist Misreading.* New York: St Martin's, 1989.

Bell, Michael. *D. H. Lawrence: Language and Being.* Cambridge: Cambridge University Press, 1992.

Bonds, Diane S. *Language and the Self in D. H. Lawrence.* Ann Arbor, MI: UMI Research Press, 1987.

Brown, Keith, ed. *Rethinking Lawrence.* Philadelphia: Open University Press, 1990.

Cowan, James C. *D. H. Lawrence: Self and Sexuality.* Columbus: Ohio State University Press, 2002.

Daleski, H. M. *The Forked Flame: A Study of D. H. Lawrence.* London: Faber, 1965.

Fernihough, Anne. *D. H. Lawrence: Aesthetics and Ideology.* Oxford: Clarendon Press, 1993.

———, ed. *The Cambridge Companion to D. H. Lawrence.* Cambridge: Cambridge University Press, 2001.

Greiff, Louis K. *D. H. Lawrence: Fifty Years on Film.* Carbondale: Southern Illinois University Press, 2001.

Holderness, Graham. *D. H. Lawrence: History, Ideology and Fiction.* Dublin: Gill and Macmillan, 1982.

Hyde, G. M. *D. H. Lawrence.* London: Macmillan, 1990.

Kermode, Frank. *Lawrence.* Suffolk, UK: Collins Fontana, 1973.

Leavis, F. R. *D. H. Lawrence: Novelist.* London: Chatto and Windus, 1955.

Lewiecki-Wilson, Cynthia. *Writing Against the Family: Gender in Lawrence and Joyce.* Carbondale: Southern Illinois University Press, 1994.

Marsh, Nicholas. *D. H. Lawrence: The Novels.* New York: St. Martin's, 2000.

Millett, Kate. *Sexual Politics.* New York: Ballantine, 1969.

Moynahan, Julian. *The Deed of Life: The Novels and Tales of D. H. Lawrence.* Princeton, NJ: Princeton University Press, 1963.

Pinkney, Tony. *D. H. Lawrence and Modernism.* Iowa City: University of Iowa Press, 1990.

Poplawski, Paul, ed. *Writing the Body in D. H. Lawrence: Essays on Language, Representation, and Sexuality.* Westport, CT: Greenwood Press, 2001.

Ross, Charles L., and Dennis Jackson, eds. *Editing D. H. Lawrence: New Versions of a Modern Author.* Ann Arbor, MI: University of Michigan Press, 1995.

Ruderman, Judith. *D. H. Lawrence and the Devouring Mother: The Search for a Patriarchal Ideal of Leadership.* Durham, NC: Duke University Press, 1984.

Sanders, Scott. *D. H. Lawrence: The World of the Major Novels.* London: Vision, 1973.

Schapiro, Barbara Ann. *D. H. Lawrence and the Paradoxes of Psychic Life.* Albany: State University of New York Press, 1999.

Scheckner, Peter. *Class, Politics, and the Individual: A Study of the Major Works of D. H. Lawrence.* London and Toronto: Associated University Presses, 1985.

Schneider, Daniel J. *D. H. Lawrence: The Artist as Psychologist.* Lawrence: University Press of Kansas, 1984.

Simpson, Hilary. *D. H. Lawrence and Feminism.* De Kalb, IL: Northern Illinois University Press, 1982.

Sklenicka, Carol. *D. H. Lawrence and the Child.* Columbia: University of Missouri Press, 1991.

Smith, Anne, ed. *Lawrence and Women.* New York: Barnes and Noble, 1978.

Spilka, Mark. *The Love Ethic of D. H. Lawrence.* Bloomington: Indiana University Press, 1955.

Stewart, Jack. *The Vital Art of D. H. Lawrence: Vision and Expression.* Carbondale: Southern Illinois University Press, 1999.

Storch, Margaret. *Sons and Adversaries: Women in William Blake and D. H. Lawrence.* Knoxville: University of Tennessee Press, 1990.

Trotter, David. *The English Novel in History 1895–1920.* London: Routledge, 1993.

Weiss, Daniel A. *Oedipus in Nottingham: D. H. Lawrence.* Seattle: University of Washington Press, 1962.

Williams, Linda Ruth. *Sex in the Head: Visions of Femininity and Film in D. H. Lawrence.* Detroit, MI: Wayne State University Press, 1993.

Williams, Raymond. *The English Novel from Dickens to Lawrence.* London: Chatto and Windus, 1970.

Worthen, John. *D. H. Lawrence and the Idea of the Novel.* Totowa, NJ: Rowman and Littlefield, 1979.

———. *D. H. Lawrence.* London: Edward Arnold, 1991.

Selected Individual Articles and Essays on *Sons and Lovers*

Baron, Helen. 'Lawrence's *Sons and Lovers* versus Garnett's'. *Essays in Criticism,* Vol. 42, No. 4 (October 1992): 265–78.

Delany, Paul. '*Sons and Lovers*: The Morel Marriage as a War of Position.' *D. H. Lawrence Review,* Vol. 21 (1989): 153–65.

Eggert, Paul. 'Edward Garnett's *Sons and Lovers*'. *Critical Quarterly,* Vol. 28, No. 4 (1986): 51–62.

Littlewood, J. C. F. 'Son and Lover'. *The Cambridge Quarterly* (autumn–winter 1969–70): 323–61.

Martz, Louis L. 'Portrait of Miriam: A Study in the Design of *Sons and Lovers*'. In *Imagined Worlds: Essays on Some English Novels and Novelists in Honour of John Butt,* edited by Maynard Mack and Ian Gregor. London: Methuen, 1968.

Schorer, Mark. 'Technique as Discovery'. *Hudson Review,* Vol. 1 (spring 1948): 67–87.

Van Ghent, Dorothy. 'On *Sons and Lovers*'. In her *The English Novel: Form and Function.* New York: Holt, Rinehart, and Winston, 1953.

Worthen, John. 'Lawrence's Autobiographies'. In *The Spirit of D. H. Lawrence: Centenary Studies,* edited by Gāmini Salgādo and G. K. Das. Totowa, NJ. Barnes, 1988.

Index

'DHL' signifies D. H. Lawrence, 'Frieda' signifies Frieda von Richthofen, Frieda Weekley, Frieda Lawrence and Frieda Ravagli. For individual entries on Lawrence's works, *see* Lawrence, David Herbert, WORKS. Boldface numbers denote essays in the volume by the individuals named.